PHYTOARCHAEOLOGY

Robert R. Brooks and Dieter Johannes

This book introduces an exciting new cross-disciplinary study: Phytoarchaeology attempts to describe the relationships between vegetation and archaeology. This first monograph proposes several different areas for further exploration and research: the survival of ancient crops; plant introductions as evidence of ancient trade contact; specific plants associated with archaeological remains; the presence of pollen or plant opal phytoliths indicating the nature of ancient environments; plants associated with ancient mines and mining activity; and the aerial discovery of archaeological remains by vegetational indicators.

For example, copper artifacts from the Kabambian culture of Central Africa have been uncovered by studying the distribution of the "copper flower," *Haumaniastrum katangense,* colonizing the overlying soil that had become rich in copper following smelting operations by this ancient culture. Similarly, it has been possible to trace ancient trading routes by studying the distribution of plants originating from a single source but colonizing ports of call along the routes.

This pioneering work covers all of the continents form the high Arctic to southern Oceania, and encompasses a variety of cultures from the "primitive" hunter-gatherer societies of Australia to the sophisticated civilizations of Greece and Rome. The authors present the basic theory of each topic with case histories and provide an up-to-date reference list of the most important literature. Drawing as it does on chemistry, palynology, statistics, aviation technology, photography, history, remote sensing, history of trade routes, pedology, and agronomy as well as archaeology and botany, **Phytoarchaeology** is an exciting synthesis of many disciplines that will form a sure basis for further research.

PHYTOARCHAEOLOGY

PHYTOARCHAEOLOGY

by

Robert R. Brooks

and

Dieter Johannes

Historical, Ethno- & Economic Botany Series
VOLUME 3
Theodore R. Dudley, Ph.D., General Editor

DIOSCORIDES PRESS
Portland, Oregon

© 1990 by Dioscorides Press
(an imprint of Timber Press, Inc.)

ISBN 0-931146-16-X
Printed in Hong Kong

Dioscorides Press
9999 S.W. Wilshire
Portland, Oregon 97225

Library of Congress Cataloging-in-Publication Data

Brooks, R. R.
    Phytoarchaeology / by Robert R. Brooks and Dieter Johannes.
        p.   cm.
    Includes bibliographical references.
    ISBN 0-931146-16-X
    1. Plant remains (Archaeology) 2. Aerial photography in
archaeology.   I. Johannes, Dieter.   II. Title.
    CC79.5.P5B76   1990
    930.1--dc20   89-17019
                                                     CIP

CONTENTS

PREFACE

It was the unusual vegetation at two very different sites thousands of kilometers apart that led the first author of this book (R. R. B.) to a study of the subject herein described. The first of these sites is situated in the suburbs of Bastia in Corsica and is covered with a unique stand of a perennial herb named *Alyssum corsicum*. The plant covers only a few hectares over a nickel-rich ultramafic (serpentine) soil. Although it was originally thought to be endemic to Corsica, it apparently originated from Turkey as weed seed in a consignment of grain brought to Corsica by the Venetians (or even earlier traders). The plant had clearly traced ancient trade routes across the Mediterranean region.

The second site was investigated in Shaba Province, Zaïre as a consequence of studies on the copper/cobalt tolerant flora of this part of Africa. Open clearings dominated by the "copper flower" *Haumaniastrum katangense* were found to contain pre-colonial artifacts such as copper crosses (croisettes) used as currency by the local Kabambian culture. It transpired that native artisans had brought copper ore to the sites for smelting over termite hills near rivers that provided water, and had abandoned the sites after a few years. The residual copper had left a phytotoxic soil that only the copper flower could colonize. This flower was clearly an indicator of buried archaeological remains. We originally coined the term *phytoarchaeology* to describe this occurrence.

The interest evoked by these two isolated examples led to a literature survey that uncovered a vast literature of other events and occurrences that could also be classified under the term phytoarchaeology: i.e., the relationship between vegetation and archaeology. These include such diverse subjects as: survival of ancient crops, specific plants associated with archaeological remains, the presence of pollen or plant opal phytoliths indicating the nature of ancient environments, plants associated with ancient mines and mining activities, and, not the least, the vast literature on aerial discovery of archaeological remains by vegetational changes (which we have termed *aerial phytoarchaeology*).

To the second author of this book (D. J.) the interest in phytoarchaeology stemmed from studies of vegetation over mineralized areas in the Harz Mountains of Germany. There, mining has been carried out for many centuries, even in pre-medieval times, and there are abundant archaeological signs of this early exploitation of the mineral riches of the region. He has also an abiding interest in archaeology and montane history.

This was a difficult book to write because of the wide range of disciplines covered and the wide dissemination of the literature in several languages. We felt that there was a need to encapsulate the whole field in a single volume, the first to appear on this important and fascinating subject. Although this is the world's first book on phytoarchaeology, we hope it will not be the last, and that we will have succeeded in stimulating fresh interest in the field and will have encouraged others to follow in our footsteps and send us details of new case histories.

This work would not have been possible without the help and cooperation of many people who took the trouble to write to us following a letter that we sent to university departments and institutions of anthropology, archaeology, geology, botany and others, in Europe and elsewhere. Numerous correspondents gave us a bibliography as well as fresh leads to follow in our search for new knowledge in a literature that was often as well hidden as the archaeological features that it described. We thank these helpful persons who supplied us not only with references, but with manuscripts and illustrations as well. We regret not being able to name them individually as they are far too numerous to list, but have gratefully acknowledged illustrative material in the legends in this book. We thank these correspondents as a whole. They were the foundations upon which this book was created.

Robert R. Brooks,
Palmerston North,
New Zealand.

Dieter Johannes
Bonn, West Germany.

January, 1989.

PART I

GENERAL PRINCIPLES

Chapter 1
GENERAL INTRODUCTION

Despite the traditional belief that mankind first appeared on earth in 4004 B.C., the emergence of man and his precursors from the lower animals can now be traced back for several million years. It is the essence of man that he adapted materials for his own use and shaped his environment to his own convenience. He fashioned tools and utensils, made shelters, formed the surface of the earth, and left behind not only his own remains, but also artifacts associated with his occupancy of the land.

Archaeology serves to provide evidence for the story of man, particularly in those periods where there was no written record. For much of Europe the written record was contemporaneous with the Roman occupation, but even so, little would have been known about life at that time had it not been for the activities of later archaeologists whose efforts have uncovered so much evidence about the past.

Serious archaeology as opposed to simple grave robbing, had its beginnings in the 18th Century. It may be called the collecting period, an important era even though marked by an attitude that would today be described as dilettantism. The archaeologist was then principally a collector of *objets d'art* for museums or private collections. The period had its zenith at the turn of the 18th Century when Napoleon plundered the treasures of Ancient Egypt and brought many of them back to Paris.

Scientific archaeology began in the middle of the 19th Century and opened up vast new horizons of hitherto unknown civilizations principally in the Middle East and Asia Minor. The work of early scientific archaeologists was rendered easy when there were obvious surface indications of archaeological features; e.g., Egyptian pyramids—to take an extreme example. Elsewhere in the Middle East where sites had been occupied for thousands of years, the erection of new buildings upon the ruins of the old, resulted in the build-up of artificial hills or mounds known as tells, which were easily recognizable.

The task of the archaeologist has become much more difficult now that the most easily recognizable sites have been discovered and explored. Reliance is being made increasingly on more sophisticated approaches to the problem. In this modern era when man has made such enormous changes to his environment, there is a tendency to believe that ancient man had little or no influence in this respect. This is not so however. Even the so-called most primitive and ancient of societies (e.g., the Australian aborigines) were able to affect their environment to a degree sufficient to leave traces still present today.

One of the most important anthropogenic modifications of the environment is changes in vegetation by advertent or inadvertent human activities. It is the different kinds of relationships between vegetation and archaeology which is the dominant theme of this book.

We have coined the term *phytoarchaeology* to describe these relationships; it embraces a wide variety of different themes, all of which are discussed. These are: the vegetation of ancient mine workings, chemical analysis of vegetation to detect ancient archaeological sites, the influence of trade routes on plant distributions, plant indicators of anthropologically-modified soils, present-day survival of ancient crops, plant remains used for reconstruction of ancient environments and climates, vegetation changes over specific archaeological· sites, plant mapping and statistical treatment of data, and finally, aerial phytoarchaeology. It is in aerial work that phytoarchaeology has perhaps achieved its greatest refinement. Airmen in both World Wars noticed that banks, ditches, lynchets, barrows, and buried foundations of roads and buildings became visible from the air due to changes in vegetation (crops or wild plants) caused by changes in the substrate. There is now a vast literature on the subject.

In a work of relatively modest length it is clearly impossible to present all aspects of phytoarchaeology and its extensive literature. The approach that we have adopted is to present the basic theory of each topic, give a few case histories, and present an up-to-date reference list of the most important literature at the end of each chapter so that the reader can do follow-up study if desired. This approach is particularly important for aerial archaeological work where the literature is so vast.

A problem encountered by the English-speaking student of phytoarchaeology and its related fields is that much of the literature is in foreign languages, notably German and French. Much of this literature has been translated and its elements incorporated in this book.

Part I is concerned with all aspects of phytoarchaeology except remote sensing, which is dealt with in Part II. The treatment of aerial phytoarchaeology is by region and is clearly biased towards those parts of the world, primarily Europe and the Americas, where so much of this work has been carried out.

The assembling of data for this book was difficult because there is no centralized index source such as *Chemical Abstracts* and *Biological Abstracts* which are so useful for chemists and biologists in non-archaeological fields. We had to rely on letters sent to relevant experts, institutions, and university departments in the fields of archaeology, botany, geology, anthropology, etc. throughout Europe and elsewhere. Inevitably, some references will have been left out, but this is the price we must pay for attempting to write a single-volume book on a multidisciplinary subject.

The information in this book covers all the continents from the high Arctic to southern Oceania, and encompasses a variety of cultures from the "primitive" hunter-gatherer societies of Australia to the sophisticated civilizations of Greece and Rome. The time span of the work is from about 20 000 B.P. (before present) up to the 19th Century. The emphasis, is however, on prehistoric or classical cultures rather than on those of medieval or more recent periods. Each time frame does deserve some mention since each has lessons in terms of techniques of discovery and cultural evaluation.

This book is interdisciplinary in its scope, and should be of practical scientific interest to teachers, and students, scientists, hobbyists, and workers in underdeveloped countries. It should also be of practical interest to exploration geologists concerned with rediscovering old mines and re-exploiting them. The book covers a wide range of fields including archaeology, botany, chemistry, palynology, statistics, aviation technology, photography, history, remote sensing, history of trade routes, pedology and agronomy. It is also hoped that the book will be appreciated not only by non-scientists but also by workers in unrelated scientific fields. In this era of scientific specialization where few dare to stray beyond the confines of their own disciplines, we hope the readers of this book will pause to see the whole picture rather than just a small part of it. If we can achieve this broader appreciation, we will be well satisfied.

Chapter 2

GEOBOTANY AND EXPLOITATION
OF ANCIENT MINES

2.1 INTRODUCTION

Geobotanical methods of exploration have been used for many centuries and have been reviewed by Brooks (1983, 1986). The technique depends on identification of vegetation patterns associated with a specific type of mineralization or mine site.

It has been known since Roman times, that natural vegetation reflects to some extent the presence of minerals or water beneath the surface of the terrain, and the early prospectors for ores in China and Europe, have been aware for at least 400 years that there is a relationship between vegetation and its substrate. Though some of the early writings on plant indicators of ores and minerals contained fanciful or far-fetched material, many of these early observations are as valid today as they were several centuries ago. For example we can quote Agricola (1556) observing that:

> . . . in a place where there is a multitude of trees, if a long row of them at an unusual time lose their verdure, and become black and discoloured, and frequently fall by the violence of the wind, beneath this spot there is a vein. Likewise along a course where a vein extends, there grows a certain herb of fungus which is absent from adjacent space, or sometimes even from the neighborhood of the veins. By these signs of nature a vein can be discovered.

In geobotanical methods of prospecting, the interpretation of the significance of the vegetation cover is carried out in a number of ways. These are: studying the nature and distribution of plant communities; observing the nature and distribution of individual indicator plants; studying morphological changes in vegetation (e.g., color changes); examining of any of the above by aerovisual observations, by aerial photography, or by satellite imagery.

One of the problems of geobotany as opposed to biogeochemistry (chemical analysis of vegetation), is that although the latter can be carried out quite easily by someone not possessing botanical knowledge, the same is not true for geobotanical methods of prospecting. An expert geobotanist should have some knowledge of a wide range of disciplines such as biochemistry, biogeography, botany, chemistry, ecology, geology and plant physiology. Few persons will have expertise in more than a few of these disciplines so that often a team will be desirable for field work.

Although the main aim of geobotanical studies has usually been the discovery of new mineral deposits, the technique is equally well suited to the discovery of ancient mine workings together with their associated artifacts. In many cases, the presence of ancient workings is indicated by mine tips that the passage of time has not been able to eradicate, so that the use of geobotanical indicators is unnecessary. There are cases, however, where only geobotany has been able to reveal the presence of mining sites and the technique has clearly shown its value for this purpose.

2.2 METHODS OF GEOBOTANICAL PROSPECTING

2.2.1 Plant Indicators of Minerals and Mining Sites

Indicator plants are species found over mineralized ground and are of two main types: local and universal. Local indicators have only local indicating properties and at other sites they may also grow over non-mineralized ground. By contrast, universal indicators indicate minerals at all sites where they occur and therefore are of great use in exploration.

Indicator plants have been known for many years, the 17th century copper miners of Scandinavia were guided to their targets by the local indicator *Viscaria alpina*, which was known as the "kisplante" (pyrite plant) and which even today is found over the ancient copper mines of Røros in central Norway (Vogt, 1942).

The study of indicator plants has been hindered by the existence of a persistent folklore on the alleged indicating ability of some species. A myth once established, is often perpetuated by a string of review articles which merely quote previous reviewers. A good example of this is furnished by the work of Nemec et al. (1936) who alleged that the horsetail, *Equisetum palustre*, in Czechoslovakia contained 610 mg/kg (ppm) gold in its ash. Subsequent work by Cannon et al. (1968) indicated that the ash never contained more than 1 mg/kg. It is not suggested that Nemec et al. falsified their data, but they do appear to have been mistaken in that they precipitated sulphides from solutions of plant material, weighed the precipitate and assumed it was all gold. In fact, as we now know, copper, arsenic, and lead, all of which form insoluble sulphides are much more common in horsetails than is gold. In a later paper, Brussell (1978) claimed to have discovered gold in the emission spectrum of the ash of *E. hyemale* from the United States, but the spectral lines used were weak lines of gold subject to massive interference from other elements in the plant material.

The myth of gold accumulation by *Equisetum* species was finally laid to rest by the work of Brooks et al. (1981) who found massive quantities of arsenic (781 mg/kg in dried material) in horsetails growing over gold mines in Nova Scotia. In no case was gold detectable in the samples. However, since arsenic is often associated geochemically with gold, horsetails can still be indicators of old gold mines, discussed below.

A list of indicator plants for mineral deposits (Brooks, 1986) is given in Table 2.1 and is an update of data from Brooks (1983). The table is conservative in that it does not include some of the "classical" indicators unless modern work has confirmed their status. A feature of the table is the very large number of taxa which indicate copper. This is because of the importance and extent of the copper/cobalt deposits of Central Africa which support a diverse copper/cobalt tolerant flora described in more detail by Brooks and Malaisse (1985).

TABLE 2.1 Plant indicators of mineral deposits.

Species	Family	Locality	References
BORON			
Eurotia ceratoides (L)	Chenopodiaceae	USSR	1
Limonium suffruticosum (L)	Plumbaginaceae	USSR	1
Salsola nitraria	Chenopodiaceae	USSR	1
COBALT			
Crassula alba (L)	Crassulaceae	Zaïre	2
Crotalaria cobalticola (U)	Fabaceae	Zaïre	3,4
Haumaniastrum robertii (U)	Lamiaceae	Zaïre	5
Silene cobalticola (U)	Caryophyllaceae	Zaïre	4
COPPER			
Acalypha cupricola (U)	Euphorbiaceae	Zaïre	38
A. dikuluwensis (U)	Euphorbiaceae	Zaïre	6
Aeollanthus biformifolius (U)	Lamiaceae	Zaïre	7
Anisopappus hoffmanianus (U)	Asteraceae	Zaïre	6
Armeria maritima (L)	Plumbaginaceae	Wales	8,9,10
Ascolepis metallorum (U)	Cyperaceae	Zaïre	6

Species	Family	Locality	References
Becium empetroides (U)	Lamiaceae	Zambia	38
B. homblei (L)	Lamiaceae	Zaïre/Zambia	11
B. peschianum (U)	Lamiaceae	Zaïre	6
Bulbostylis barbata (U)	Cyperaceae	Australia	12
B. burchelli (L)	Cyperaceae	Australia	13
Commelina zigzag (U)	Commelinaceae	Zaïre	6
Crotalaria cobalticola (U)	Fabaceae	Zaïre	4
C. francoisiana (U)	Fabaceae	Zaïre	6
Cyanotis cupricola (U)	Commelinaceae	Zaïre	6
Ecbolium lugardae (L)	Acanthaceae	S.W. Africa	13,14
Elsholtzia haichowensis (L)	Lamiaceae	China	15
Eschscholzia mexicana (L)	Papaveraceae	USA	16
Gladiolus actinomorphanthus (U)	Iridaceae	Zaïre	6
G. klattianus subsp. angustifolius (U)	Iridaceae	Zaïre	6
G. peschianus (U)	Iridaceae	Zaïre	6
G. tshombeanus subsp. parviflorus (U)	Iridaceae	Zaïre	6
Gutenbergia cuprophila (U)	Asteraceae	Zaïre	6
Gypsophila patrini (L)	Caryophyllaceae	USSR	17
Haumaniastrum katangense (U)	Lamiaceae	Zaïre	6
H. robertii (U)	Lamiaceae	Zaïre	5,6
Helichrysum leptolepis (L)	Asteraceae	S.W. Africa	13,14
Impatiens balsamina (L)	Balsaminaceae	India	18
Lindernia damblonii (U)	Scrophulariaceae	Zaïre	6
L. perennis (U)	Scrophulariaceae	Zaïre	6
Lychnis alpina (L)	Caryophyllaceae	Fennoscandia	19,20
Minuartia verna (L)	Caryophyllaceae	UK	8
Pandiaka metallorum (U)	Amaranthaceae	Zaïre	6
Polycarpaea corymbosa (L)	Caryophyllaceae	India	21
P. spirostylis (L)	Caryophyllaceae	Australia	22,23
Rendlia cupricola (U)	Poaceae	Zaïre	6
Sopubia metallorum (U)	Scrophulariaceae	Zaïre	6
S. neptunii (U)	Scrophulariaceae	Zaïre	6
Sporobolus stelliger (U)	Poaceae	Zaïre	6
S. deschampsioides (U)	Poaceae	Zaïre	6
Tephrosia s. nov. (L)	Poaceae	Queensland	12
Vernonia cinerea (L)	Asteraceae	India	21
V. ledocteanus (U)	Asteraceae	Zaïre	6

IRON

Species	Family	Locality	References
Acacia patens (L)	Fabaceae	Australia	24
Burtonia polyzyga (L)	Fabaceae	Australia	24
Calythrix longiflora (L)	Myrtaceae	Australia	24
Chenopodium rhadinostachyum (L)	Chenopodiaceae	Australia	24
Eriachne dominii (L)	Poaceae	Australia	24
Goodenia scaevolina (L)	Goodeniaceae	Australia	24

LEAD

Species	Family	Locality	References
Alyssum wulfenianum (U)	Brassicaceae	Austria/Italy	25
Thlaspi rotundifolium subsp. *cepaeifolium* (U)	Brassicaceae	Austria/Italy	25

Species	Family	Locality	References
	MANGANESE		
Crotalaria florida			
var. *congolensis* (L)	Fabaceae	Zaïre	4
Maytenus bureauvianus (L)	Celastraceae	New Caledonia	26
	NICKEL		
Alyssum bertolonii (U)	Brassicaceae	Italy	27
A. pintodasilvae (U)	Brassicaceae	Portugal	28
A. spp. of Section			
Odontarrhena (U)	Brassicaceae	S. Europe	29
Hybanthus			
austrocaledonicus (U)	Violaceae	New Caledonia	30
H. floribundus (L)	Violaceae	Australia	31,32
Lychnis alpina			
var. *serpentinicola* (L)	Caryophyllaceae	Fennoscandia	33
	SELENIUM AND URANIUM		
Aster venustus (L)	Asteraceae	USA	34
Astragalus albulus (L)	Fabaceae	USA	34
A. argillosus (L)	Fabaceae	USA	34
A. confertiflorus (L)	Fabaceae	USA	34
A. pattersoni (U)	Fabaceae	USA	34
A. preussi (U)	Fabaceae	USA	34
A. thompsonae	Fabaceae	USA	34
	ZINC		
Armeria halleri (L)	Plumbaginaceae	Pyrenees	35
Hutchinsia alpina (L)	Brassicaceae	Pyrenees	35
Minuartia verna (L)	Caryophyllaceae	W. Europe	36
Thlaspi calaminare (U)	Brassicaceae	W. Europe	36
Thlaspi ssp. (U)	Brassicaceae	S. Europe	37
Viola calaminaria (U)	Violaceae	W. Europe	36

L—local indicator
U—universal indicator

References:
1 Buyalov and Shvyryayeva (1961)
2 Malaisse et al. (1979)
3 Brooks et al. (1977)
4 Duvigneaud (1959)
5 Brooks (1977)
6 Duvigneaud and Denaeyer-De Smet (1963)
7 Malaisse et al. (1978)
8 Ernst (1969b)
9 Farago et al. (1980)
10 Henwood (1857)
11 Howard-Williams (1970)
12 Nicolls et al. (1965)
13 Cole (1971)
14 Cole and Le Roex (1978)
15 Se Sjue-Tzsin and Sjuj Ban-Lian (1953)
16 Chaffee and Gale (1976)
17 Nesvetaylova (1961)
18 Aery (1977)
19 Brooks and Crooks (1980)
20 Brooks et al. (1979b)
21 Ventakesh (1964)
22 Brooks and Radford (1978)
23 Skertchly (1897)
24 Cole (1965)
25 Reeves and Brooks (1983a)
26 Jaffré (1977)
27 Minguzzi and Vergnano (1948)
28 Menezes de Sequeira (1969)
29 Brooks et al. (1979a)
30 Brooks et al. (1974)
31 Cole (1973)
32 Severne and Brooks (1972)
33 Rune (1953)
34 Cannon (1957)
35 Pulou et al. (1965)
36 Ernst (1968b)
37 Reeves and Brooks (1983b)
38 Brooks et al. (1980)

2.2.2 Plant Communities Indicative of Minerals and Mining Sites

The Russian geologist Karpinsky (1841) was one of the first to recognize that different plant associations exist on varying geological substrates such as sandstones, clays, limestones etc., and that this distribution might be used to characterize the geology of the area concerned. Karpinsky concluded that reliance should be placed on an examination of the whole community rather than on one or two characteristic plants within it. His classical work ultimately led to the science of indicator geobotany which is a division of botany concerned with plant distributions and their relationship to the geological and ecological environment.

Indicator geobotany has been brought to a particularly high state of development by workers in the Soviet Union. Indicator communities or characteristic floras will not necessarily indicate mineralization but will often serve to characterize regions where certain types of mineralization are likely to occur. An example of this is the use of serpentine floras for locating ancient chromite mines.

The relationship between plants and bedrock (mineralized or otherwise) is affected by a number of factors including climate, geomorphology, and edaphic variables such as soil pH and composition. It is obvious that a favorable climate will tend to nullify the adverse effects of toxic elements in the substrate. For this reason geobotany tends to be a more powerful tool in semi-arid areas or in Mediterranean-type climates where there is a prolonged dry summer so that the elemental content of the soil moisture gradually increases to an unsupportable level. A further advantage of working in semi-arid areas is that plant mapping is much simpler in a region of light vegetation cover than in thick bush or tropical forest.

The science of indicator geobotany as applied to archaeology has been stimulated by two significant developments during the last decade. The first of these is satellite imagery (see Part II). The second is the development of sophisticated computer-assisted techniques which allow thorough statistical treatment of the raw data in order to evaluate very subtle variations in the composition of the plant community.

2.2.3 Characteristic Floras and Mining Sites

Apart from species changes in vegetation over mining sites compared to plants growing over the surrounding background, certain types of mineralization have a characteristic flora that can be identified readily without mapping procedures. These include basiphilous (limestone), halophyte, selenium, serpentine, cupricolous, and zinc (*galmei*) floras (Brooks, 1983; 1987). Not all of these are really relevant to the search for ancient mining activities but some, particularly zinc and cupricolous floras, are. Use of these heavy-metal floras will be discussed under specific case histories below.

2.2.4 The Elements of Phytosociology

Many of the European studies of vegetation over mineral deposits and ancient mining sites have used the technique of *phytosociology* to classify and describe the flora of these sites. Phytosociology is based on the fundamental work of Braun-Blanquet (1932) in France and is commonly used and studied in most of continental Europe though not in the English-speaking world. Some mention of the basic elements of this science will now be made as it is referred to extensively in the remainder of this chapter and elsewhere in the book.

Phytosociology is a branch of phytogeography and is concerned with the classification of plant communities found at specific types of site in a given region or even worldwide. The system is hierarchical with the *Class* being at the top of the system. The Class is followed by the *Order, Alliance, Association,* and *Subassociation.* The phytosociological units have been capitalized throughout this book in order to avoid confusion with non-phytosociological nouns of the same name.

The most commonly recorded phytosociological unit is the Association as shown in Tables 2.2, 2.3, and 2.4. The Association has its own character species and is subdivided into

Subassociations defined by the so-called *differentials*. It is also usual to list *companions* commonly found in the Associations or Subassociations. The higher units of the hierarchy also have their character species.

By convention, the first word of each phytosociological unit has a specific type of ending as follows. The Class has the ending -etea as for example *Violetea*, the Order ends with -alia as in *Violetalia*, the Alliance ends with -ion as in *Thlaspion*, and the Association has an -etum ending as in *Thlaspietum*. These forms are shown in Tables 2.2, 2.3, and 2.4.

It must be emphasized that the Class is a very far-reaching classification governing many Orders, Alliances and Associations. For example, it has been suggested by Ernst (1974) that all of the metal-tolerant plants of Europe belong to the Class Violetea.

The system of phytosociological classification used by European scientists can be extremely complicated and confusing. For the sake of clarity, we have simplified the system when it is described in this book.

TABLE 2.2   The Thlaspietum cepaeifolii Association (Ernst 1964).

Height above sea level: 580–2100 m
Percentage cover: 30–90
Character species of the Association:
          Thlaspi rotundifolium subsp. *cepaeifolium*
Character species of the Alliance Galio-Minuartion:
          Poa alpina
          Galium anisophyllum
          Dianthus sylvestris
Character species of the Class Violetea:
          Minuartia verna
          Silene cucubalus
Companions:
          Thymus polytrichus
          Molinia caerulea
          MOSSES
          Tortella tortuosa
          Cephaloziella starkei
          Bryum caespitosum
          Racomitrium canescens
          LICHEN
          Cladonia pyxidata

After: Ernst (1974) by courtesy of Gustav Fischer Verlag, Stuttgart.

TABLE 2.3   The Minuartio-Thlaspietum alpestris Association (Koch, 1932).

Height above sea level: 170–610 m
Percentage cover: 50–100
Character species of the Association:

 Thlaspi alpestre
 Minuartia verna

Character species of the Cochlearia Subassociation:

 Cochlearia officinalis

Character species of the Plantago Subassociation:

 Plantago lanceolata
 Anthoxanthum odoratum
 Achillea millefolium
 Leontodon autumnalis
 Lotus corniculatus
 Leontodon hispidus
 Rhytidiadelphus squarrosus

Character species of the Order Violetalia:

 Festuca ovina
 Agrostis tenuis

Character species of the Class Violetea:

 Minuartia verna
 Silene cucubalus

Companions:

 Rumex acetosa
 Euphrasia nemorosa
 Thymus serpyllum
 Campanula rotundifolia
 Linum catharticum
 Cerastium fontanum
 Galium saxatile
 Viola riviniana
 V. lutea
 Ranunculus acris
 Hieracium pilosella
 Arabis hirsuta
 Carex caryophyllea
 MOSSES
 Weissia viridula
 Bryum caespitosum
 Pohlia nutans
 Pleurozium schreberi
 Eurhynchium swartzii
 LICHENS
 Cladonia rangiformis
 C. pyxidata
 C. mitis
 C. coccifera
 Peltigera canina
 Cornicularia aculeata

After: Ernst (1974) by courtesy of Gustav Fisher Verlag, Stuttgart.

TABLE 2.4 The Violetum calaminariae rhenanicum Association (Ernst, 1969b).

Height above sea level: 140–330 m
Percentage cover: 50–100
Character species of the Association:

  Viola calaminaria subsp. *calaminaria*
  Armeria maritima var. *calaminaria*

Character species of the Alliance Thlaspion calaminaris

  Thlaspi alpestre

Character species of the Order Violetalia

  Festuca ovina
  Agrostis tenuis

Character species of the Class Violetea

  Minuartia verna
  Silene cucubalus

Companions

  Rumex acetosa
  Pimpinella saxifraga
  Polygala vulgaris
  Euphrasia stricta
  Thymus serpyllum
  Campanula rotundifolia
  Potentilla erecta
  Ranunculus acris
  Cerastium fontanum
  Galium mollugo
  Linum catharticum
  Hieracium umbellatum
  Lotus corniculatus
  Trifolium pratense
  T. repens
  MOSSES
  Weissia viridula
  Bryum caespitosum
  Ceratodon purpureus
  Cephaloziella starkei
  Pohlia nutans
  Pleurozium schreberi
  Pohlia annotina
  Eurhynchium swartzii
  Rhytidiadelphus squarrosus
  Climacium dendroides
  LICHENS
  Cladonia rangiferina
  C. chlorophaea
  C. subulata
  C. furcata
  Peltigera canina
  Stereocaulon nanodes

After: Ernst (1974) by courtesy of Gustav Fisher Verlag, Stuttgart.

2.3 CASE HISTORIES OF GEOBOTANICAL INDICATORS OF ANCIENT MINE SITES

2.3.1 Central Africa

The copper/cobalt deposits of Zaïre and Zambia are the largest in the world with some 100 outcrops spread over an area of about 25,000 km². One of the best known of the "copper flowers" is *Haumaniastrum robertii*, a member of the mint (Lamiaceae) family, found to the west of the Shaban Copper Arc (see Fig. 2.1) in Zaïre. It is found primarily in the region between Kolwezi and Likasi. To the east of the Shaban Copper Arc, near Lubumbashi, this species is replaced by its close relative *H. katangense*. In spite of its reputation as a "copper flower", *H. robertii* is probably an indicator of cobalt rather than copper. It can accumulate up to 1% cobalt in its dried leaves (Brooks, 1977). *H. katangense* is an indicator of copper and grows exclusively on copper-rich soils (Brooks et al. 1980, 1987). It can contain a maximum of 0.20% cobalt and 0.84% copper (Brooks et al. 1987). The distribution of *H. katangense* has lead to important and exciting discoveries (Plaen et al. 1982).

Haumaniastrum katangense has escaped from its original habitat and is found on man-made substrates which are lightly or heavily mineralized in copper. Such substrates include sites of furnaces, traditionally used in precolonial days for the production of small copper crosses; sites of exploitation of copper minerals during the early decades of colonization; and the verges of dirt roads which have been dressed with gangue from mining activities (the copper content of this gangue can sometimes approach 3%).

The full distribution of *H. katangense* has been described by Malaisse and Brooks (1982). We will here only discuss its distribution over sites of ancient precolonial mining and smelting. These sites can be identified by dense carpets of *H. katangense* (and occasionally *H. robertii*) which grow over them. Only at one locality (Luisha) are the two species found together. They tend to occupy separate and complementary ecological niches, *H. robertii* preferring rocky debris such as the lower slopes of excavated material, and *H. katangense* preferring level ground with slightly compressed soils where stagnant water is found during the rainy season.

During the precolonial period (14th century), the Kabambian culture developed in Zaïre (Maret, 1979). One of the most important artifacts of this culture is copper in the form of *croisettes* (crosses) used originally as ingots and later as currency. In the course of the Kabambian, the crosses diminished in size and became more uniform. They gradually evolved into an all-purpose unit of value. These copper crosses, which are well dated, provide a valuable clue for dating other sites in Zaïre. The artisans used copper smelters which were located at rather specialized sites. The furnaces were backed onto abandoned termite hills which thereby provided a gradient suitable for the flow of molten copper. They were surrounded by earth walls about a meter high which must have contaminated the molds and smelting conduits. The furnaces were situated near *dambos* (periodically-inundated savanna) or near rivers which provided the necessary water. The sites were also near stands of *Pterocarpus tinctorius* which were used to produce charcoal. A reconstructed smelter is shown in Plate 2.1.

The old sites discovered along the Luano, Ruashi, Kilobelobe, or Kafubu rivers (Fig. 2.2) have the same common characteristics: the adjacent open forest has disappeared; there are few species growing on the summits of the termite mounds; *H. katangense* grows in a dense circle along the base of the mounds (Plate 2.2). These sites are sometimes arranged in groups of 30 along 5 km of river bank, as is the case at Ruashi. Each occurrence of *H. katangense* faithfully delineates a subsoil containing an archaeological horizon linked to a copper smelter. Within a radius of three or four meters, this horizon furnishes remains of conduits, molds and rejected copper crosses, together with abundant smelter waste. This waste is composed of partially-melted malachite, or copper amalgamated with the earth of the retaining walls, and also includes scoria and charcoal. Typical artifacts from these sites are shown in Fig. 2.3.

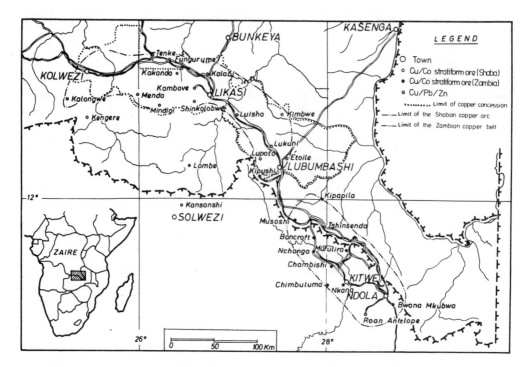

Fig. 2.1 Map of Central Africa showing the Shaban Copper Arc and Zambian Copperbelt.

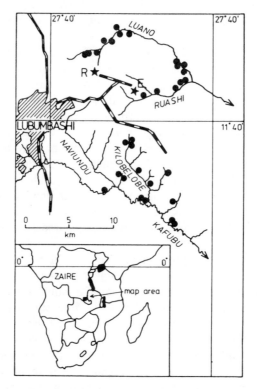

Fig. 2.2 Site of ancient copper smelters near Lubumbashi, Shaba Province, Zaïre Source: Plaen et al. (1982). By courtesy of Pergamon Press, Oxford.

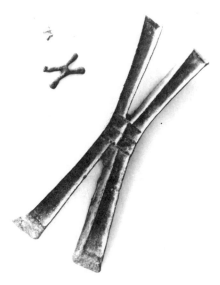

Fig. 2.3 Typical artifacts from ancient Kabambian copper smelting sites in Shaba Province, Zaïre.

Detailed analysis of the contents of one of the sites (near Kilobelobe) has been carried out. Beneath an overburden of humic soil not exceeding 10 cm in depth, layers of 5–9 cm thickness contained metallurgical residues. One typical excavation of 2 m^2 area and 10–20 cm depth, revealed 200 g of charcoal and copper slag, 350 g of fragments of burnt clay from furnaces and conduits; 160 g of malachite and 150 g of copper.

A phytosociological study of the Kilobelobe site shows a carpet dominated by *Haumaniastrum katangense* and *Bulbostylis mucronata*. Along the periphery *Nephrolepis undulata* and *Arthraxon quartinianus* are well developed. Several clumps of *Alectra sessiliflora* var. *senegalensis*, *Antherotoma naudinii* and *Polygala* sp. have been observed.

Study of the above stratigraphy and the quantity of waste, showed that activity had been brief and had been confined to a single season. About 200 of these precolonial sites have now been discovered and have led to excavations resulting in the unearthing of many copper crosses ranging in weight from a few grams up to 36 kg. *Haumaniastrum katangense* does not indicate the presence of ancient smelting activities when the remains are buried beneath a thick non-metalliferous surface layer. It should also be noted that not all archaeological sites have been revealed by the presence of *H. katangense* alone. Nevertheless, without the aid of this "copper flower", the number of discoveries would have been only about one third of those so far recorded.

Haumaniastrum katangense is not necessarily unique in Shaba Province in relation to its ability to function as a phytoarchaeological indicator species. The same property is possessed to a lesser degree by *H. robertii* and *Bulbostylis mucronata*. The latter is also found over ancient copper workings at Seruwila, Sri Lanka. Many of these sites appear on aerial photographs (Anon., 1970a) since vegetation is more vigorous over previously-worked terrain and less vigorous over old furnace sites.

2.3.2 Plant Indicators of Ancient Gold Mines

Among the myths that exist in the rich folklore of geobotany is the alleged uptake of gold by species of horsetail (*Equisetum*). A drawing of the common field horsetail (*E. arvense*) is shown in Fig. 2.4. There is some evidence, however, that horsetails frequently do grow over ancient gold mines since these plants appear to favor disturbed ground and are tolerant of arsenic (a frequent companion of gold), an element normally very toxic to plants.

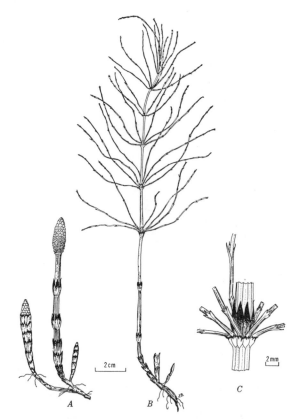

Fig. 2.4 Drawing of a horsetail (*Equisetum arvense* L.). A—fertile stems with spore-producing cones; B—sterile stems with part of rhizome; C—node of sterile stem. Source: Cannon et al. (1968).

The question of the association of horsetails with gold has been investigated by Brooks et al. (1981) who determined gold, arsenic and antimony (all these elements are associated together geochemically) in horsetails growing over abandoned gold mining sites in Nova Scotia, eastern Canada. Six of the 25 species of horsetail were analyzed: *E. arvense, E. fluviatale, E. hyemale, E. palustre, E. scirpioides,* and *E. sylvaticum*. In no case did the gold content of the horsetails exceed 1 mg/kg (ppm) in sharp contrast to the very high values obtained by Nemec et al. (1936). Of particular interest, however, was the very high arsenic content of the samples. Concentrations of this element in the phyllodes ranged from 41–738 mg/kg, accompanying antimony contents of 4–77 mg/kg.

Background arsenic levels in horsetails in Nova Scotia were of the order of 3 mg/kg, a value far higher than for vegetation in general (0.2 mg/kg; Brooks, 1983).

The high arsenic levels in Nova Scotian horsetails result from the highly-arseniferous nature of the Meguma Series rocks covering most of the southern part of Nova Scotia. The rocks are so arseniferous that in many places, such as Montague Mines near Halifax, mining activities have resulted in extensive contamination of water supplies by arsenic.

The tolerance of horsetails to arsenic when combined with the frequency of their occurrence over auriferous mine tailings, leads to the conclusion that the genus *Equisetum* contains species that are in fact local indicators of the gold with which the arsenic is associated. The original mythology may therefore have some basis of fact, albeit based on an *indirect* local association with gold rather than accumulation of this element by the plants.

The gold mines of Nova Scotia date back only to the 19th century and these sites are hardly archaeological in the true sense of the word. However, the research carried out at these sites has served to shed light on the role of horsetails as indirect indicators of gold mineralization. This information is clearly of use in suggesting a way of discovering ancient gold mines from the horsetails growing upon them.

A species of onion (*Allium* sp.) also appears to have the reputation of being an indicator of gold or silver mineralization. Boyle (1979) reports that early Chinese records of the 9th century A.D. describe the association of *A. fistulosum* with silver and *A. bakeri* with gold. This association may be indirect due to the presence of sulphur which is found both in onions and in sulphide minerals which often contain both silver and gold. *Allium* like *Equisetum* also has the reputation of accumulating arsenic and it may well be that both genera are indirect indicators of noble metals via the link with arsenic.

2.3.3 Northern Italy and Southern Austria

Medieval Mining Sites

The Cave del Predil (formerly Raibl) region of northern Italy (Fig. 2.5) is the site of a complex of large and small mines that have been operating since medieval times. The first evidence for lead mining in the region dates back to 1506 A.D., although a manuscript from 1456 A.D. mentions sulphide mining near Raibl. The area near this mine, and the river terraces downstream, are populated by an extraordinary plant with an unusual capability to tolerate and hyperaccumulate lead and zinc. This plant is *Thlaspi rotundifolium* subsp. *cepaeifolium*; its ecology and biogeochemistry have been investigated by Reeves and Brooks (1983a) and Ernst (1974).

The river Silizza (Schlitza) flows from Lago del Predil adjacent to the mines and descends via Tarvisio (Tarvis) into the Gailtal and then via Villach into the Drau River. On the west bank of the Silizza near Cave del Predil and extending into the lower slopes of Monte Re

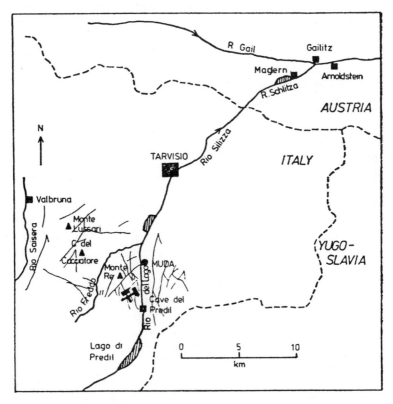

Fig. 2.5 Map of the Cave del Predil area of northern Italy showing medieval and modern lead/zinc mine workings. Source: Reeves and Brooks (1983a). By courtesy of Elsevier Applied Science Publishers, Barking.

(Königsberg) are numerous mine workings which are found as far north as the confluence of the Freddo (Kaltwasser) and Silizza Rivers (Fig. 2.5). The tailings from the workings have been transported into the river where the fluvial sediments and gravels have become stained with dark ore-rich material. The tailings have been transported some distance by the river and have accumulated at various sites downstream such as at Arnoldstein in Austria near the confluence of the Gail and Schlitza rivers. The metallophytes are often found in these accumulations. Their local distribution is therefore from Lago del Predil to Arnoldstein with intermediate occurrences at Muda (Mauth) on the west bank of the Silizza between the Freddo River and Tarvisio, and at Maglern a short distance upstream from Arnoldstein. At the last locality there is also a zinc mine whose tailings make some contribution to the contaminated gravels at this site.

Thlaspi rotundifolium subsp. cepaeifolium is one of the dominant members of a heavy metal plant community described by Ernst (1974) that includes a metal-resistant ecotype of Minuartia verna. Ernst did not include Alyssum wulfenianum (an accumulator of lead) in this community, probably because of its much more restricted distribution to Cave del Predil and its general vicinity. The Thlaspi metallophyte is found at scattered mineralized and contaminated localities from Jauken in Austria some 55 km to the northwest of Cave del Predil to Pecnik-Peca in Jugoslavia some 105 km to the east.

According to Ernst (1974), the soils supporting this Thlaspi subspecies have lead contents ranging from 0.06% (Bleiberg ob Villach) to 0.4% (Jauken), and zinc contents ranging from 0.7% (Crna) to 14.6% (Jauken), together with small amounts of copper (0.01%).

The heavy-metal community associated with the Raibl Mine is known as the Thlaspietum cepaeifolii Association (Ernst, 1964, 1974—see Table 2.2). The physiognomy of this species-poor community is characterized by dark-green cushions of Thlaspi rotundifolium subsp. cepaeifolium and light-green cushions of an ecotype of Minuartia verna that is particularly resistant to heavy metals. The latter is one of the most characteristic plants of sites contaminated by waste from ancient and modern mining activities. The Thlaspietum cepaeifolii Association includes a low-growing Silene cucubalus and scattered dwarf forms of Galium anisophyllum and Poa alpina.

The above community gives the impression of a typical plant assemblage of scree slopes despite the fact that the mineralized soils are level, stable, and finely-divided.

Bronze Age Smelter Sites

Northern Italy is the site of numerous Bronze Age smelter sites (Fig. 2.6) which utilized the nearby copper ores and which were positioned near stands of beech which make the best charcoal for the purpose. Preuschen (1965, 1968) has reported the discovery of several such smelters in the Trento-Lavarone region. Many of these sites were discovered by the absence of vegetation caused by the phytotoxicity of the ores or slags. This toxicity still remains after 3000 years. Preuschen (1968) has catalogued some 35 smelter sites and has recorded that Silene inflata serves as a never-failing indicator of slags left behind by these early Bronze Age smelterers. Other signs of subterranean slags include the stunted physiognomic appearance of the overlying forest.

The use of vegetation in indicating the presence of ancient slag heaps and smelters has been further investigated by Preuschen (1964). He has observed that such sites are often covered with a sward of Vaccinium and Myrtillus shrubs and by a specific community of indicator plants dominated by Silene inflata. He noted that the sites were also covered with specialized mosses, lichens and algae whose identity has not yet been established. When the slags are found below meadowland, the poisonous salts leach from the slags and produce recognizable changes in crops, such as reduction in fruit size and early withering of annuals. Local farmers describe these sites as "Braunflecken" (brown spots) and have noted that top-dressing with nitrogenous fertilizers does nothing to improve crop yields, although the addition of lime does help somewhat.

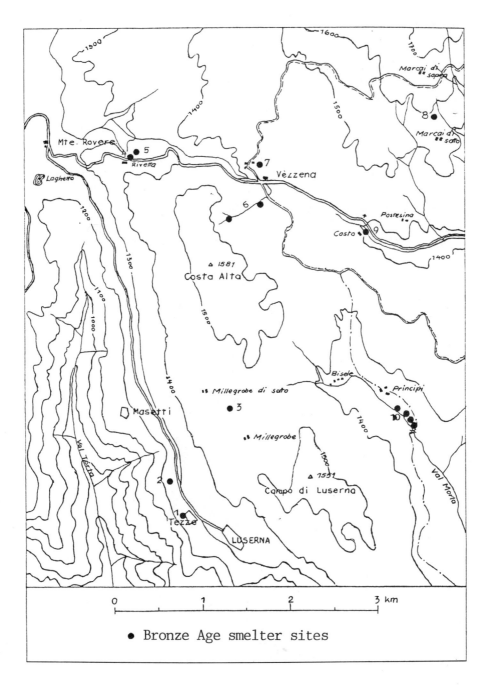

Fig. 2.6 Bronze Age smelter sites in Northern Italy. Some of these were discovered from the nature of their vegetative cover. Source: Preuschen (1965). By courtesy of the editor of *Der Anschnitt*.

2.3.4 The British Isles

Introduction

The Pennine Range of northern England, the Mendips of southwest England, and the mountains of North Wales contain a large number of base metal (lead/zinc/copper) mining sites which in many cases have been worked since Roman times. The spoil heaps and mine tailings of these workings are still in evidence today and provide an environment extremely hostile to both plants and animals. For example, Chisnall and Markland (1971) found that cattle and horses were still dying from lead poisoning by contaminated water (2–5 mg/L lead) adjacent to old Roman mine tips near Matlock in the Pennines.

The location of abandoned lead mines in the British Isles is given in Fig. 2.7. A more detailed maps of these sites in the southern Pennines is given in Fig. 2.8. It is this latter region which has been the most thoroughly studied botanically (e.g. Hajar, 1987).

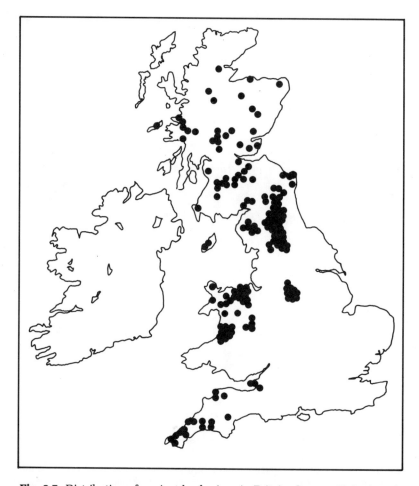

Fig. 2.7 Distribution of ancient lead mines in Britain. Source: Hajar (1987).

Phytosociology of the Flora of Ancient Mine Workings in Britain

The metal-tolerant flora of lead/zinc/copper mineralization has been classified by Ernst (1976) within the phytosociological class Violetea calaminariae. Within the Pennines, Mendips and North Wales is an Association known as the Minuartio-Thlaspietum alpestris (Koch, 1932; Shimwell, 1968; Ernst, 1974). A simplified representation of this important Association is given in Table 2.3 and is based on data from Ernst (1974).

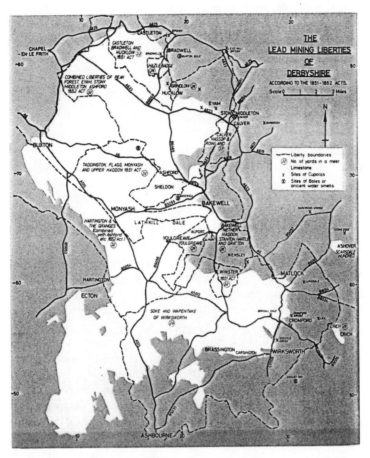

Fig. 2.8 Distribution of lead mines in the southern Pennines. Source: Ford and Rieuwerts (1983). By courtesy of the Peak District Mines Historical Society.

Compared with the heavy-metal communities of western Europe, the Minuartio-Thlaspietum Association is impoverished in numbers of species. Above all, there is a complete absence of *Armeria maritima* and a somewhat rare appearance of *Silene cucubalus*. The plant communities in Britain have furthermore been greatly disturbed by active mining subsequent to the original Roman exploitation.

In addition to the character species of the Class (*Minuartia verna*) and that of the Alliance and local Association (*Thlaspi alpestre*), there are metal-resistant ecotypes of *Festuca ovina* (Wilkins, 1960), *Agrostis tenuis* = *A. capillaris* (Bradshaw et al. 1965), *Rumex acetosa,* and *Euphrasia nemorosa* (Ernst, 1968a).

The Thlaspietum Association can be subdivided into several Subassociations including that of *Cochlearia officinalis* in the higher elevations (470–610 m) of the northern Pennines. The *Plantago lanceolata* Subassociation is found mainly over the less mineralized soils of the southern Pennines. This community is found not only in Britain but also over zinc/lead deposits in Osnabrück in West Germany.

Lead Mines and Vegetation of the Pennine Range

Introduction and history. The lead mines of the Pennine Range of northern England have been worked since before Roman times (Ford and Rieuwerts, 1983). Their distribution in Derbyshire is given in Fig. 2.8. The workings are virtually confined to metalliferous veins in the Carboniferous limestone of the Peak District in Derbyshire. The mineralization is largely galena (lead sulphide) with associated sphalerite (zinc sulphide). The average lead content is about 5% in the veins capable of being worked. It is estimated that some 3–6 million tonnes of lead ores have been recovered since mining began over 2000 years ago. Zinc production is estimated at 250 000–500 000 tonnes. The mines ceased operation by the early 20th century and have been replaced by other mines producing large amounts of barite (barium sulphate), calcite (calcium carbonate), and fluorite (fluorspar). All of these minerals had been discarded as waste during the lead mining period.

Lead ore was probably exploited in the Peak District even in the pre-Roman period, though there is not definite proof of this. It is known however, that there is evidence of Roman exploitation in the shape of lead "pigs" (ingots). At least 27 of these have been recovered and were distinguished by the letters LVT, LVTVD, or LVTVDARES. These refer to the settlement of Lutudarum where the smelting was carried out at a site near Matlock in the southern Pennines.

Very few Roman artifacts have been recovered from the mine sites because of subsequent disturbance, although some objects associated with lead mining operations have been discovered at Elton, Crich, and Longstone Edge. More recently an opencast lead vein bridged by a Roman wall has been discovered at Roystone Grange near Ballidon (Ford and Rieuwerts, 1983). In the Matlock Museum there is a Roman smelting hearth (L. Willies pers. comm.) operated with foot bellows, and is one of only three or four so far discovered in Britain.

After the withdrawal of the Romans, the Saxons and Danes continued mining on a small scale in the 600 years before the Norman Conquest.

The Domesday Survey undertaken in 1086, some 20 years after the Norman Conquest, lists 7 lead smelters at Bakewell, Ashford, Crich and Matlock. The lead was used mainly for castles and numerous religious houses in the 11th, 12th and 13th Centuries.

The period from 1700 to 1750 was one of particularly active mining. Thereafter production remained relatively constant until the middle of the 19th century when a steady decline began. The last operation to close was the Mill Close Mine in Darley Dale. This ceased operations just before World War II.

Vegetation of the Pennine lead mines. The vegetation of spoil heaps and outcrops of the Pennine lead mines has been studied by several workers including Clarke and Clark (1981), Shaw (1984), Shimwell and Laurie (1972), Baker (1987), and Hajar (1987). The vegetation is influenced by a number of unfavorable edaphic factors in addition to the toxic effects of heavy metals such as lead, cadmium and excess zinc. These factors include surface instability, low organic status of the soil, and severe deficiency of plant nutrients such as nitrogen and potassium. The process of colonization is slow and is governed initially by species capable of giving rise to specialized races or ecotypes capable of successful growth and reproduction on otherwise phytotoxic substrates.

Among the most important of the plants that grow on Pennine mine sites are *Minuartia verna* and *Thlaspi alpestre* (Plate 2.3). These are normally considered to be alpine taxa in many parts of Europe, but in Britain they are strongly associated with soils contaminated by heavy metals. This association was noted as early as in the 16th century (Thalius, 1588) in the case of *M. verna,* and in the 19th century (Windsor, 1865) for *T. alpestre.* The distribution of these two metallophytes in the British Isles in relation to the location of lead mines is shown in Fig. 2.9. Within the southern Pennines the distribution of both species (Fig. 2.10) is strongly correlated with the location of local lead mines (Fig. 2.8).

From experiments carried out by Hajar (1987), it appears that *T. alpestre* tends to be more commonly associated with bare soil than does *M. verna,* but the latter is found over a wider range of soil pH values. Both species occupy similar ecological niches (Hajar, 1987); i.e. infertile but somewhat disturbed sites with broken vegetation on metalliferous mining spoil heaps.

In making a general comparison of the above species, Hajar (1987) came to the following conclusions: 1) *T. alpestre* has a more restricted distribution in Europe and the

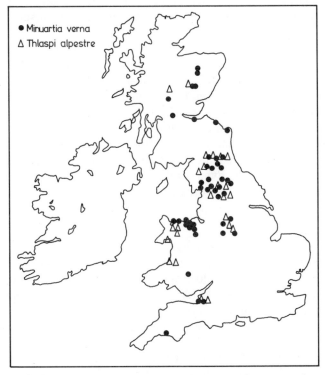

Fig. 2.9 Distribution of *Minuartia verna* and *Thlaspi alpestre* in the British Isles. Compare with Fig. 2.7 for location of lead mines. Source: Hajar (1987).

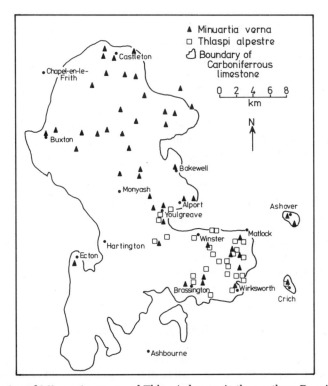

Fig. 2.10 Distribution of *Minuartia verna* and *Thlaspi alpestre* in the southern Pennines. Compare with Fig. 2.8 for location of lead mines. Source: Hajar (1987).

British Isles than does *M. verna;* 2) In Derbyshire, *M. verna* is found over a wider range of soil pH values; 3) *T. alpestre* is particularly associated with high exposures of bare soil; 4) *T. alpestre* may be less restricted to north-facing slopes.

Many other plant species are found over lead-contaminated soils in the Pennine Range. Some of these are listed in Table 2.3. Plants frequently found along with *T. alpestre* and *M. verna* are: *Festuca ovina, F. rubra, Thymus praecox* subsp. *arcticus, Galium sterneri, Koeleria macrantha, Linum catharticum, Campanula rotundifolia, Rumex acetosella, Cerastium fontanum,* and *Trifolium repens.* In the Derbyshire lead mining region, the positions of most of the main veins have been known for several hundred years. There may be cases however, where the distribution of *Minuartia verna* and *Thlaspi alpestre* might indicate the presence of hitherto unrecorded lead veins or outcrops together with associated medieval or even Roman artifacts. Even if this turns out not to be the case, the story of the relationship between vegetation and mine sites this interesting region is still well worth recording.

The Mendip Lead Mining District

Introduction and history. The lead mines of the Mendip Hills of southwest England are situated some 20 km south of the city of Bristol. The mines were known to be in operation in 49 A.D. (6 years after the Roman conquest) and there is some evidence that mining activities began as far back at the 3rd century B.C. (Anon., 1970b). Evidence for mining during Roman times has been afforded by the discovery of 23 dated "pigs" of lead as far afield as St. Valery-sur-Somme in France. Thereafter, the record became obscure until Richard I gave permission for lead mining in 1189 A.D. The Mendip area was divided into four districts (Fig. 2.11) known as the "Charterhouse," "Harptree", "Chewton", and "Wells" Liberties.

The lead mining industry gradually declined due to flooding in the lower levels of the mines, exhaustion of surface workings, and increased competition from foreign ores. All mining operations had ended by 1850. The slags and wastes however, were so rich in lead, and were of such a vast extent, that companies sprang up to reprocess waste material. Silver was also mined and some 3000 ounces had been produced by the end of the 19th century. The reprocessing plants gradually shut down as the price of lead fell: the Waldegrave works in 1876, and the St. Cuthberts works in 1910. These works were once combined under the name of "Priddy Minery" (Fig. 2.12). They offer a rich harvest of interesting remains including smoke flues, ruined buildings, and spoil heaps. Roman remains are also to be found at the site.

The area around the old Priddy smelter is so heavily contaminated that conifers planted in recent years have failed to flourish over the site and its immediate environs (this and other mining sites of the same area are described in the standard work on the subject by Gough, 1967).

Vegetation of the Mendip mining region. The vegetation of the Mendip mining area has not been studied to the same degree as that of the southern Pennines. However, Foster (1970) has noted that in the Mendips the lead-rich areas:

> . . . can often be identified by characteristic types of vegetation. Coarse tussock grass, mosses and heather often form the basis of the plant community. The number of species of flowering plants is limited, but includes common plants such as violets (*Viola* sp.), willow herb (*Epilobium* sp.), and orchid (*Orchis*) species. One unusual plant found in surprising numbers is moonwort (*Botrychium lunaria*).
> The type of vegetation is influenced by four main factors: the topography of the surface, the type of soil, the lead content, and man's activities.
> The surface of the ground often determines the plant types. Where it is rough with steep slopes, soil creep is seen, and the plants found will often include *Calluna* patches, mosses and fungi. The drier south- and west-facing slopes have a more open community with *Orchis mascula* among the grasses.

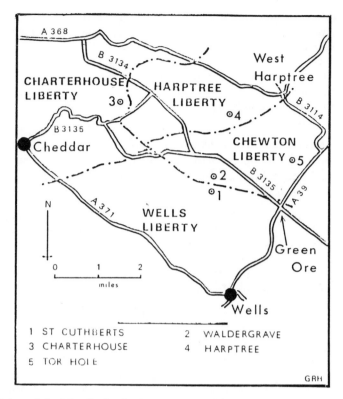

Fig. 2.11 Map of the Mendip lead mines, near Bristol, England. Source: Anon. (1970b)

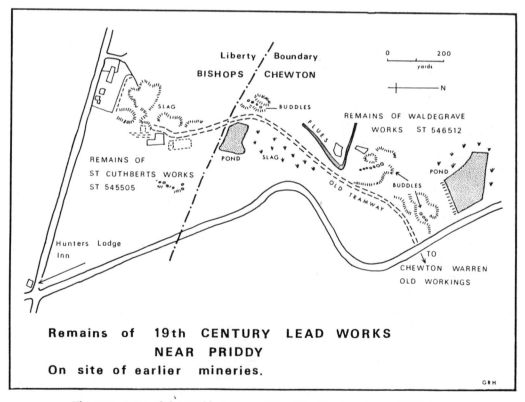

Fig. 2.12 Map of the Priddy Minery, Mendips. Source: Anon. (1970b).

Flat open land tend to have hummocks composed of the larger species of grasses with patches of *Calluna* scrub. Foliose lichens and some thallose lichens (e.g. *Peltigera canina*) are found.

Land used for the mining works has often been colonised by common weeds, possibly because there is normal soil underneath the surface debris.

Much of the soil is coarse, and plants tends to be drought-resistant species, but some areas are liable to flooding, giving a suitable habitat for rushes (*Juncus* sp.) and even marsh marigolds (*Caltha palustris*).

Baker (1974) has studied the occurrence of heavy metal-tolerant plants in the Mendip mining area. Among these is *Silene maritima* which had previously been recorded in the vicinity of old Mendip mine workings by Murray (1896), White (1912), and Marshall (1914). Baker found this species at five stations in the area and his observations were as follows:

[1]—*Blackmoor,* near Charterhouse-on-Mendip . . . 'where also a large number of intermediate forms occurs connecting this species with *Silene cucubalus*' (Murray, 1896). Confirmed by Marsden-Jones and Turrill (1957) and by the author (i.e. A. J. M. Baker) in 1971. The *Silene maritima* population was confined to a small area of vitrified lead slag which also supported a large population of *Thlaspi alpestre*. Many plants showed hybrid characters. Ernst (1968a) visited this area and recorded *S. cucubalus* but not *S. maritima*.

[2]—*Priddy*. *S. maritima* is found about old lead workings (White, 1912) and is plentiful at the Mineries (Murray, 1896). This was confirmed by Marsden-Jones and Turrill (1957) and by the author (A. J. M. B.) in 1970. A large population extended over an area of vitrified lead slag (as at Charterhouse) to short grassy turf off the metal-contaminated soil. Hybrid plants were found growing in association with the taller vegetation as found by Marsden-Jones and Turrill (1957). *Minuartia verna* also occurs at this site. Another site is recorded by Marshall in Murray (1896) as 'on a wall near Priddy'.

[3]—*Silene maritima* has been found '. . . by the streamlet in Long Bottom under Blackdown in no great quantity . . ." (White, 1912) and ". . . by a stream at the foot of Blackdown . . ." (Murray, 1896).

[4]—*Between Shipham and Rowberrow. Silene maritima* was abundant on old mining ground (White, 1912; Marshall, 1914). There is now very little evidence of the calamine workings in this area. One site was inspected by the author (A. J. M. B.) in 1971 just north of Shipham. The workings are largely covered over with a grassy turf. Rocky outcrops where visible, probably mark the location of shallow calamine pits. A few plants of *S. maritima* were recorded at the periphery of these outcrops along with *Thlaspi alpestre*.

[5]—*Between Star and Shipham. S. maritima* was found on ground left hummocky by former calamine workings, now calcareous pasture. The species was found in small quantity here and was associated with *Thlaspi alpestre, Genista tinctoria* and *Anthyllis vulneraria*. Plants were found along the periphery of calamine pits as above, and also on more rocky limestone cliffs. First recorded by Burton in 1963 and confirmed by the author (A. J. M. B.) in 1972."

Dolfrwynog in North Wales

Introduction and history. The copper bog of Dolfrwynog in North Wales (Fig. 2.13) lies in the middle of a district with a long history of mining of copper, gold, silver, and other metals (Andrew, 1910). The ancient Britons and Welsh were fully aware of the precious metals which lay within their hills. Three Welsh chieftains are known to have possessed chariots of gold, and it is inferred that this gold was derived from the mines which the Welsh worked at an early date. Many gold ornaments have been unearthed from time to time, and as their style differs entirely from that of the Christian period, they are believed to predate that period. It is known that the Romans under Julius Caesar worked minerals in various parts of the British Isles and there are many indications of Roman mine workings where gold

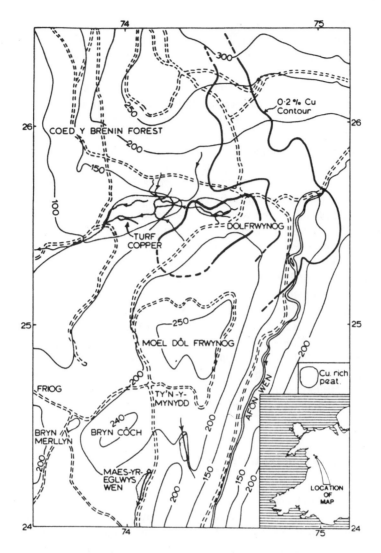

Fig. 2.13 Map of the Coed-y-Brenin area, North Wales, showing the location of cupriferous bogs. Source: Andrews and Fuge (1986). By courtesy of the editor of *Applied geochemistry*.

must have been the principal metal sought. One of the most remarkable of these is outside Merionethshire ai Ogofau in Carmarthen where there are undoubted traces of Roman occupancy. Another such locality in Merioneth is at the banks of the All-y-Wenallt.

Gold was also mined near Dolfrwynog in the 17th century by Thomas Bushell, who rented royal mines and erected a mint at Aberystwyth to produce coins for the Royalists during the Civil War. His was the only mint outside the control of the Parliamentarians. During the war he lent Charles I some 1 500 000 pounds. It is believed that Bushell worked the mines mainly for gold and paid the king one-tenth as a royalty.

Dean (1844) reported the existence of gold at Dolfrwynog and mining began in the same year. In 1847 the North Wales Silver Lead Copper and Gold Mining Co., with a capital of 150 000 pounds, was floated in order to work the lodes at Dolfrwynog and at nearby sites. Some 300 tonnes of ore were milled and produced 7.75 lbs. of gold then worth 350 pounds sterling. The second half of the 19th century witnessed a boom in Welsh gold mining which finally ended by the outbreak of World War I. Most of the gold came from the Dolgellau Gold Belt of which Dolfrwynog is a part.

Porphyry copper was reported by Rice and Sharp (1976) from the eastern flanks of the Harlech Dome where Cambrian sediments have been intruded by diorite sills, stocks and minor dykes. The copper mineralization consists of veinlets of chalcopyrite occurring in both the diorites and sediments.

The Dolfrwynog Bog contains a compressed peat with an average copper content of just under 1%. During the early decades of the 19th century, the peat was dried and burnt and the ash, containing about 2.5% copper, was sent to Swansea for smelting. The project was abandoned in the 1820s due to economic factors (Henwood, 1857).

Vegetation of the Dolfrwynog Bog. The vegetation of the Dolfrwynog Bog has been described by Baker (1974) and Farago et al. (1980). The main indicator species are: *Silene maritima, Armeria maritima, Minuartia verna, Agrostis capillaris, Rumex acetosa,* and *Calluna vulgaris.* Species such as *Vaccinium myrtillus* and *Ulex gallii,* though common in the general area, are completely absent where copper concentrations in the substrate are high.

Ernst (1969a) has carried out a pollen survey of the copper-rich peat of Dolfrwynog and has shown that the copper-resistant population of *Armeria maritima* and *Minuartia verna* has been in existence since the 12th century A.D., though copper mining in the 1820s caused a severe depletion in the numbers of these two taxa.

The heavy metal vegetation of Dolfrwynog differs from that of the Pennine lead mines in that it belongs to a different phytosociological Association: the Sileno-Armerietum maritimae metallicolae. Braun-Blanquet and Tüxen (1952) have classified this community within the Armerion maritimae Alliance.

Ernst (1974) has included the following species within the Association: *Silene maritima* and *Armeria maritima* (character species of the Association); *Agrostis capillaris* (differential of the Order Violetalia); *Minuartia verna* (character species of the Class Violetea calaminariae); the companions *Thymus praecox* subsp. *arcticus,* and *Calluna vulgaris.*

2.3.5 The Eastern Harz Region (East Germany)

Introduction and History

Space does not permit a full recording of all ancient and medieval mining sites and their associated vegetation in Europe, but special mention must be made of the base metal (mainly copper) deposits of the eastern Harz. The Mansfeld copper deposits (Fig. 2.14) are situated in East Germany and have been described by Schubert (1953/54) and by Mahn et al. (1986). These deposits lie in the form of a basin with most of the mining shafts and spoil heaps along the perimeter (see Fig. 2.14).

The heavy metal plant communities over these mine wastes are influenced by the age of these wastes which date back to well before the 12th century A.D. By the 16th century, copper mining and smelting were in full swing in the vicinity of Eisleben. An illustration from Agricola (1556) (Fig. 2.15) portrays these activities.

Schubert (1953/54) has divided the spoil heaps of the Mansfeld region into five groups according to their age:

1) Pre-1200 A.D. These ancient spoil heaps have now weathered so extensively that they are no longer visible on the surface. The sites can however, be identified by chemical analysis of the ore-rich surface material.

2) 1200–1400 A.D. These mine tips are scarcely 1 m high and follow a contour about 100 m wide between Wolferode and Gerbstedt (Fig. 2.14). Between Hettstedt and Wolferode the band is 500 m wide.

3) 1400–1670 A.D. This period contains remnants of 35 smelters located along small rivers. The mining activity was carried out along a contour some 700 m wide. The mine tips are larger than before and have a height of up to 4 m. They are partially or completely vegetated. Adits are also present and have been dated to the period 1575–1671 A.D.

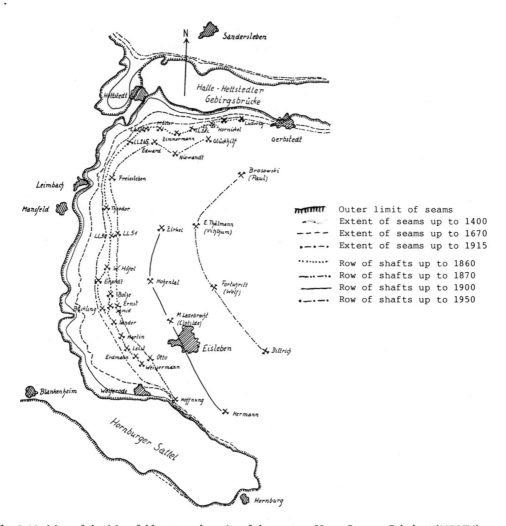

Fig. 2.14 Map of the Mansfeld copper deposits of the eastern Harz. Source: Schubert (1953/54).

Fig. 2.15 Copper smelting near Eisleben (eastern Harz) during the 16th Century. Source: Agricola (1556).

4) 1671–1815 A.D. This period yields a number of smelters whose spoil heaps are still unvegetated today. The heaps are much larger than those of earlier periods and are up to 8 m in height. There are numerous adits and other workings in the contour band.

5) 1815-present. The smelters cease to be confined to running streams. With the steady removal of the Kupferschiefer (copper slate), the row of shafts moves progressively away from the outer rim of the basin as shown in Fig. 2.14.

Vegetation of the Mansfeld Copper Ores

The vegetation of the Mansield copper ores is included in the Armerietum halleri Association, one of three within the Armerion halleri Alliance (Schubert, 1953/54; Ernst, 1974). The physiognomy of the community is defined by large cushions of red flowers of *Armeria maritima* subsp. *halleri* (Plate 2.4) as well as by white flowers of *Silene cucubalus* and *Minuartia verna* subsp. *hercynica*. Companion species are *Rumex acetosa*, *Campanula rotundifolia*, *Thymus serpyllum*, *Ceratodon purpureus*, *Pimpinella saxifraga* and *Euphrasia cyparissias*. The occurrence of *Minuartia verna* on metalliferous ground in this area has been known since the 16th century (Thalius, 1586).

Plant succession in colonization can be studied very well in the Mansfeld mine dumps (one of the world's finest natural laboratories for this purpose) because so many of the sites can be dated quite accurately.

One of the first colonists of mine tips is *Silene cucubalus* (= *S. vulgaris*) var. *humilis*; it is often the only species found on the steep slopes of such tips. This is because of its very extensive root system which can reach 2 m below the surface even though the aerial parts of the plant seldom exceed 10 cm in height. This stage of plant succession has been named the *Silene* stage by Schubert (1953/54); it is shown in Fig. 2.16. In places where the mine tips are less steep or where *S. cucubalus* var. *humilis* has already stabilized the terrain, *Minuartia verna* subsp. *hercynica* and *Alyssum montanum* are the first colonists. Colonization by the former is known as the *Minuartia* stage (Fig. 2.16). Both species have extensive root systems which stabilize the soil so that *Rumex acetosa* and *Festuca ovina* can establish themselves. The result of this later colonization is often the extinction of *M. verna* subsp. *hercynica* due to competition.

The consolidation of the soil results in an accumulation of fine-earth particles and an improvement in the water-holding capacity. This leads to the colonization of the site by *Festuca ovina*, *Scabiosa canescens*, *Euphrasia stricta*, *Rumex acetosa*, *Centaurea scabiosa*, and *Agrostis stolonifera*. This is known as the *Euphrasia* stage (Fig. 2.16). In the damp valleys of the region, the *Euphrasia* stage is replaced by a lichen stage dominated by species of *Cladonia*.

In locally favorable climatic zones, the next stage in the succession is the *Armeria* stage (Fig. 2.16). Here the character species of the Association have their maximum development because the plant cover is not yet so thick as to hinder the growth of shade-sensitive and competition-sensitive species. It is here that *Armeria halleri*, which, with its less extensive root systems, cannot tolerate the extreme dryness and toxicity of the substrates of the earlier stages, first appears. This stage also marks the first appearance of *Scabiosa ochroleuca*, *Achillea millefolium*, *Potentilla verna*, *Ononis spinosa*, *Thymus serpyllum*, *Centaurea scabiosa*, *Ranunculus bulbosus*, *Hieracium pilosella*, *Potentilla heptaphylla*, *Plantago lanceolata*, and *Galium verum*.

Because of the few bare sites which now exist, the plant community changes and is characterised by extensive nanism. In comparison with the early stages, a distinct zoning of soil horizons becomes apparent, with a humic horizon of about 5 cm overlying the slaty substrate.

At the base of the mine tips where the fine soil fractions and toxic salts accumulate due to rainfall and where the vitality of other plants is hindered by the toxicity of the substrate, the *Armeria* stage gives way to the *Brachypodium* stage (Fig. 2.16). It represents a terminal

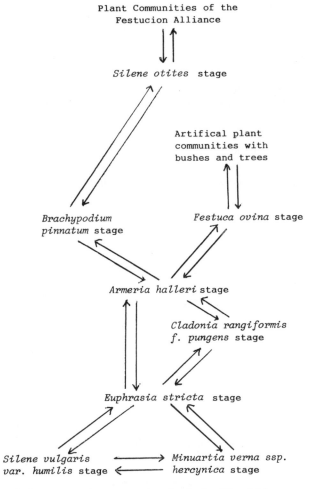

Plant Communities of the
Festucion Alliance

Silene otites stage

Artifical plant
communities with
bushes and trees

Brachypodium
pinnatum stage

Festuca ovina stage

Armeria halleri stage

Cladonia rangiformis
f. pungens stage

Euphrasia stricta stage

Silene vulgaris
var. humilis stage

Minuartia verna ssp.
hercynica stage

Fig. 2.16 Diagram of plant successions over mine tips in the Mansfeld copper mining region, eastern Harz. Source: Schubert (1953/54).

stage of the development of heavy metal plant communities in this region and is dominated by *Brachypodium pinnatum*. Other colonisers in this stage of the succession are: *Eryngium campestre*, *Seseli annuum*, *Prunella grandiflora*, *Salvia pratensis*, *Botrychium lunaria*, *Helianthemum nummularium*, and *Odontites, lutea*.

In damper locations and at the base of younger mine tips more deficient in heavy metal salts, the *Armeria* stage gives way to the *Festuca* stage dominated by *Festuca ovina* and other grasses (Fig. 2.16). The ground is completely covered at this stage and excludes plants such as *Minuartia verna*. The 20-cm thick fine soil fraction with its good water-retention capacity is favorable for mosses such as *Cirriphyllum piliferum* or even *Mnium cuspidatum* and often shrubs such as *Rosa rubiginosa*, *R. canina*, *Prunus spinosa* and *Lycium halmifolium*. There is often a ring-like growth of bushes around the base of old mine tips where the plants are able to penetrate to non-contaminated ground upon which the mine debris had been placed.

The climax stage of the Festucion Alliance is the *Silene otites* community composed of this species and *Adonis vernalis*, *Astragalus danicus*, *Erophila verna*, *Cerastium semi-decandrum*, and *Carex humilis*. This community often occupies an area of several thousand square meters.

The plant successions show a steady increase in the minimal area needed to encompass all species. For the first stages, 0.5 m^2 is sufficient and increases to 8 m^2 for the *Cladonia* community. In the final climax stages, a minimum area of 8 m² is required.

The relationship between the age of the mine tips and the extent to which vegetational succession has occurred is very marked. Spoil heaps of the first period (1200–1400 A.D.) are virtually completely vegetated (Fig. 2.17) and show bare patches only in exposed locations. The heaps are flat and low and the copper ore is widely disseminated. Depending on the geomorphology, the foot of the tips is colonised by the *Festuca* or *Brachypodium* communities (Fig. 2.17). The *Euphrasia* and *Cladonia* stages appear in the few bare areas.

In the case of spoil heaps of the second period (1400–1671 A.D.), the successional stages are somewhat different from those of the first period. The heaps are now much steeper and the initial stage is that of the *Silene* community with the *Brachypodium* stage not far from the heaps. The mine tips of the second period are of two types. In the first (Fig. 2.17) the outline is rounded, and in the second there is a depression at the summit. In the latter case, the *Armeria* or even the *Festuca* stages can develop. On the rounded heaps, only the *Minuartia* or *Euphrasia* stages can develop.

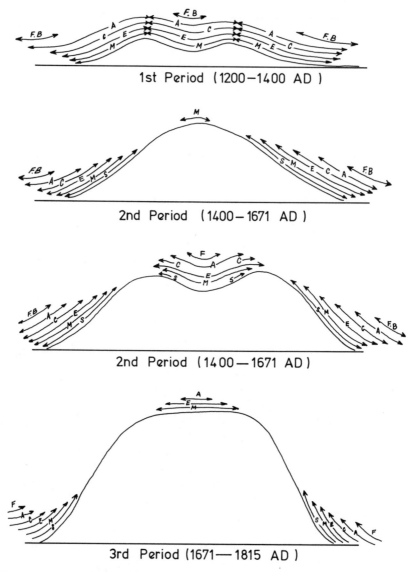

Fig. 2.17 Plant successions over mine tips of different ages in the Mansfeld copper mining region, eastern Harz. Source: Schubert (1953/54).

For spoil heaps of the third period (1671–1815 A.D.) (Fig. 2.17), the *Festuca* stage is less developed than in the second period due to action of rain causing the movement of fine earth fractions. Many of the successional stages are missing over such heaps so that the *Euphrasia* stage leads directly to the *Festuca* or even to the *Silene* stages if the slopes of the heaps are very steep. In the course of time the older mine heaps can be colonised with a dense shrub layer developed as a result of seeding of such plants as *Prunus spinosa*, *Rosa canina*, and *Lycium halmifolium*. Even trees such as *Quercus robur* and *Prunus avium* can colonise these sites.

Brief mention must be made of an important paper by Schubert (1954) that describes the metal-resistant vegetation of the Bottendorfer Höhen over the Kupferschiefer deposits of this region. Mining commenced here prior to 1689. The most characteristic plant of the region is the endemic *Armeria maritima* subsp. *bottendorfensis*.

2.3.6 The Western Harz Region (West Germany)

Introduction and History

The western Harz region is one of the greatest of the European mineral provinces (Fig. 2.18). Some useful historical introductions to mining in the region have been given by authors such as Bode (1928) and Bornhardt (1943). Bode has catalogued the location of 191 medieval mine sites, smelters, and slag heaps in the region, and many more have been recorded since that date.

Many of these are easily recognizable from the sparse and xerophytic nature of the overlying vegetation. After establishment of these sites, a continuous layer of vegetation occurs only after leaves or needles have built up a layer of humus. Even then, leaching of phytotoxic salts to the surface results in the appearance of a characteristic plant community.

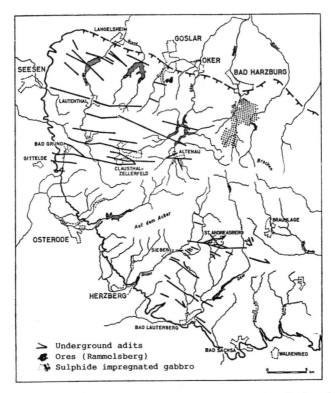

Fig. 2.18 Map of the western Harz showing mining areas. Source: Gundlach and Steinkamp (1973). By courtesy of the editor of *Zeitschrift der Deutschen Geologischen Gessellschaft*.

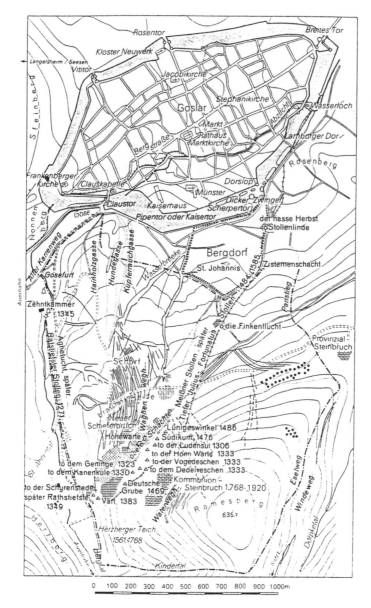

Fig. 2.19 Map of medieval mine sites and smelters near Goslar. Note medieval names (e.g. Ramesberg = Rammelsberg). Source: Denecke (1978). By courtesy of the editor of *Archaologisches Korrespondenzblatt* (Mainz).

According to Bode (1928), there were already 38 mines and smelters in operation near Goslar (Fig. 2.19) by the year 1311 A.D. Mining in this region was carried out principally at the Rammelsberg (Fig. 2.20), one of the great mineral treasure houses of medieval Europe.

The origin of the name Rammelsberg according to medieval legends (as reported by Sudhof, 1982) is as follows: The Saxon king Otto I lived nearby at what is now Bad Harzburg and sent his chief huntsman, a certain Herr Ramm, to kill boar for the royal table. Whilst chasing his quarry, Ramm found that his horse could not cross an intervening ravine and left it tethered to a tree. Upon his return, and history does not record whether he had been successful in the hunt or not, Ramm discovered that his horse had impatiently removed the soil cover with his hooves and had uncovered the rock substrate whose golden streaks of sulphide ores glistened in the sun. This is a good example of a legend that could have led to a

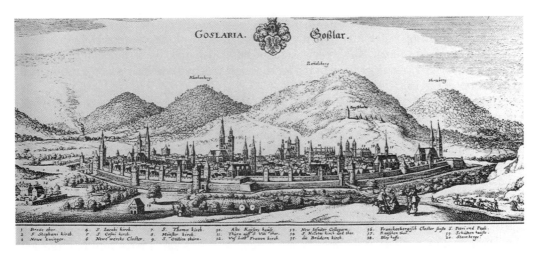

Fig. 2.20 17th century engraving of Goslar with the Rammelsberg in the background. Engraving by M. Merian reproduced by courtesy of the Goslar Museum (City Archives of Goslar).

subsequent discovery.

Mining operations in the western Harz began some time in the 4th century and continued under the Saxon Kings in the 11th century. Mining reached a peak in the first half of ihe 14th century when the town of Goslar (then an important center) was surrounded by numerous valleys supporting many small mines and smelters. It declined later in the century due to water inflow into the mines and to the plague that decimated the local population. There was an upswing in activity in the middle of the 15th century stimulated by dewatering of the mines and the creation of shareholding societies. Following these reforms initiated by Duke Julius of Brunswick, there was (apart from the disturbance of the Thirty Years War from 1618–1848) a steady increase in the prosperity of the region. Mining and smelting became widespread beyond the immediate area of Goslar and involved control by rich landowners and even monasteries such as that at Walkenried.

The Rammelsberg ores are rich in lead, zinc and copper but are low in noble metals, though about 1 kg of gold was produced annually from the Rammelsberg during the 15th century. Most of the smelters had only 2–4 furnace units (Fig. 2.21).

Bornhardt (1943) has recognised two main periods of mining in the western Harz. The first, the medieval period, extended from around 1300 A.D. to the beginning of the more recent period, from the middle of the 16th century right up to the present time.

Fig. 2.21 Medieval smelter in the Goslar area. Source: Cited by Denecke (1978). By courtesy of the editor of *Archaologisches Korrespondenzblatt* (Mainz).

Plant Indicators of Medieval Mines and smelters

A description of vegetation patterns and smelter sites in the western Harz has been given by Heimhold (1982). The species composition depends on a number of factors, including aspect and degree of slope of the terrain, height above sea level, and the nature and composition of the soil.

In the case of the Rammelsberg itself, the most thoroughly studied of the Harz zones of mineralization, the northern slopes facing Goslar receive the first buffeting from the northern air currents so that the microclimate near the ground has much less significance than on the southern slopes. The northern slopes are therefore somewhat impoverished in species. At the higher altitudes they are colonized mainly by spruce (*Picea* sp.) (reinforced by afforestation) and mountain ash (*Sorbus aucuparia*) because these two species are highly weather-resistant. Birch and willow (*Betula* sp. and *Salix* sp.) are found at the base of the mountain.

In addition, because the weathered Middle Devonian Wissenbach slate provides an acid soil poor in nutrients, the northern slopes of the Rammelsberg do not support a rich vegetation (except perhaps at the foot of the mountain where cattle have fertilized the soil with nitrogenous manure).

The mine tips from Maltermeisterturm to Ramseck (Fig. 2.19) appear to be virtually devoid of vegetation, with neither trees nor shrubs but only a sparse cover of herbs, mosses and lichens. The slag heaps carry an extraordinary range of lichens. Plantations of conifers between Maltermeisterturm and the youth hostel grow over mining terrain of great antiquity.

The heavy metals locked up in the rocks and the presence of sulphides have led to a sparse tree cover. The acid humus layer does little to improve the vegetation, though there is proliferation of a moss (*Mielichhoferia nitida*) found only over copper deposits in the Harz and elsewhere in Europe.

The spruce plantations above the meadows give sufficient protection for the development of a herb layer in the more open areas. This layer is dominated by *Deschampsia flexuosa*, a grass which always indicates soils poor in nutrients. In early summer, the tender green leaves of *Trientalis* sp. brighten the terrain, and in sites sheltered from the wind, there are stands of foxglove (*Digitalis* sp.) and belladonna.

In the higher parts of the Rammelsberg, from Ramseck to the brow of the mountain on the side facing Goslar, there is a spruce forest of uneven quality. The ground is here enriched by the presence of *Galium verum* with cushions resembling feather pillows among masses of *Polygala vulgaris*.

Specialized plants have developed everywhere the Harz rivers have deposited sands and gravels derived from mineralized outcrops or mining and smelting activities. In these sites there is a lack of competition from species which cannot grow over the toxic soils.

The sulphide minerals, smelters slags and mine tips on the Rammelsberg support a community which is part of the Armerietum halleri Association (Libbert, 1930), mistakenly called a "galmei flora" by Heimhold (1982). The character species of this Association is *Armeria maritima* subsp. *halleri* which is also found in the eastern Harz over the Mansfeld copper deposits (see above). Other prominent plants of this Association are: *Minuartia verna* subsp. *hercynica, Silene vulgaris* subsp. *humilis, Cardaminopsis halleri,* and *Viola tricolor.* This community is extremely rare in Europe, and is a result not only of the natural environment but also of anthropogenic modification of mineralized terrain.

Shrubs are rare over mineralized parts of the Rammelsberg and consist mainly of *Sambucus nigra* and *S. racemosa.* Where the nutrient status of the soil is improved, *Luzula* sp. is found among the grasses below the mixed broadleaved beech forest which still survives on the southern flanks of the mountain.

Along the edges of grassy or gravelly paths are found several species of *Carex* (including *C. distans*), together with the sylvan horsetail *Equisetum sylvaticum.*

In damp places, the white cushions of peat moss appear together with isolated specimens of the swamp violet (*Viola palustris*) and *Lycopodium clavatum*.

Three species of fern (*Asplenium septentrionale*, *Dryopteris oreopteris*, and *Polypodium vulgare*) are common throughout the region rather than being confined to the Rammelsberg alone.

2.3.7 The Zinc Deposits of Western Germany and Eastern Belgium

Introduction and History

The zinc deposits of western Germany and eastern Belgium are situated near Aachen. Their geology has been described by Schwickerath (1931) and Gussone (1961). The zinc rich soils extend in a wide southwest to northeast-trending band (Fig. 2.22) from just east of Aachen to southeast of Le Rocheux in eastern Belgium. The deposits are found within strips of limestone and dolomite and are characterized by numerous prospecting shafts and adits, spoil heaps, and ruined buildings from earlier mining activities. These give a desolate appearance enhanced by the surrounding limestone hills which are almost completely denuded of trees and shrubs.

It is clear that mining activity at Aachen dates back to Roman times, because Roman coins (1st century A.D.) and implements have been found at mine sites and spoil heaps near Gressenich and Breinigerberg. Plinius (77 A.D.) reports mining activity in "Germania" where an ore known as *cadmia* was extracted. There is no evidence however, for a continuous period of ore extraction after withdrawal of the Romans up to the first record of Middle Ages activity in 1344 A.D.—a gap of about 1000 years.

One of the most important of the early mining sites was in the area bounded by Maubach, Stolberg, Busbach and Breinig (Fig. 2.22). The last of the mines to operate was at Diepenlinchen near Maubach where operations ceased at about the time of World War I. The number of previously-operated mines is very large and some of these were of great importance. In more recent times, some of the mine tips were reworked to remove more of their remaining lead and zinc.

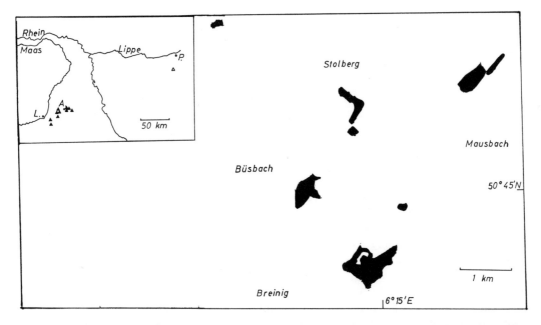

Fig. 2.22 Approximate distribution in 1970 (solid areas) of the galmei flora of the Aachen region, West Germany. Inset—solid triangles—Violetum calaminariae rhenanicum: open triangles—Violetum calaminariae westfalicum. Source: Ernst (1974). By courtesy of Gustav Fischer Verlag, Stuttgart.

The lead/zinc ore deposits of the region are associated with limestones of the Devonian and Lower Carboniferous periods. These ores are often accompanied by sulphides and more frequently by marcasite (white iron pyrites). Copper mineralization is scarce.

One of the earliest mines to be developed was on the Brockenberg where galmei, a collective name for carbonates and silicates of zinc (sometimes erroneously called calamine), was mined. Evidence is found in numerous ancient mine workings. Mining activity at the Breinigerberg is likewise very ancient and has been traced back to Roman times. Operations here ceased in the 1870s due to the high cost of draining the mines.

Vegetation of Ancient Mining Sites.

A vegetation community confined to ore-rich soils in the region is known as a galmei flora and has been described by Schwickerath (1931), Savelsbergh (1976) and Kremer (1982). The community includes such famous metallophytes as *Thlaspi calaminare*, which is the first to appear in the spring. Other members of the community include *Viola calaminaria* (Plate 2.5), *Minuartia verna* var. *caespitosa*, *Armeria maritima* subsp. *elongata*, and *Silene vulgaris* subsp. *humilis*. The last particularly favors collapsed mine shafts or other depressions known locally as "Pingen." The mixture of colors afforded by the rose-red *Armeria* and yellow *Viola* gives the tone to this community which is known as the Violetum calaminariae rhenanicum Association (Ernst, 1969b). A summary of this Association is given in Table 2.4.

Table 2.5 presents a summary of the European plant Associations within the three Alliances of the Order Violetalia calaminariae and Class Violetea calaminariae.

TABLE 2.5 Phytosociological classification of metal-tolerant plants found over central European Roman and medieval mining sites.

Category	Character species	Occurrence
Class—Violetea calaminariae	*Silene vulgaris*	
Order—Violetalia calaminariae	*Minuartia verna*	
Alliance 1—Galio anisophylli- Minuartion vernae		Alpine distribution
Alliance 2—Thlaspion- calaminaris	*Thlaspi calaminare* *Cardaminopsis halleri*	
Association 1—Violetum calaminariae rhenanicum	*Viola calaminaria* (yellow form)	Zinc ores west of the Rhine
Association 2—Violetum calaminariae westfalicum	*Viola calaminaria* (violet form)	Zinc ores east of Rhine
Alliance 3—Armerion halleri		
Association 1—Armerietum halleri		Harz and northern foothills

The range of galmei plants is being reduced by industrial development in the region and is now only a fraction of its original extent. There are very few undisturbed sites supporting this community except in eastern Belgium near Le Rocheux. Ernst (1974) has described another galmei community situated in Westphalia. Here the Violetum calaminariae rhenanicum Association is replaced by the Violetum calaminariae westfalicum Association. *Viola calaminaria* var. *westfalicum* with its reddish violet flowers dominates the community from May to October.

The origin of the Aachen community is of some interest. The flora is of Quaternary origin and is probably a relic of the Ice Ages, certainly in regard to *Viola calaminaria*, *Minuartia verna*, and *Thlaspi alpestre*. Most of their companions are found elsewhere only in alpine regions. In the late autumn, *Seseli annuum* which originates from the Black Sea littoral, appears along with *Gentiana germanica* and *G. ciliata*. It is not found in the surrounding local flora.

Further description of mine taxa over European ancient and medieval mining sites can be found in Ernst (1974).

2.3.8 Ancient Copper Mines of Daye, People's Republic of China

The Daye region of Hubei Province in central China contains large copper deposits which have been exploited for nearly 3000 years. Unlike many other mining provinces where later mining has destroyed earlier artifacts, the region still retains relics of early mining activities. After rainfall, the local mountains are often stained with *tonglü* (verdigris) due to leaching of secondary copper minerals, and are named Tonglüshan (shan = mountain). Early miners were attracted to the copper deposits not only because of the verdigris but also because of the ubiquitous presence of the "copper plant" *Elsholtzia haichowensis,* which colonises the phytotoxic soil (see Plate 2.6). A description of this plant has been given by Se Sjue-Tzsin and Sjuj Ban Lian (1953).

A fascinating description of this ancient mining province and of the "copper flower" as well as of the numerous ancient mining artifacts discovered in the region, has been given by Huangshi Museum et al. (1980).

> Found on Tonglüshan are no less than 400 000 tonnes of ancient slag, ancient shafts and drifts densely distributed underground, and remains of copper smelting furnaces built in various dynasties, all of which bear witness to the scale and skill of mining and smelting in those days.
>
> By C-14 dating of the mine posts and wooden handles of tools, as well as from pottery styles, it was found that some of the mines belong to the Spring and Autumn Period (770–479 B.C.) or earlier. Bronze and wooden implements were used in these mines. Iron and steel tools replaced bronze in the pits of the period from the Warring States to the Han Dynasty (5th century B.C. to 2nd century A.D.). Smelting furnaces and potteries of later periods have been unearthed, and are mainly of the Song Dynasty (960–1279 A.D.).
>
> Among the tools found in the ancient drifts prior to the 6th century B.C. were wooden shovels, rakes and hammers, bronze adzes, chisels and pickaxes.
>
> Cast iron was discovered in China by the end of the 6th century B.C. and in the pits of the Han Dynasty, bronze tools were replaced by iron and included axes, sledgehammers, rakes, hoes, and chisels. With these simple tools, the miners excavated shafts and drifts as deep as 50 m. The excavation depth was between 20 and 30 m in the earlier pits. The shafts and drills were supported by square morticed frames. Some timber props were cut into spears and wedged into the walls to keep them in place. Most of the walls and ceilings of the shafts and drifts were protected by panelling.
>
> Pits of the Warring States and Han Period were generally 40–50 meters deep. The shafts were propped up by stacking square frames one on top of another. Instead of panels, fine wooden sticks and bamboo mats were used for lining the walls of shafts and drifts.

The Tonglüshan area of Hubei province remains one of the best preserved sites of ancient mining activities anywhere on earth and is particularly noteworthy in that it carried the faithful copper indicator *Elsholtzia haichowensis*. It is a remarkable illustration of the concept of phytoarchaeology.

2.4 METALLICOLOUS LICHENS AND MOSSES OVER ANCIENT AND MEDIEVAL MINING AND SMELTER SITES

2.4.1 Western Harz

Cryptogams (mosses and lichens) are commonly found over abandoned mine shafts and slag heaps. In the western Harz the ecology of these primitive plants has been described by Ullrich (1977, 1982). They are found along much of the northwest face of the Rammelsberg and have been able to colonize the bare slopes of the mountain because the toxic soils have eliminated virtually all competition from flowering plants. The lichens are to a large extent substrate-specific and many favor mineralized ground. The first attempt to define a phytosociological unit for this community was made by Hilitzer (1923) who described an Acarosporetum sinopicae Association. Later this community was discovered over numerous slag heaps throughout the Harz and was renamed the Icones lichenum hercyniae Association. Lichens (and one moss) of the mineralized northern face of the Rammelsberg are listed in Table 2.6.

TABLE 2.6 Cryptogams associated with medieval slag heaps and mines on the Rammelsberg, Goslar, Western Harz

Species	Plant type	Comments
Acarospora sinopica	Lichen	Character species of the Association
A. montana	Lichen	Endemic to the Harz
Buellia sororia	Lichen	Common in Goslar area
Lecanora soralifera	Lichen	
L. subaurea	Lichen	Common on the Rammelsberg
Lecidea pilati	Lichen	
L. plana	Lichen	Rare
L. silacea	Lichen	Very rare. Endemic to Rammelsberg
Rhizocarpon oederi	Lichen	
R. furfurosum	Lichen	
Stereocaulon condensatum	Lichen	
Umbilicaria torrefacta	Lichen	
U. proboscidea	Lichen	
Mielichhoferia nitida	Moss	Copper moss confined to mineralization in Harz, Europe and South America

Source: Ullrich 1980

2.4.2 Ancient and Medieval Copper Mines of Coniston, England

The Coniston region of the English Lake District has been a center of copper mining since Roman times. Production reached a peak in the 19th century and ceased in 1942 (Shaw, 1970). Purvis and James (1985) studied the ecology and distribution of lichen communities over slag heaps in the region and found a community analogous to the Acarosporetum sinopicae of the Rammelsberg in the western Harz. They identified five lichen species new to Britain in this hostile environment: *Stereocaulon symphycheilum, Lecanora handelii, Rhizocarpon furfurosum, Lecidea atrofulva,* and *L. inops.*

Here as elsewhere, *Acarospora sinopica* appears to be restricted to rocks rich in iron pyrites.

2.5 CHAPTER SUMMARY

Geobotany is concerned with the relationship between plants and the geological substrate. It can be extended to the field of phytoarchaeology. This chapter reviews methods of plant mapping including a mention of phytosociology upon which much of this mapping is based. Some case histories include geobotanical plant indicators of ancient copper smelter sites in Zaïre. Among these is the "copper flower" *Haumaniastrum katangense* which has led to the discovery of artifacts of the 14th century Kabambian culture.

Following an account of plant indicators of old gold mines in Canada and China, there is a discussion of medieval (or earlier) mining sites in northern Italy and central Europe. Bronze Age smelter sites in the former have been identified by the distribution of the herb *Silene inflata.*

In the British Isles, the flora of ancient mine workings (mainly involving lead, copper, and zinc) has been described. Prominent among these plants are *Armeria maritima, Minuartia verna,* and *Thlaspi alpestre.*

In the Harz region of East Germany, the Mansfeld copper deposits provide an excellent phytoarchaeological record of past mining activities dating back to well before the 12th century A.D.

In the western Harz (West Germany) the base metal ores of the Goslar region provide several examples of plant species indicative of medieval (and earlier) mining activities.

The zinc deposits of western Germany (near Aachen) and eastern Belgium are covered with a highly endemic flora dominated by such metal-tolerant species as *Viola calaminaria* and *Thlaspi calaminare.* These and other plants faithfully delineate old mine workings from which artifacts as old as the Roman period have been uncovered.

The Daye region of China is noted for the occurrence of the copper-tolerant endemic herb *Elsholtzia haichowensis* which is found over these deposits that have been mined for 3000 years and which have yielded many ancient artifacts.

The chapter closes with a description of metal-tolerant lichens and mosses found over ancient and medieval mining and smelter sites.

REFERENCES

Aery, N. C. 1977. Studies on the geobotany of Zawar Mines. *Geobios (India)* 4: 225–228.

Agricola, G. 1556. *De Re Metallica.* Eng. Trans. by Hoover, H. C., and Hoover, L. H. Dover Pub. New York (1912).

Andrew, A. N. 1910. The geology of the Dolgelly Gold Belt, North Wales. *Min. Mag.* 7: 159–171.

Andrews, M. J., and Fuge, R. 1986. Cupriferous bogs of the Coed y Brenin area, North Wales, and their significance for mineral exploration. *Appl. Geochem.* 1: 519–525.

Anon, 1970a. Téchniques rurales en Afrique. 11. *Manuel de Photointerpretation.* Secrétariat d'Etat aux Affaires Etrangères République Française, Paris.

Anon, 1970b. The Mendip lead industry. *Fieldworker* 1: 132–137.

Baker, A. J. M. 1974. *Heavy Metal Tolerance and Population Differentiation in Silene maritima* With. Ph.D. Thesis, University of London.

———— 1987. Metal tolerance. *New Phytol.* 106 (Suppl.): 93–111.

Bode, A. 1928. Reste alter Hüttenbetriebe im West- und Mittelharze. *Jb. Dt. Geogr. Ges.* 1928: 141–197.

Bornhardt, W. 1943. Der Oberharzer Bergbau im Mittelalter. *Arch. Landes-Volkskunde Niedersachs.* 1943: 449–502.

Boyle, R. W. 1979. The geochemistry of gold and its deposits. *Geol. Surv. Can. Bull.* 280: 580 pp.

Bradshaw, A. D., McNeilly, T. S., and Gregory, R. P. G. 1965. Industrialization, evolution and the development of heavy metal tolerance in plants. In, *5th Brit. Ecol. Soc. Symp. Oxford,* 327–343.

Braun-Blanquet, J. 1932. *Plant Sociology.* McGraw-Hill, New York.

Braun-Blanquet, J., and Tüxen, R. 1952. Irische Pflanzengesellschaften der Pflanzenwelt Irlands. *Ver. Geobot. Inst. Rübel. (Zürich)* 25: 224–420.

Brockner, W., and Kolb, H. E. 1986. Archäometrische Untersuchungen an Erz-und Schlack-funden der Grabung Düna. In, *Düna/Osterode—ein Herrensitz des frühen Mittelalters.* Arbeitshf. Denkmalpflege Niedersachs. #6.

Brooks, R. R. 1977. Copper and cobalt uptake by *Haumaniastrum* species. *Pl. Soil,* 48: 541–545.

_____ 1983. *Biological Methods of Prospecting for Minerals.* Wiley, New York.

_____ 1986. Present status of botanical exploration using higher plants. In, D. Carlisle et al. [eds.] *Mineral Exploration, Biological Systems and Organic Matter.* Prentice-Hall, Englewood Cliffs. 98–132.

_____ 1987. *Serpentine and its Vegetation: a Multidisciplinary Approach.* Dioscorides Press, Portland.

Brooks, R. R., and Crooks, H. M. 1980. Studies on uptake of heavy metals by the Scandinavian "kisplanten" *Lychnis alpina* and *Silene dioica. Pl. Soil* 54: 491–495.

Brooks, R. R., Holzbecher, J., and Ryan D. E. 1981. Horsetails as indirect indicators of gold mines. *J. Geochem. Explor.* 16: 21–26.

Brooks, R. R., Lee, J., and Jaffré, T. 1974. Some New Zealand and New Caledonian plant accumulators of nickel. *J. Ecol.* 62: 523–529.

Brooks, R. R., and Malaisse, F. 1985. *The Heavy Metal-Tolerant Flora of Southcentral Africa.* Balkema, Rotterdam.

Brooks, R. R., McCleave, J. A., and Malaisse, F. 1977. Copper and cobalt in African species of *Crotalaria* L. *Proc. Roy. Soc. Lond. Sec. B* 197: 231–236.

Brooks, R. R., Morrison, R. S. Reeves, R. D., Dudley, T. R., and Akman, Y. 1979a. Hyperaccumulation of nickel by *Alyssum* Linnaeus (Cruciferae). *Proc. Roy. Soc. Lond. Sec. B* 203: 387–403.

Brooks, R. R., Naidu, S. D. Malaisse, F., and Lee, J. 1987. The elemental content of metallophytes from the copper/cobalt deposits of Central Africa. *Bull. Soc. Roy. Bot. Belg.* 119: 179–191.

Brooks, R. R., and Radford, C. C. 1978. An evaluation of background and anomalous copper and zinc concentrations in the "copper plant" *Polycarpaea spirostylis* and other Australian species of the genus. *Proc. Australas. Inst. Min. Metall.* 268: 33–37.

Brooks, R. R., Reeves, R. D. Morrison, S. M., and Malaisse, F. 1980. Hyperaccumulators of copper and cobalt—a review. *Bull. Soc. Roy. Bot. Belg.* 113: 166–172.

Brooks, R. R., Trow, J. M., and Bølviken, B. 1979b. Biogeochemical anomalies in Fennoscandia: a study of copper, lead and zinc in *Melandrium dioicum* and *Viscaria alpina. J. Geochem. Explor.* 11: 73–87.

Brussell. D. 1978. *Equisetum* stores gold. *Phytologia* 38: 469–473.

Buyalov, N. I., and Shvyryayeva, A. M. 1961. Geobotanical methods in prospecting for salts of boron. *Int. Geol. Rev.* 3: 619–625.

Cannon, H. L. 1957. Description of indicator plants and methods of botanical prospecting for uranium deposits on the Colorado Plateau. *U.S. Geol. Surv. Bull.* 1030M: 399–516.

Cannon, H. L., Shacklette, H. T., and Bastron, H. 1968. Metal absorption by *Equisetum* (horsetail). *U.S Geol. Surv. Bull.* 1278A: 1–21.

Chaffee, M. A., and Gale, C. W. 1976. The California poppy (*Escholtzia mexicana*) as a copper indicator plant—a new example. *J. Geochem. Explor.* 5: 59–63.

Chisnall, K. T., and Markland, J. 1971. Contamination of pasture land by lead. *J. Ass. Pub. Analysts* 9: 116–118.

Clarke, R. K., and Clark, S. C. 1981. Floristic diversity in relation to soil characteristics in a lead mining complex in the Pennines, England. *New Phytol.* 87: 799–815.

Cole, M. M. 1965. *Biogeography in the Service of Man.* Inaug. Lect. Bedford College, London: 59 pp.

_____ 1971. The importance of environment in biogeographical/geobotanical and biogeochemical investigations. *Can. Inst. Min. Metall. Spec. Vol.* 11: 414–425.

_____ 1973. Geobotanical and biogeochemical investigations in the sclerophyllous woodland and shrub associations of the Eastern Goldfields area of Western Australia with particular reference to the role of *Hybanthus floribundus* (Lindl.) F. Muell. as a nickel indicator and accumulator plant. *J. Appl. Ecol.* 10: 269–320.

Cole, M. M., and Le Roex, H. D. 1978. The role of geobotany, biogeochemistry, and geochemistry in mineral exploration in South West Africa and Botswana: a case history. *Trans. Geol. Soc. S. Africa* 81: 277–317.

Dean, J. T. 1844. *Rep. Brit. Ass. Trans. Sec.*: 56.

Denecke, D. 1978. Erzgewinnung und Hüttenbetriebe des Mittelalters im Oberharz und im Harzvorland. *Arch. Korrespondenzbl.* 8: 77–85.

Duvigneaud, P. 1959. Plantes cobaltophytes dans le Haut Katanga. *Bull. Soc. Roy. Bot. Belg.* 91: 111–134.

Duvigneaud, P., and Denaeyer-de Smet 1963. Cuivre et végétation au Katanga. *Bull. Soc. Roy. Bot. Belg.* 96: 93–231.

Ernst, W. 1964. Ökologisch-soziologische Untersuchungen in den Schwermetallgesellschaften Mitteleuropas unter Einschluss der Alpen. *Abh. Landesmus. Naturkunde, Münster,* 27: 1–54.

_____ 1968a. Zur Kenntnis der Soziologie und Ökologie der Schwermetallvegetation Grossbritanniens. *Ber. Dt. Bot. Ges.* 81: 116–124.

_____ 1968b. Das Violetum calaminariae westfalicum eine Schwermetallpflanzengesellschaft bei Blankenrode in Westfalen. *Mitt. Flor.-Soz. Arbgem. N.F.* 13: 263–268.

_____ 1969a. Pollenanalytischer Nachweis eines Schwermetallrasens in Wales. *Vegetatio* 18: 394–400.

_____ 1969b. *Die Schwermetallvegetation Europas.* Habilschrift, Math. Nat. Fak. Univ. Münster: 184 pp.

_____ 1974. *Schwermetallvegetation der Erde.* Fischer, Stuttgart.

_____ 1976. In, R. Tüxen [ed.] *Prodrome of the European Plant Communities.* R3. *Violetea calaminaria.* Cramer, Vaduz (Liechtenstein).

Farago, M. E., Mullen, W. A. Cole, M. M., and Smith, R. F. 1980. A study of *Armeria maritima* (Mill) Willdenow growing in a copper-impregnated bog. *Environ. Pollut.* 21: 225–244.

Ford, T. D., and Rieuwerts, J. H. 1983. *Lead Mining in the Peak District, 3rd ed.* Peak Park Joint Planning Board, Bakewell.

Foster, B. T. 1970. Some observations on the flora of the Mendip mining region. *Fieldworker* 1: 137.

Gough J. W. 1967. *Mines of Mendip.* David and Charles, Bristol.

Gundlach, H., and Steinkamp, K. 1973. Geochemische Prospektion im Oberharz, einem alten Bergbaugebiet. *Z. Dt. Geol. Ges.* 124: 37–49.

Gussone, R. 1961. Die Blei-Zinkerz Lagerstätten der Gegend von Aachen. In, *Mineralogische und Geologische Streifzüge durch die Nördliche Eifel.* V.F.M.G., Heidelberg pp. 19–25.

_____ 1985. Der Metallerzbergbau im Aachener Raum und seine Geschichte. *Schriftenreihe Ges. Dt. Metallhütten Bergl, Clausthal-Zellerfeld* 42: 19–33.

Hajar, A. S. M. 1987. *The Comparative Ecology of Minuartia verna (L.) Hiern. and Thlaspi alpestre L. in the Southern Pennines with Special Reference to Heavy Metal Tolerance.* Ph.D. Thesis, University of Sheffield.

Heimhold, W. 1980. Pflanzen im Bereich des Rammelsberger Erzbergbaues. In, *Über 1000 Jahre Erzbergwerk Rammelsberg.* Harzer Knappenverein, Goslar: 26–28.

Henwood, W. J. 1857. Notice of the copper turf of Merioneth. *Edin. New Phil. J.* 5: 61–63.

Hilitzer, A. 1923. Les lichens des roches amphiboliques aux environs de Vseruby. *Cas. Narod. Mus.* 1923: 1–14.

Howard-Williams, C. 1970. The ecology of *Becium homblei* in Central Africa with special reference to metalliferous soils. *J. Ecol.* 58: 745–752.

Huangshi Museum, et al. 1980. *Tonglüshan (Mt. Verdigris), Daye—A Pearl Among Ancient Mines.* Cultural Relics Publishing House, Beijing.

Jaffré, T. 1977. Accumulation du manganèse par les espèces associées aux terrains ultrabasiques de Nouvelle Calédonie. *C. R. Acad. Sci. Paris Sér. D* 284: 1573–1575.

Karpinsky, A. M. 1841. Can living plants be indicators of rocks and formations on which they grow and does their occurrence merit the particular attention of the specialist in structural geology ? (in Russ.). *Zhur. Sadovodstva*, Nos. 3

Koch, C. 1932. Die Vegetationsverhältnisse des Silberberges im Hüggelgebiet bei Osnabrück. *Mitt. Naturwiss. Ver. Osnabrück* 22: 117–149.

Kremer, B. 1982. Schwermetallpflanzen und Galmeiflur. *Rhein. Heimatpfl.* 19: 34–38.

Libbert, W. 1930. Die Vegetation des Fallsteingebietes. *Mitt. Flor. Soz. Arbgem.* 2: 1–66.

Mahn, E. G., Schubert, S., and Weinert, E. 1986. Exkursionsführer Mansfelder Hügelland. In, *Anthropogene Vegetationskomplexe des Mansfelder Hügellandes*. Martin Luther University, Halle.

Malaisse, F., and Brooks, R. R. 1982. Colonisation of modified metalliferous environments in Zaïre by the copper plant *Haumaniastrum katangense*. *Pl. Soil*, 64: 289–293.

Malaisse, F., Grégoire, J., Brooks, R. R., Morrison, R. S., and Reeves, R. D. 1978. *Aeolanthus biformifolius* De Wild.: a hyperaccumulator of copper from Zaïre. *Science* 199: 887–888.

Malaisse, F., Grégoire, J., Morrison, R. S., Brooks, R. R., and Reeves, R. D. 1979. Copper and cobalt in vegetation in Fungurume, Shaba Province, Zaïre. *Oikos* 33: 472–478.

Maret, P. de 1979. Luba roots: the first complete Iron Age sequence in Zaïre. *Current Anthropol.* 20: 233–234.

Marsden-Jones, E. M., and Turrill, W. B. 1957. *The Bladder Campions*. Royal Society, London.

Marshall, E. S. 1914. *Supplement to the Flora of Somerset*. Somerset Archaeological and Natural History Society, Taunton.

Menezes de Sequeira, E. 1969. Toxicity and movement of heavy metals in serpentinic soils (north eastern Portugal). *Agron. Lusit.* 330: 115–154.

Minguzzi, C., and Vergnano, O. 1948. Il contenuto di nichel nelle ceneri di *Alyssum bertolonii*. *Mem. Atti. Soc. Tosc. Sci. Nat.* 55: 49–74.

Murray, R. P. 1896. *The Flora of Somerset*. Somerset Archaeological and Natural History Society, Taunton.

Nemec, B., Babicka, J., and Oborsky, A. 1936. The occurrence of gold in horsetails (in Ger.). *Bull. Int. Acad. Sci. Bohême* 1–7: 1–13.

Nesvetaylova, N. G. 1961. Geobotanical investigations for prospecting for ore deposits. *Int. Geol. Rev.* 3: 609–618.

Nicolls, O. W., Provan, D. M. J., Cole, M. M., and Tooms, J. S. 1965. Geobotany and biogeochemistry in mineral exploration in the Dugald River area, Cloncurry district, Australia. *Trans. Inst. Min. Metall. Sec. B* 74: 695–799.

Plaen, G. de, Malaisse. F., and Brooks, R. R. 1982. The copper flowers of Central Africa and their significance for archaeology and mineral prospecting. *Endeavour*, 6: 72–77.

Plinius, 77 A.D. *Historia Naturalis*. 34/2.

Preuschen, E. 1964. Kupfererzbergbau und Vegetationsstörungen. Arch. Ur-Frühgesch. Bergbauforsch. *Arch. Austriaca* 35: 87–88.

———— 1965. Das urzeitliche Kupfer-Verhüttungsgebiet von Lavarone (Trentino). *Der Anschnitt* 17: 8–13.

———— 1968. Bronzezeitlicher Kupfererzbergbau im Trentino. *Der Anschnitt* 20: 3–15.

Pulou, R., Gramont, X. de, Magny, J., and Carles, J. 1965. Deux plantes indicatrices des gisements de zinc et de plomb dans les Pyrénées. *Bull. Soc. Hist. Nat. Toulouse* 100: 465–468.

Purvis, O. W., and James, P. W. 1985. Lichens of the Coniston copper mines. *Lichenologist* 17: 221–237.

Reeves, R. D., and Brooks, R. R. 1983a. Hyperaccumulation of lead and zinc by two metallophytes from a mining area in central Europe. *Environ. Pollut.* 31: 277–287.

———— 1983b. Nickel and zinc hyperaccumulation by European species of *Thlaspi* L. (Cruciferae). *J. Geochem. Explor.* 18: 275–283.

Rice, R., and Sharp, G. J. 1976. Copper mineralization in the forest Coed-y-Brenin, North Wales. *Trans. Inst. Min. Metall. Sec. B*, 85: 1–13.

Rune, O. 1953. Plant life on serpentine and related rocks in the north of Sweden. *Acta Phytogeogr. Suec.* 31: 1–135.

Savelsbergh, E. 1976. Die Vegetationskundliche Bedeutung und Schutzwürdigkeit des Breinigerberges bei Stolberg (MTB 5203) unter Berücksichtigung geologischer und geschichtlicher Aspekte. *Gött. Flor. Rundbr.* 9: 127–133.

Schubert, R. 1953/54. Die Schwermetallpflanzengesellschaften des östlichen Harzvorlandes. *Wiss. Z. Martin-Luther-Univ. Halle-Wittenberg Math. Nat. Kl.* III: 51–70.

———— 1954. Die Pflanzengesellschaften der Bottendorfer Höhen. *Wiss. Z. Martin-Luther-Univ. Halle-Wittenberg Math. Nat. Kl.* III, 99–128.

Schwickerath, M. 1931. Das Violetum calaminariae der Zinkböden in der Umgebung Aachens. Eine pflanzensoziologische Studie. *Beitr. Naturdenkmalpfl.* 14: 463–503.

Se Sjue-Tszin and Sjuj Ban-Lian 1953. *Eschscholzia haichowensis* Sun—a plant that can reveal the presence of copper-bearing strata. *Dichzi Sjuozheo* 32: 360–368.

Severne, B. C., and Brooks, R. R. 1972. A nickel accumulating plant from Western Australia. *Planta* 103, 91–94.

Shaw, S. C. 1984. *Ecophysiological Studies on Heavy Metal Tolerance in Plants Colonising Tideswell Rake, Derbyshire.* Ph.D. Thesis, Sheffield Univ.

Shaw, W. T. 1970. *Mining in the Lake Counties.* Dalesman Publishing Co. Clapham.

Shimwell, D. W. 1968. Notes on the distribution of *Thlaspi alpestre* L. in Derbyshire. *Proc. Bot. Soc. Brit. Is.* 7: 373–376.

Shimwell, D. W., and Laurie, A. E. 1972. Lead and zinc contamination of vegetation in the Southern Pennines. *Environ. Pollut.* 3: 291–301.

Skertchly, S. B. J. 1897. The copper plant (*Polycarpaea spirostylis* F. von Mueller). *Qld. Geol. Surv. Pub.* 119: 51–53.

Sudhof, A. 1980. Das Erzbergwerk Rammelsberg und Goslar. In, *Über 1000 Jahre Erzbergwerk Rammelsberg.* Harzer Knappenverein, Goslar: 29–31.

Thalius, J. 1588. *Sylva Hercynica, Sive Catalogus Plantarum Sponte Nascentium in Montibus et Locis Vicinis Hercyniae.* Frankfurt (Main).

Ullrich, H. 1977. G. F. W. Meyer als Entdecker des Acarosporetum sinopicae (Hil.) Schade im Harz. In, *125 Jahre Naturwissenschaftlicher Verein Goslar.* Goslar, 21–24.

———— 1980. Die Flechten-Vegetation der Berghalden am Nordwesthang des Rammelsberges bei Goslar. In, *Über 1000 Jahre Erzbergwerk Rammelsberg.* Harzer Knappenverein, Goslar: 45–47.

Ventakesh, V. 1964. Geobotanical methods of mineral exploration in India. *Indian Miner* 18:101.

Vogt, T. 1942. Geokjemisk og geobotanisk malmeleting. II. *Viscaria alpina* (L.) G. Don som "kisplante". *Kong. Norsk. Videns. Sels. For.* 15: 5–8.

White, J. W. 1912. *The Flora of Bristol.* J. Wright and Sons, Bristol.

Wilkins, D. A. 1960. The measurement and genetical analysis of lead tolerance in *Festuca ovina. Rep. Scot. Soc. Res. Pl. Breed.* 1960: 85–98.

Windsor, J. 1865. On *Thlaspi alpestre. The Naturalist* 2: 108–110.

Chapter 3

BIOGEOCHEMICAL STUDIES OVER ANCIENT MINE SITES AND WORKINGS

3.1 INTRODUCTION

Biogeochemical methods of prospecting involve the chemical analysis of soils and vegetation in order to provide evidence for the presence of minerals below the surface of the terrain (Brooks, 1972, 1983; Malyuga, 1964; Kovalevsky, 1987). Soils are included in the definition of biogeochemical prospecting because they contain biological material such as humus. Although the technique was developed for the express purpose of mineral exploration, it is but a short step to extend its scope to include detection of archaeological sites. These may be uncovered wherever the chemical composition of vegetation or soils reflects the presence of an anomalous metal content in the substrate. This anomaly could be caused by anthropogenic modification of the environment, or by the presence of minerals carried to the site or mined *in situ* by ancient human communities.

Biogeochemical studies have been greatly facilitated by developments in analytical chemistry during the past 25 years. The first of these was the appearance of atomic absorption spectrometry (AAS) during the early 1960s. It became possible to determine many elements with good sensitivity and precision in rocks, soils, vegetation and other samples. The next milestone was the development of inductively-coupled plasma (ICP) emission spectrometry in the late 1970s. Now it was possible to determine over 20 elements simultaneously with precision and sensitivity equal to, or better than, AAS. Another recent development is the technique of ICP mass spectrometry (ICP-MS) which provides the possibility of determining individual isotopes as well as elements.

Although the use of biogeochemistry in archaeological prospecting has been somewhat limited in the past and is less important than geobotanical methods (see Chapter 2), it has a place in the armory of the archaeologist—as will be seen from the following case histories.

3.2 BIOGEOCHEMICAL EXPLORATION OF THE MANSFELD COPPER DEPOSITS, EAST GERMANY

The chemical analysis of soils and vegetation can often be the only indication of ancient mine workings below the surface. A good example is provided by the famous Mansfeld copper deposits of the eastern approaches of the Harz Mts. in East Germany (DDR). These deposits have been worked for probably 1000 years (Schubert, 1954/55—see also Chapter 2). Mine tips predating the 15th century have now weathered to ground level and only chemical analysis of the soil for copper can indicate the original sites.

Ernst (1966) has described biogeochemical investigations on soils and vegetation at some of the mining sites of the Mansfeld "Early Period" (1200–1400 A.D.) (Table 3.1). The stages of plant succession are well delineated by heavy metal concentrations in soils and vegetation (see also Chapter 2). It is clear that the plant distribution is influenced not only by the copper content of the soil but also by the presence of anomalous zinc concentrations.

TABLE 3.1 Heavy metals in plants and soils near shafts of the "First Mining Period" (1200–1400 A.D.) in the Mansfeld Copper Mining Region, East Germany.

	A	B	C	D	E	F	G
pH of soil	7.7	8.1	7.9	7.8	7.4	6.9	5.3
Cu (%) in soil	1.63	0.98	1.07	1.03	0.81	0.35	0.04
Zn (%) in soil	0.86	0.46	0.56	0.44	0.42	0.32	0.06
Silene cucubalus var. *humilis*							
Cu content (mg/kg)	—	293	318	194	47	41	—
Zn content (mg/kg)	—	255	342	324	153	353	—
Minuartia verna subsp. *hercynica*							
Cu content (mg/kg)	—	—	282	328	81	93	—
Zn content (mg/kg)	—	—	433	432	130	260	—
Armeria maritima subsp. *halleri*							
Cu content (mg/kg)	—	—	—	278	82	84	—
Zn content (mg/kg)	—	—	—	342	127	156	—
Rumex acetosa							
Cu content (mg/kg)	—	—	—	377	—	—	—
Festuca ovina							
Cu content (mg/kg)	—	—	—	237	—	—	—

A—uncolonised center of mounds, B—*Silene* stage, C—*Minuartia* stage, D—Armerietum halleri typicum community, E—Armerietum halleri cladonietosum community, F—Armerietum halleri achilletosum community, G—Desiccated grass. Source: Ernst (1966). By courtesy of Gustav Fischer Verlag, Jena.

3.3 PRECOLONIAL COPPER WORKINGS IN SHABA PROVINCE, ZAIRE

Copper has been mined in Shaba Province, Zaïre for well over 500 years (see also Chapter 2), dating back to the 14th century Kabambian culture of Central Africa. There are numerous precolonial mine workings particularly in the Mindigi area (Fig. 2.1) some 100 km west of Likasi. The area is also highly cobaltiferous with the mining centered around Mindigi Hill. Fig. 3.1 represents two transects across this site. The hill itself is relatively lightly mineralized with about 800 mg/kg copper and 400 mg/kg cobalt in the soils. It supports an open forest (*forêt claire*) dominated by *Brachystegia floribunda* (A), and *Uapaca* spp. (B). On the lower slopes (2) there is a steppe formation dominated by *Loudetia simplex* and *Cryptosepalum dasycladum*. It is in the lower parts of the transect (3,4) that anthropogenic activity is most pronounced. The area is riddled with pre-European workings. The highly-toxic soils above these workings (3700 mg/kg copper and 1900 mg/kg cobalt) support a carpet of *Eragrostis boehmii* and several highly metallicolous species, e.g., members of the genera *Ascolepis*, *Icomum*, *Vernonia*, *Triumfetta* etc.

3.4 PRECOLONIAL SMELTER SITES IN SHABA PROVINCE, ZAIRE

There was mention in Chapter 2 of the detection of precolonial smelter sites in Shaba by the presence of cupricolous plants over these sites in which the original smelters (on termite hills) have weathered to ground level, and where the soil has been poisoned by ores brought to the site so that only metal-tolerant plants can grow there. A feature of these sites (Figs. 2.2 and 2.3) is the high proportion of copper and cobalt available to the plants. The content of these two elements in plants at these sites is considerably greater than in similar species growing over copper/cobalt ores elsewhere (Table 3.2). It is thereby possible to differentiate between smelter sites with potential for archaeological discoveries, and sites where natural non-anthropogenic minerals occur (Brooks and Malaisse, 1985; Plaen et al. 1982; Malaisse and Brooks, 1982).

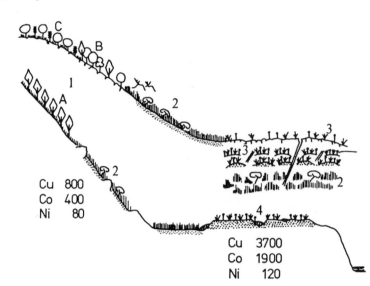

Fig. 3.1 Transects across mineralized hills at Mindigi, Shaba Province, Zaïre.

1—open forest over non-mineralized terrain: A—open forest dominated by *Brachystegia floribunda*; B,C—open forest with *Uapaca* sp. *Monotes katangensis* and *Philippia benguelensis*.

2—Slope with light mineralization (Cu/Co) comprising a shrubby steppe with *Loudetia simplex*, *Tristachya helenae* and *Protea goetzeana*.

3—deposit rich in cobalt and copper with accompanying tailings covered by a carpet of *Eragrostis boehmii*.

4—Spoil tip rich in copper and cobalt supporting a carpet similar to 3 above. Values for elemental concentrations are in mg/kg (ppm). Source: Duvigneaud (1959). By courtesy of Société Royale Botanique de Belgique, Brussels.

TABLE 3.2 Copper concentrations (mg/kg) in soils and vegetation over ancient copper smelter sites in Shaba Province, Zaïre.

Material	n	Copper concentrations		
		Smelter sites	Naturally-mineralized ground	Non-mineralized ground
Soil 0–5 cm	2	9150, 20850	5000	50
100 cm	2	520, 220	5000	50
200 cm	2	140, 220	5000	50
Alectra sessiliflora	10	588	13–170	10
Antherotoma naudinii	10	717	27	20
Arthraxon quartinianus	10	101	36	30
Haumaniastrum katangense	10	561	166–2135	30
Nephrolepis undulata	10	120	365	30
Vernonia petersii	10	753	1487	100

3.5 BIOGEOCHEMICAL INVESTIGATIONS OF ANCIENT BRITISH MINING SITES

Biogeochemical investigations over ancient and medieval mining sites in Great Britain have served to complement geobotanical studies over the same sites. There has already been some mention of the copper bogs of Wales (Dolfrwynog) which were a source of copper ore in the 1820s and which may have been exploited as far back as Roman times. A thorough geobotanical and biogeochemical study of the area has been carried out by Farago et al. (1980). They reported up to 15,350 mg/kg (1.53%) copper in roots and leaves of the copper indicator *Armeria maritima* which grew on soils containing up to 3% of this metal. This is compared to only 14 mg/kg in bulk samples of the same species growing nearby on non-mineralized ground containing only 23 mg/kg copper.

The lead and zinc content of two typical metal-tolerant plants colonising ancient and medieval mining sites (*Minuartia verna* and *Thlaspi alpestre* in Great Britain have been reviewed by Hajar (1987) (Table 3.3). It is clear that while both of these indicator plants restrict lead uptake, probably at their root systems, both, particularly *Thlaspi alpestre,* readily accumulate zinc. The latter can contain up to 2.5% zinc in dried leaves and in this respect closely resembles its near relative *T. calaminare* found over zinc deposits in western Germany (see Chapter 2).

The ability of the genus *Thlaspi* to hyperaccumulate (> 1% in dried material) zinc has been reported by Reeves and Brooks (1983). They identified ten species with this capability, including *Thlaspi rotundifolium,* subsp. *cepaeifolium* from mining sites in the Cave del Predil (Raibl) area of northern Italy. Specimens from this region can contain up to 1.73% zinc (see also Rascio, 1977).

It is quite clear that the heavy metal content of vegetation growing over ancient and medieval mining sites is a good indicator of the presence of past mining activities. Exploration of such sites can lead to the uncovering of archaeological artifacts.

TABLE 3.3 Lead and zinc concentrations (%) in *Minuartia verna* (MV), *Thlaspi alpestre* (TA) and soils over ancient and medieval mining sites in Great Britain.

Location	Lead			Zinc			Ref
	MV	TA	Soils	MV	TA	Soils	
S. Pennines	0.006–0.05	0.01–0.27	1.30–9.50	0.11–0.75	0.12–2.50	0.15–18.1	1
Tideslow Rake	0.50	—	4.00–5.33	0.07	—	0.42–0.46	2
Slaley	0.002	0.009	0.03	0.22	1.90	3.60	3
Grinton	—	—	—	0.17	1.13	—	3
Grizedale	0.02–0.04	0.03–0.06	0.006–0.13	0.03–0.16	0.55–0.84	0.05–1.47	3
Copperthwaite	—	—	—	0.13	1.13	—	3
Langthwaite	0.004	0.004	0.03	0.08	0.81	0.44	3,4
Grassington	0.02	0.008	0.82–7.81	0.32	2.32	0.46–0.89	3
Mendips	—	—	0.24–0.85	0.08	0.57	1.00–4.00	3
Trelogan	0.07–0.16	—	0.05	0.22–0.32	—	0.22	5
Black Rocks	0.26	0.06	8.49	0.36	1.91	1.62	6
Bonsall Moor	0.07	0.02	1.74	0.05	1.30	2.01	6
Bradford Dale	0.14	0.02	5.92	0.13	2.11	1.07	6
Dirtlow Rake	0.10	—	5.55	0.04	—	0.36	6
Whites Rake	0.17	0.02	2.80	0.16	1.75	0.59	6
Grattondale	0.02	—	0.77	0.07	—	2.57	6
Wensleydale	0.01	0.006	0.83	0.11	1.62	1.47	6

1—Shimwell and Laurie (1972), 2—Shaw (1984), 3—Ernst (1968), 4—Clark and Clarke (1981), 5—Johnston and Proctor (1977), 6—Hajar (1987).

3.6 VEGETATION AND COPPER MINES IN SRI LANKA

Brooks et al. (1985) have carried out geobotanical and biogeochemical studies over the Seruwila copper deposit some 20 km southeast of the town of Trincomalee. The copper has been mined for over 1000 years and there are numerous copper workings in the area (Plate 3.1). Soil and plant samples were collected along a 180 m transect across the ore body near a gossanous outcrop at Kollan Kulam (Fig. 3.2). Eighteen elements were determined in plant foliage and soil samples. The data showed that the ore pathfinders Ca, Co, Mg, Mn, Mo, Ni and P in soils and vegetation were indicative of mineralization in the area. Indicator plants included *Glycosmis mauritiana* and *Pterospermum canescens*. The investigations have not yet led to discovery of ancient artifacts due in part to the emphasis on mineral exploration and also to the unstable political situation (Tamil separatists have been active in this part of the country).

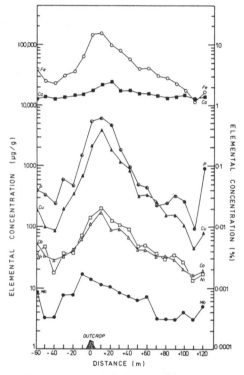

Fig. 3.2 Elemental concentrations in soils (Ca, Fe in %: others in æg/g) along a transect of a copper-magnetite ore body near Seruwila, Sri Lanka. The site is the scene of ancient copper workings. Source: Brooks et al. (1985). By courtesy of Elsevier Science Publishers, Amsterdam.

3.7 THE HEAVY METAL CONTENT OF MOSSES AND LICHENS FOUND OVER ANCIENT AND MEDIEVAL MINING SITES AND SMELTERS

There has already been a discussion in Chapter 2 of the association of cryptogams (mosses and lichens) with ancient and medieval mining sites and slag heaps from smelters in the western Harz. Several biogeochemical investigations on the heavy metal content of lichens from these sites have been carried out (e.g., Noeske et al., 1970; Lange and Ziegler, 1963). Attention has been centered around the Acarosporetum sinopicae Association

(Hilitzer, 1923) which belongs to the Acarosporion fuscatae Alliance (Klem, 1950). The copper and iron content of 10 species of this Association growing over mine tips and smelter slags in the western Harz has been determined by Lange and Ziegler (1963) (Table 3.4).

The iron content of *Acarospora sinopica* distinguishes this species from all other lichens in the community, and serves as a means of identification of this difficult-to-resolve species. Noeske et al. (1970) have also studied the metal content of lichens over medieval mining sites in the Harz. They determined not only the total metallic burden of the plants but also the localization of selected elements in specific plant organs. Their main findings were that five species (*Acarospora smaragdula*, *Lecanora hercynica*, *Lecidea macrocarpa*, *Stereocaulon denudatum* and *S. nanodes*) growing over 14th century slag heaps had a high elemental content compared with a control species (*Cornicularia aculeata*) growing over Middle Triassic carbonate rocks. The iron content of the five species ranged from 4875 to 14 409 mg/kg (ppm) compared with 563 mg/kg for the control.

TABLE 3.4 **Mean iron and copper contents (mg/kg dry weight) in lichens growing over medieval slag heaps on the Rammelsberg, Western Harz, East Germany. Data for the rock substrate are also included.**

	Iron		Copper	
# Species or substrate	Slags	Rock	Slags	Rock
1 *Acarospora sinopica*	44330	62500	1100	940
2 *A. smaragdula* var.	15100	—	60	—
3 *A. montana*	15400	1770	89	29
4 *Leconora epanora*	5832	3164	220	27
5 *Rhizocarpon oederi*	5833	—	1670	—
6 *Lecidea macrocarpa*	14580	—	160	—
7 *Stereocaulon dactylophyllum*	6000	250	80	35
8 *S. vesuvianum*	8300	450	100	15
9 *Cladonia arbuscula*	1070	558	80	15
10 *Cornicularia aculeata*	424	270	37	25
Slag* (1–4)	30000	—	9800	
(7,8)	34000	—	5400	—
(9,10)	—	—	9000	
Sandstone (1–4)	—	45000	—	<100
Basalt** (7,8)	120000	—	—	—

**Basalt from Mt Meissner, Hassia, E. Germany. * Slags found at sites where Rammelsberg ore had been smelted or is supposed to have been smelted. Source: Lange and Ziegler (1963). By courtesy of Floristisch-soziologische Gemeinschaft, Göttingen.

3.8 BIOGEOCHEMICAL MAPPING OF TERRAIN CONTAINING ANCIENT AND MEDIEVAL MINING SITES

The question arises as to whether biogeochemical prospecting for ore deposits would also lend itself to archaeological prospecting. Pape (1981) made the premise that the chemical composition of conifer needles and evergreen leaves would reflect the nature of the geological substrate. He determined 23 elements in leaves and needles from plants (*Calluna*, *Juniperus* and *Picea*) growing over a titanium deposit in southern Norway, and in leaves (*Picea* and *Calluna*) from the Harz region of Lower Saxony. He established that elemental concentrations, as well as combinations of them, gave a key to the nature of the substrate.

Different types of rock, mineralization, and anthropogenic workings, were identified by anomalous elemental concentrations in the plant material. This indicates the possibility of the usefulness of such procedures in archaeological prospecting.

In a comprehensive study, Johannes and Krause (1985) developed computer-generated maps of the northwestern Harz and its environs (600 km) based on data from the concentrations of 23 elements in pine needles and leaves of *Calluna*. The work involved mathematical treatment of concentration intervals in a procedure different from that of Pape (1981). The maps were prepared for individual elements rather than for combinations of them, because reworking of geological material in the ancient Harz mining region (mining had been carried out for 1500 years) has been so extensive, and the effects on plant physiology so profound, that the former method of data presentation provided no clear picture.

These elemental concentration interval maps gave an indication not only of ore deposits, but also of medieval and later metal-rich mine dumps derived from mines, ore treatment, and smelting operations. There also indications were of former ore carriageways (from pieces of ore that had fallen from moving transport wagons), sites of particulate emission such as smelting hearths, and anthropogenically-contaminated stream sediments. During the sampling program, special attention was paid to the presence of indicator plants (metallophytes and calciphile plants) as well as to morphological changes in the vegetation such as *dwarfism, chlorosis, necrosis,* and the presence of barren areas. Indications of the presence of montane areas of historical interest were in most cases signaled by the geobotanical and biogeochemical investigations.

In some cases the biogeochemical method could be used to identify unknown and previously-known locations of ancient mine dumps from which the slag had long since disappeared. At these sites anomalous elemental concentrations in leaves still gave some indication of the original operations at the location.

3.9 CHAPTER SUMMARY

This chapter is concerned with the use of biogeochemistry (chemical analysis of vegetation) to detect archaeological remains. Case histories include chemical analysis of pre-15th century mine dumps at Mansfeld in East Germany. Weathering to ground level has rendered these dumps non-recognizable topographically even though they support a specialized metal-tolerant flora. Chemical analysis of the soils confirms the identity of these structures.

In Zaïre, chemical analysis of "copper flowers" such as *Haumaniastrum katangense* enables a distinction to be made between plants growing over mineralized sites and those growing over metal-rich smelter sites containing buried artifacts of the precolonial period. Similar work was carried out using various metal-tolerant plant species in Britain such as *Minuartia verna, Thlaspi alpestre,* and *Armeria maritima.*

The use of chemical analysis of lichens to identify mining sites in Britain and Germany has also been discussed.

Perhaps one of the most effective methods of biogeochemical prospecting has been reported from the western Harz region of West Germany. Spruce (*Picea* sp.) needles and leaves of *Calluna* sp. have been analyzed for 23 elements. A statistical treatment of the data using a form of discriminant analysis has been used to identify geological substrates that could contain old mine workings together with their associated artifacts.

REFERENCES

Brooks, R. R. 1972. *Geobotany and Biogeochemistry in Mineral Exploration.* Harper Row, New York.

_____ 1983. *Biological Methods of Exploration for Minerals*. Wiley, New York.

Brooks, R. R., Baker, A. J. M., Ramakrishna, R. S., and Ryan, D. E. 1985. Botanical and geochemical exploration studies at the Seruwila copper-magnetite prospect in Sri Lanka. *J. Geochem. Explor.* 24: 223–235.

Brooks, R. R., and Malaisse, F. 1985. *The Heavy Metal—Tolerant Flora of Southcentral Africa*. Balkema, Rotterdam.

Clark, R. K., and Clarke, S. C. 1981. Floristic diversity in relation to soil characteristics in a lead mining complex in the Pennines, England. *New Phytol.* 87: 799–815.

Duvigneaud, P. 1959. Plantes 'cobaltophytes' dans le Haut Katanga. *Bull. Soc. Roy. Bot. Belg.* 91: 111–134.

Ernst, W. 1966. Ökologisch-soziologische Untersuchungen an Schwermetallgesellschaften Südfrankreichs und des östlichen Harzvorlandes. *Flora (Jena)* 156: 301–318.

_____ 1968. Zur Kenntnis der Soziologie und Ökologie der Schwermetallvegetation Grossbritanniens. *Ber. Dt. Bot. Ges.* 81: 116–124.

Farago, M. E., Mullen, V. A., Cole, M. M., and Smith, R. F. 1980. A study of *Armeria maritima* (Mill.) Willdenow growing in a copper-impregnated bog. *Environ. Pollut.* 21: 225–244.

Hajar, A. S. M. 1987. *The Comparative Ecology of Minuartia verna (L.) Hiern., and Thlaspi alpestre L. in the Southern Pennines with Special Reference to Metalliferous Soils*. Ph.D. Thesis, University of Sheffield.

Hilitzer, A. 1923. Prispevky k lisejnikum Sumavy a Posumavy. *Cas. Nar. Mus. Praha 97.*

Johnston, W. R., and Proctor, J. 1977. A comparative study of metal levels in plants from two contrasting lead-mine sites. *Pl. Soil* 46: 251–257.

Johannes, D., and Krause, H. 1985. Ergebnisse biogeochemischer Untersuchungen im Bereich des Nordwestharzes. *Erzmetall* 38: 432–440.

Kovalevsky, A. L. 1987. *Biogeochemical Exploration for Mineral Deposits*. VNU Science Press, Utrecht.

Lange, O. L., and Ziegler, H. 1963. Der Schwermetallgehalt von Flechten aus dem Acarosporetum sinopicae auf Erzschlackenhalden des Harzes. *Mitt. Flor.-soz. Arbgm.* 10: 156–177.

Malaisse, F., and Brooks, R. R. 1982. Colonisation of modified metalliferous environments in Zaïre by the copper plant *Haumaniastrum katangense*. *Pl. Soil* 64: 289–293.

Malyuga, D. P. 1964. *Biogeochemical Methods of Prospecting*. Consultants Bureau, New York.

Noeske, O., Lauchlii, A., Lange, O. L., Vieweg, G. H., and Ziegler, H. 1970. Konzentration und Lokalisierung von Schwermetallen in Flechten der Erzschlackenhalden des Harzes. *Flechtensymp. 1969, Vorträge Gesamtgebiet Bot. N.F.* 4: 67–69.

Pape, H. 1981. *Development of a Geochemical Mapping Method for the Prospecting Deposits, Environmental Research and Regional Planning on the Basis of Multielement Investigations of Plant Ashes*. Gebrüder Borntraeger, Berlin.

Plaen, G. de, Malaisse, F., and Brooks, R. R. 1982. The copper flowers of Central Africa and their significance for archaeological and mineral prospecting. *Endeavour* 6: 72–77.

Rascio, N. 1977. Metal accumulation by some plants growing on zinc-mine deposits. *Oikos* 29: 250–253.

Reeves, R. D., and Brooks, R. R. 1983. Hyperaccumulation of lead and zinc by two metallophytes from a mining area in Central Europe. *Environ. Pollut.* 31: 277–287.

Schubert, R. 1953/54. Die Schwermetallpflanzengesellschaften des östlichen Harzvorlandes. *Wiss. Z. Martin Luther Univ. Halle-Wittenberg Math. Nat. Kl.* III 1953/1954: 51–70.

Shaw, S. C. 1984. *Ecophysiological Studies on Heavy-metal Tolerance in Plants Colonising Tideslow Rake, Derbyshire*. Ph.D. Thesis, University of Sheffield.

Shimwell, D. W., and Laurie, A. E. 1972. Lead and zinc contamination of vegetation in the Southern Pennines. *Environ. Pollut.* 3: 291–301.

Chapter 4

THE INFLUENCE OF ANCIENT TRADE ROUTES ON ANTHROPOGENIC MODIFICATION OF VEGETATION

4.1 INTRODUCTION

In an excellent review of the subject of anthropogenic modification of world floras, Jäger (1977) has shown that such changes can be classified under the following headings:

1) preservation of relic species that would otherwise have become extinct. An example of this is the persistence in open areas of heliophile post-glacial plants that would have been threatened by natural reforestation after the Ice Ages. Man has preserved the open environment by deforestation for agriculture.

2) areal expansion of certain species by colonization of previously inaccessible ecological niches made available by human activities such as eliminating competing species or creating new environments that a given species may colonise successfully.

3) development of new strains and cultivars of plants. New subspecies can develop naturally, once geographical barriers have been removed by human activities such as trade. These activities are related to inadvertent actions (e.g. establishment of weeds in certain areas) or to advertent colonization of new areas by crop plants.

4) areal reduction of species distribution by agriculture or by over-utilization of certain plants for food, timber or medicinal uses. Other human activities producing this effect are drainage and eutrophy.

5) extinction of plants. For example in the Hawaiian islands, 700 endemic species have already been rendered extinct, primarily by agriculture.

There is little doubt that improved trade links have greatly facilitated the areal expansion of plants. In the more advanced countries, new species introductions reached a peak in the middle of the 19th century coincident with the development of sophisticated railroad networks. This has now been surpassed by species extinctions. Fig. 4.1 shows dates for the first appearance of new taxa in Germany (Rothmaler, 1976).

A study of anthropogenic modification of floras can lead to the identification of ancient trade routes and trails, as the following case histories demonstrate.

4.2 AREAL EXPANSION OF PLANTS BY SEA ROUTES

There is a stand of *Alyssum corsicum* (Plate 4.1) in the suburbs of the city of Bastia in Corsica. The site consists of a few hectares of ultramafic (serpentine) soil, a substrate extremely unfavorable for most plants because of its high content of nickel and magnesium and its low nutrient status. These ultramafic soils usually carry a highly specific and unusual flora (Krause, 1958; Brooks, 1987) characterized by a paucity of species, a high degree of endemism, and the appearance of abnormal and stunted forms.

Alyssum corsicum was discovered early in the 19th century (Duby, 1828) and at that time was thought to be endemic to Corsica. It is endemic to ultramafic rocks and requires this type of substrate for growth and seed germination. However, in the 1950s, D. Huber-Morath discovered that this plant was widespread in western Anatolia, Turkey in an area that had been an important source of grain in antiquity.

It appears that *A. corsicum* was brought to Corsica inadvertently as weed seed in grain

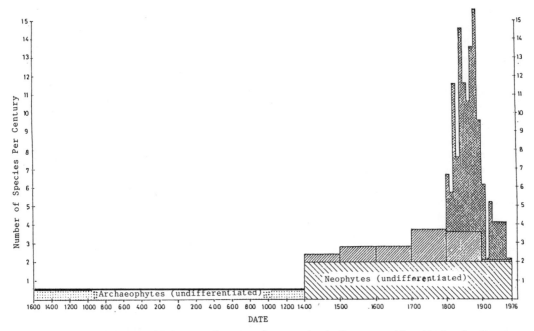

Fig. 4.1 Date of first establishment of native plant species in Germany. After: Rothmaler (1976).

shipments from Anatolia. Fortuitously, there was a small outcrop of ultramafic rocks near the port where the grain and its "weeds" fell literally upon "stony ground" so that a small colony of the plants became established and remains to this day.

The traders who brought *Alyssum corsicum* to Corsica have been thought to have been either the Phoenecians or the Venetians. It is true that Phoenecians visited Corsica in the 6th century B.C. from their strongholds in Sicily and Sardinia, but the only port in Corsica at that time was Alalia (Aleria), some 60 km south of the present site of Bastia. Corsica was at that time controlled by the Greek Phocaeans who were conquered later in the same century by the Etruscans. It is therefore unlikely that the Phoenecians brought *A. corsicum* to Corsica.

It is probable that the Venetians brought the grain and its "weeds" from Anatolia because they had important trading links between western Anatolia (a source of grain) and Corsica (a source of timber).

The fate of the only colony of *Alyssum corsicum* in the western Mediterranean now hangs in the balance since developers are keen to build over this unique site to extend the city (which can be clearly seen in the background of Plate 4.1). Conservationists, led by Madame Marcelle Conrad of Miomo near Bastia are trying hard to halt the march of "progress" and it is hoped that 20th century man will not succeed in destroying a fascinating piece of evidence concerning trade routes of the early Middle Ages.

4.3 AREAL EXPANSION OF PLANTS ALONG NATIVE TRAILS

4.3.1 Indian Trails in Kansas, U.S.A.

Blasing (1986) has studied Indian trails near Flint Hills, Kansas. The trails belong to the Late Ceramic period and are delineated by numerous clues including the presence of burial mounds, quarries, collection stations, and workshops. These are common everywhere where the trail passes near chert outcrops; chert was used by the early Indians for knives, scrapers and other tools.

Botanical evidence for the location of the ancient trails is provided by the presence of certain plant species such as the native pawpaw (*Asimina triloba*) with its highly prized and edible fruit. At Deep Creek, in the Flint Hills, this species is close to the extreme edge of its habitat. It prefers a moister climate and is found only where the trail passes near shady areas well watered by springs. The fruit was eaten by these early Indians and the seeds thrown away. The seeds are large and heavy so that it was difficult for them to spread any distance by natural means other than being eaten by animals and spread by this means. Blasing (1986) found pawpaw trees in four valleys of the Deep Creek area. Three of these were at Shane Creek, Hackberry Creek, and Pawpaw Glen. The fourth was a tributary directly south of Pillsbury Crossing (Fig. 4.2). It is likely that the collection localities were part of the trail; the three valleys would have given excellent access to or from the uplands.

4.3.2 Indian Trails in North Dakota, U.S.A.

In North Dakota, Beckes et al. (1982) found an unusual concentration of limber pine (*Pinus flexilis*) along an ancient Indian trail. The seeds of this tree were a prehistoric food source. Since the stands were outside the normal range for this species, it was inferred that they had spread downslope from Indian camp sites along the trail where seeds had been dropped as prehistoric groups passed through the area.

The stand is located on U.S. Federal land about 20 km north of Marmarth (Fig. 4.2), North Dakota. It occurs on a series of low scoria-capped hills near the confluence of the Little Missouri River and Cannonball Creek. The average elevation of the site is about 870 m. A detailed ecological analysis of the stand was carried out by Potter and Green (1964) who concluded from dendrochronological measurements that the oldest trees were 238 years old.

Loendorf (1978) carried out archaeological reconnaissance in the vicinity of the stand and found five prehistoric sites ranging from sparse lithic scatters to a more extensive camp-site, such as at Gulley Egg, where multiple fire hearths, butchered bones, and numerous stone artifacts were discovered. Extensive research in other areas (Frison, 1978) has demon-strated the association of limber pine stands with archaeological sites at several high-altitude locations in northern Wyoming.

From dendrochronological studies at the Little Missouri Badlands site, Beckes et al. (1982) suggested a maximum age of 600 years for the stand. The stand was clearly anthro-pogenic rather than natural, since it occurred at an altitude 1500 m below its normal range and was separated by a distance of 250–400 km from its next nearest neighbors.

It seems that the limber pine stand is related to native trails, since natural pathways or routes of least resistance were heavily utilized by the prehistoric inhabitants of southwestern North Dakota. The Little Missouri River and Cannonball Creek confluence forms a vertical intersection of two natural transportation corridors. The former originates in the vicinity of Devils' Tower, Wyoming, and was a well known route for prehistoric and early historic groups travelling between the Black Hills and the Missouri River. Cannonball Creek is one of the major western tributaries of the Little Missouri, and is a natural access route to the Powder River Basin. Late prehistoric groups travelling from the Black Hills or the Powder River country around 1300 A.D. are the most likely candidates for the accidental or inten-tional propagation of this stand.

4.3.3 Native Trails in Africa

The delineation of native trails in central Africa has been studied by Plaen (1988) who has found a good example for trade routes between Shaba Province, Zaïre, and Ruanda. He has noted negative indications of the routes as evidenced by the disappearance of vegetation along 15th century east-west trails, caused by mechanical trampling of the vegetation by many thousands of feet. Traces of these ancient trails are very obvious in the Marangu Mts. of Shaba.

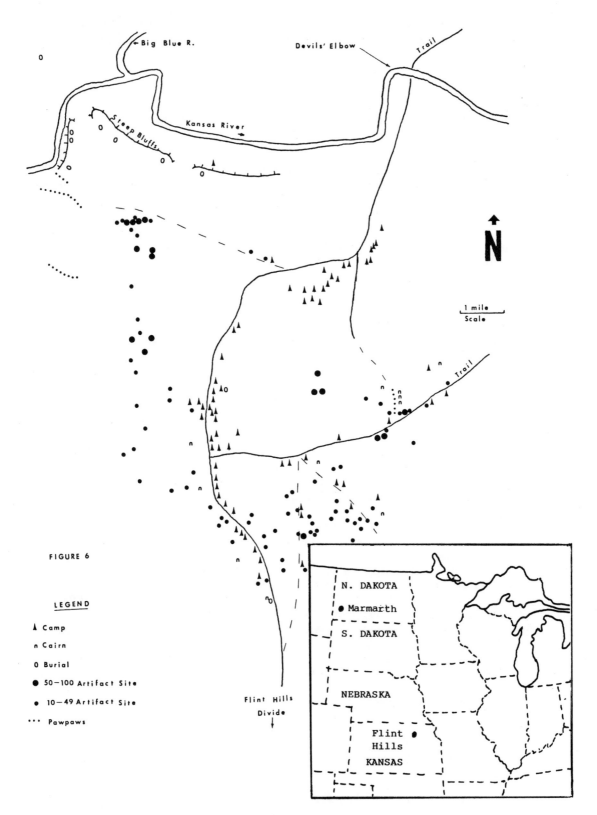

Fig. 4.2 Map of Indian trails in the Deep Creek Drainage area, Kansas, U.S.A. The site of stands of pawpaw (*Asimina triloba*) is shown. Source: Blasing (1986). By courtesy of the author.

A positive indication of human activity along the trails has been afforded by the presence of numerous ancient copper smelter sites along the routes (see Chapters 2 and 3).

4.4 CHAPTER SUMMARY

This chapter is concerned with the influence of ancient trade routes upon the distribution of plant species. Anthropogenic modification of world floras has been achieved in several main ways. Among these is the areal colonization of previously-inaccessible ecological niches rendered available by human activity. A striking example of this is afforded by the presence of the nickel-accumulating herb *Alyssum corsicum* in a very restricted area on the island of Corsica. The stand is found on a few hectares of nickel-rich ultramafic (serpentine) soil at the outskirts of the port of Bastia. It transpires that the plants had been brought to the site as weed seed in a shipment of grain brought from western Turkey by Venetian traders.

Native trails in North America have also been responsible for the movement of many plant species away from their normal habitat. An example of this is the distribution of the native paw paw (*Asimina triloba*) in Kansas, and the limber pine (*Pinus flexilis*) in North Dakota.

Native trails in Central Africa are characterized by a deficiency of several plant species (an example of negative phytoarchaeological indicators) due to mechanical trampling under foot and their utilization as food. The precolonial copper smelters (see Chapters 2 and 3) with associated stands of the "copper flower" *Haumaniastrum katangense* are commonly found along these ancient trails.

REFERENCES

Beckes, M. R., Jagler, B. K., Burge, T. L., and Love, T. G. 1982. Possible cultural origin of an isolated stand of *Pinus flexilus* in the Little Missouri Badlands. *Unpublished paper presented at 39th Annual Plains Anthropological Conference*, Bismarck, North Dakota.

Blasing, R. 1986. Archeological survey of the Upper Deep Creek Drainage, Kansas. *Dep. Anthrop. Report Wichita State Univ. Wichita.*

Brooks, R. R. 1987. *Serpentine and its Vegetation: a Multidisciplinary Approach.* Dioscorides Press, Portland.

Duby, J. E. 1828. *Alyssum corsicum.* In, De Candolle [ed.] *Botanica Gallica* 1: 34.

Frison, G. 1978. *Prehistoric Hunters of the High Plains.* Academic Press, New York.

Krause, W. 1958. Andere Bodenspezialisten. In W. Rühland [ed.] *Handbuch der Pflanzenphysiologie,* v.4. Springer, Berlin: 755–806.

Jäger, E. J. 1977. Veränderungen des Artenbestandes von Floren unter den Einfluss des Menschen. *Biol. Rundsch.* 15: 287–300.

Loendorf, L. L. 1978. An evaluation of 100 archeological and historical sites in the Little Missouri grasslands of North Dakota. *Report to U.S. Forest Service, Dickinson, North Dakota.*

Plaen, G. de 1988. Les Indices Phytoarchéologiques. *In, La Métallurgie Ancienne au Shaba.* A.C.C.T. Paris.

Potter, L. D., and Green, D. L. 1964. Ecology of the northeastern outlying stand of *Pinus flexilis. Ecology* 45: 866–868.

Rothmaler, W. 1976. *Exkursionsflora für die Gebiete der D.D.R. und B.R.D.* Volk und Wissen V.E.B., Berlin.

Chapter 5

PLANT INDICATORS OF ANCIENT ANTHROPOGENIC MODIFICATION OF SOILS

5.1 INTRODUCTION

From time immemorial, man has modified the vegetation of his environment by various advertent and inadvertent activities. Human activity has been responsible for the preservation of some species (particularly Ice Age relics), and for the increase or decrease of the areal distribution of others. Wilmanns (1965/66) has discussed the effect of man upon the distribution of cryptogams (mosses and lichens) in Europe, and we have also shown in Chapter 2 how medieval mine tips and slag heaps have provided suitable ecological niches.

Apart from mining and smelting operations, the vegetation over ancient and medieval archaeological sites has been influenced by other human activities, not the least of which is the alteration of the nutrient status of the soils by increased levels of phosphate and nitrogen derived from human and animal remains and from their effluents.

Early agriculture also resulted in the destruction of forests and the establishment or preservation of heliophile plants and "weeds" which could not survive in a forested environment. Another contribution to the nutrient status of soils has been provided by building operations in which limestone blocks or the associated mortar have weathered to produce a calcium-rich substrate which profoundly affects the composition of the surface vegetation and provides a valuable clue to that which lies beneath the surface soil.

There are 7 main ways in which human activity can modify soils and produce changes in the vegetation above archaeological sites:

1) clearance of forests, 2) increase of the phosphate level in soils, 3) increase in nitrate and general nutrient levels in soils, 4) establishment of mine tips and slag heaps from mining activities (see Chapter 2), 5) disturbance of soils by agriculture thus allowing for introduction of weeds, 6) increase of the calcium content of soils by building activities, and 7) drainage of wetlands for agriculture.

Some of the above changes will now be considered in more detail.

5.2 ELEVATED PHOSPHATE LEVELS IN SOILS

It is well known that the soil above ancient burial mounds (barrows) is usually enriched in phosphate. This phosphate is derived not only from the bones of the corpse(s) buried therein, but also from bones of sacrificial animals (or sometimes humans) buried along with the most important occupant. Food was often buried in the barrows to give refreshment to the chieftain on his way to, and at, his final destination.

When a grave has remained undisturbed, the phosphate content of the surface soil is only slightly enriched compared to background. It is more strongly enriched if the surface soil has been excavated by grave robbers so that there has been mixture of the upper and lower soil horizons. Lorch (1951) has developed the "phosphate method" for establishing whether or not a given site is a burial mound, and if so whether it has been subjected to plundering. The method depends on analysing a statistically-significant number of samples both from the site and from adjacent "background" areas.

A specific example of this procedure has been given by Jacob (1952) for the Fürstenstand barrow on the Kreiberg near Daschendorf (Lower Franconia, West Germany). The grave has a diameter of about 20 m and a height of about 1.5 m. (Fig. 5.1). There still remains a circle of stones around the site. The depression at the top is not necessarily a result of grave-robbing because in many such mounds, the collapse of internal structures can lead to these declivities. Local tradition implies that the name Fürstenstand (Fürst = prince or sovereign) is derived from the fact that a noble of some importance was buried there in the 10th century A.D. along with many gold implements and pieces of jewellery. This gold would have been an incentive to plundering of the grave.

The phosphate content of soils from a traverse of this site (Fig. 5.1) ranged from 0.3 to 0.9 mg/g (300–900 ppm) and clearly shows that the site had been plundered in the Middle Ages or later.

Though not carried out in this case, analysis of the vegetation cover would probably have shown patterns corresponding with the range of phosphate levels encountered.

Several interesting phytoarchaeological projects have been carried out in Ghana, Africa, by M. Posnansky (pers. comm.). In 1975 and 1979 he mapped the trees round the old town of Bagho which existed between 1150 and 1800 A.D. In its heyday, Bagho was involved in the gold trade to the north. The quarters lived in by the different ethnic and occupational groups can easily be distinguished by their thick growth of elephant grass. The elephant grass grows well because of higher concentrations of phosphates and nitrates in the soil, accumulated over years of constant occupation. Around the quarters there is a fringe of trees and shrubs. These features show up well in aerial photographs.

The Furstenstand Burial Mound

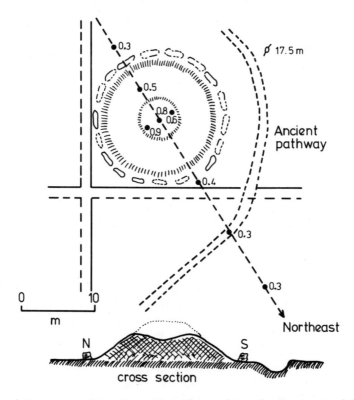

Fig. 5.1 Phosphate concentrations (mg/g) in soils overlying the Fürstenstand barrow in Lower Franconia, West Germany. Source: Jacob (1952).

In the successor village of Hani, Posnansky and his co-workers observed the same enhanced vegetation in the environs and compared the vegetation around the modern village with that around Bagho. They mapped the vegetation along transects extending one kilometer on each side of the sites. The fringe vegetation was far richer than in the surrounding savanna, with roughly double the number of tree species and large numbers of fruit trees, including citrus, silk cotton, and baobab. Some of the trees may have been planted intentionally, but Posnansky considered that most of the trees had grown from seeds contained either in household rubbish or feces. Because the land around the villages was used for rubbish disposal and sanitary purposes it was heavily enriched in plant nutrients. The larger trees, gave shade as they grew, for more delicate plants to thrive. This same phenomenon has been observed by J. Anquandah (cited by Posnansky in his pers. comm.) at other Ghanaian archaeological sites.

Posnansky carried out similar work in Jamaica and found fringe vegetation around human occupation sites that was unusually rich in both medicinal and nutritional plants. The interesting feature of the medicinal plants is that they were normally of the same plant families as those occurring around West African sites. This seems to indicate that slaves brought to Jamaica from West Africa, sought or brought with them, the same medicinal plants that had been of use to them in their former home.

5.3 ELEVATED LEVELS OF NITRATE AND OTHER NUTRIENTS IN SOILS

Human settlement invariably produces an increase in levels of nitrates and other nutrients in soils in the area. This increase follows from natural animal and plant effluents and remains, rather than from artificial fertilizers which were not used until the 19th century. The previous section concerning Ghanaian sites mentioned phosphate specifically, but it is probable that nitrate was equally important in determining their fringe vegetation.

Lohmeyer (1954) has discussed the origins of many associations of nitrophilous "weeds" in Central Europe and has shown that their distribution is largely anthropogenic in origin. This can be related to runoff from early settlements with the accumulation of nitrates along the flood banks of rivers providing an ecological niche from which plants later spread along the watercourses (Table 5.1).

TABLE 5.1   List of nitrophile weeds originally introduced into Central Europe as a result of runoff from early settlements.

Agrostis stolonifera	Alopecurus geniculatus	Arctium lappa
A. tomentosum	Artemisia vulgaris	Atriplex hastata
Bidens tripartita	Capsella bursa-pastoris	Carduus crispus
Chaerophyllum bulbosum	Chenopodium album	C. glaucum
C. polyspermum	C. rubrum	Chrysanthemum inodorum
Cirsium arvense	Convolvulus sepium	Cuscuta europaea
Galium aparine	Inula britannica	Lamium album
Lolium perenne	Panicum crusgalli	Plantago major
Poa annua	Polygonum aviculare	P. brittingeri
P. nodosum	P. persicaria	Potentilla anserina
P. reptans	Rorippa sylvestris	Rumex crispus
R. obtusifolius	Senecio fluviatilis	Stellaria media
Tanacetum vulgare		

Source: Lohmeyer (1954).

The role of nitrates and other nutrients in the pinpointing of early abandoned settlements throughout Europe has been described by Margl (1971). The species composition of such sites presents a recurring pattern of impoverishment in species numbers (Malek, 1966). In contrast to this overall impoverishment, there is an increase in the number of nitrophilous plants as well as those favoring phosphate, potassium, and calcium.

The competition from this first group of nitrophilous plants results in the elimination of many woodland species. However, the mere absence of such species is not an infallible indication of the presence of nearby early settlements.

A second group of plants whose presence indicates early abandoned settlements, includes medicinal, cultivated, and garden plants (at castles, monasteries etc.) that originated in other climatic regions and adapted well to the prevailing environmental conditions of partial shade. Fischer-Benzon (1894) has given an overview of such plants used in the Middle Ages. Table 5.2 lists nitrophilous plants and garden escapees. The latter are mainly fruit and vegetable species which have reverted to the wild state. Both groups of plants now form part of the climax stage of the deciduous *Quercus-Fagus* forest.

TABLE 5.2   Plants which may indicate the presence of abandoned early settlements in forested areas of Central Europe.

Group I—direct indicators		
Carex muricata	Chelidonium majus	Fraxinus excelsior
Galium aparine	Geranium robertianum	Geum urbanum
Lamium maculatum	Parietaria officinalis	Poa trivialis
Pulmonaria officinalis	Sambucus nigra	Torilis anthriscus
Ulmus campestris	Urtica dioica	
Group II—garden escapees		
Acer platanoides	Acorus calamus	Althaea officinalis
Aristolochia clematitis	Arum maculatum	Asarum europaeum
Euphorbia lathyrus	Hedera helix	Helleborus viridis
Melissa officinalis	Nepeta cataria	Scilla bifolia
Staphylea pinnata	Vinca minor	

Source: Margl (1971).

The reconstruction of the typical flora of an abandoned early settlement is not difficult to achieve since it can be done by comparison with the vegetation over known abandoned settlements.

In the climax woodland, the indicator flora persists for a very long time so that abandoned settlements dating from the early Middle Ages can still be identified. However, in more humid areas the nutrients leached out of the soil much faster and the time frame of discovery is thereby shortened.

Vegetation over cleared land cannot be used for the location of early settlements and other methods have to be used.

Plants whose distribution results from nutrient enrichment provide a direct and accurate pinpointing of old settlements, whereas garden escapees usually have a wider distribution and indicate general rather than specific areas where archaeological sites might be located.

Meadow thickets and the edges of forests, whose soils are enriched with nutrients from adjacent open areas, often contain a high proportion of nitrophilous species. These can be differentiated from soils covering early settlements by the absence of garden escapees.

In general, this method for locating archaeological sites is most effective where large areas of woodland are involved. According to Jäger (1977), the use of mineral fertilizers in the

19th century changed meadows to pastures that no longer provided a refuge for garden plants because of the much stronger competition from the new and more vigorous grasses which had been concomitantly introduced. We therefore cannot expect to find garden escapees over late abandoned settlements when the climax vegetation has been re-established. This is only of academic interest since the location of these settlements would hardly be unknown.

5.4 CALCIPHILOUS PLANTS AS INDICATORS OF MIDDENS AND OF ANCIENT WALLS AND BUILDINGS

5.4.1 Introduction

Calciphilous plants (limestone floras) are a readily discernable indication of limestone areas (Brooks, 1983). Calcium has a great effect on vegetation and usually carries a characteristic flora which renders the geological boundary easy to delineate.

The effect of calcium on plants depends more on its solubility than on the absolute amount present. The solubility of limestone in water is about 0.1% whereas dolomite (calcium magnesium carbonate) is about half as soluble. Many of the effects of calcium are indirect. Lime has a favorable effect on the drainage and texture of the soil and is able to coagulate many of the colloidal compounds which make a soil heavy and poorly drained. The result of this conditioning effect is that many plants that thrive in any type of soil in warm and dry climates, tend to confine themselves to calcareous soils at higher latitudes, since these are the only soils that can provide the conditions that they require. A striking example is the beech *Fagus sylvatica* which thrives everywhere in southern Europe but in its natural (more northerly) state, as for example in England, is confined to limestone.

Plant communities that thrive on calcareous soils are said to be *calciphilous* and exclude *calcifuge* plants such as the Ericaceae which require a low pH to thrive.

An anthropogenic calcareous soil can be created by one of two main activities. The first is the use of limestone blocks with associated cement or mortar for building purposes. The second, confined mainly to primitive cultures, involves rubbish dumps of shellfish (*middens*). In both cases the limestone weathers to a calcareous soil which can support a calciphilous flora readily identifiable from the surface of the terrain.

5.4.2 Ancient Walls and Buildings

Accumulation of calcium in the soil resulting from limestone and mortar used in building activities can produce a characteristic calciphilous flora with both lower and higher plants. A good example of the former has been given by Wilmanns (1965/66) who observed the colonization by calciphilous lichens of ancient vineyard soil-retaining walls on Spitzberg Mountain near Tübingen in southwestern Germany (BRD). The stones had been brought to the site from the nearest limestone area some 20 km away. They were colonised by elements of the Calophacetum arenariae Association dominated by lichens such as *Calophaca arenaria* and *Verrucaria macrostoma*.

A striking example of the colonization of ancient ruins by higher plants has been given by Rodi (1974). The *Rätischer Limes* (Plate 5.1) is a Roman boundary wall (limes) built of limestone boulders that stretches eastwards from *Schwäbisch Gmünd* in Württemberg West Germany, to the heights between Remstal and the Leintal valley. In the woods between Mögglingen and Heuchlingen (Fig. 5.2), remnants of the Rätischer Limes appear as a stone wall up to one meter in height and several meters wide. It can be traced for about one kilometer and is known locally as the *Teufelsmauer* (Devil's wall). The wall is interspersed with heavily-ruined watch towers. The stones were quarried from the Black Lower Triassic (*Schwarzer Jura*) limestone and overlay Lower Triassic clays of different types (Fig. 5.2).

The wall is now a walking track delineated not only by geology but also by the ubiquitous presence of a narrow band of *Vicia dumetorum-Quercus-Fagus* woodland. Each of the five geological formations in the figure is covered with its own characteristic vegetation. The pH of the soil directly over the wall is 7.0 and falls to 4.5 over the background where the *Luzula luzuloides* reflects the high acidity and the sea grass the variable moisture status of the clays. The Rätischer Limes carries a calciphilous community including: *Vicia dumetorum, Lathyrus vernus, Asarum europaeum, Convallaria majalis, Galium odoratum,*

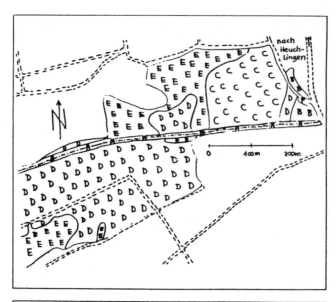

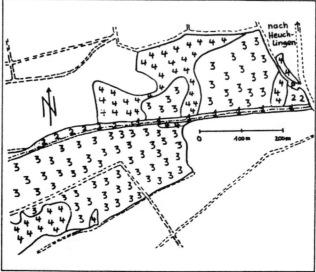

Fig. 5.2 Soil (above) and vegetation (below) maps of the *Rätischer Limes* Roman wall and its surroundings.

    A—calcareous black and brown earth over a flat limestone (wall) base
    B—marly soil over Liassic clays
    C—damp double-layered brown earth derived from surface loam over Liassic clays
    D—damp argillaceous soils over Lower and Middle Jurassic clays
    E—intermittently-damp argillaceous soils over Lower and Middle Jurassic clays
    1—*Mercurialis perennis—Quercus—Fagus* woodland
    2—*Vicia dumetorum—Quercus—Fagus* woodland
    3—*Luzula luzuloides—Quercus—Fagus* woodland
    4—*Ficaria verna—Quercus—Fagus* woodland
    The *Ratischer Limes* is shown by the symbol _ . _ . _ . _ . _ .

Lamium galeobdolon, Campanula trachelium, and *Aegopodium podagraria.* Over the eastern part of the wall there is a *Mercurialis perennis-Quercus-Fagus* woodland with accompanying calciphilous species such as *Acer campestre, Acer pseudoplatanus, Euonymus europaeus* and, dominantly *Mercurialis perennis* (Plate 5.2).

5.4.3 Middens

The presence of calcium carbonate in shell middens (rubbish dumps) established by former ancient cultures would be expected to influence the nature of the vegetation by producing a local enclave of calcareous soil. Sawbridge and Bell (1972) recognised 6 vegetation dominance types on shell middens on the coast of British Columbia. The middens had been created by the Kwatiutl Indian tribe and were from 1000–6000 years old. Although midden horizons contained high levels of exchangeable calcium (5125–14350 ppm), vegetation on adjacent areas was frequently similar to that on the middens. The authors concluded that the shell deposits had little or no influence on the vegetation of the surrounding forest. However, a community dominated by *Pseudotsuga menziesii* did appear to be associated with the occurrence of prehistoric house depressions on midden sites. Although the work of Sawbridge and Bell (1972) apparently does present largely negative data, their methodology was basically very sound and should be emulated by others wishing to discover the presence of shell middens elsewhere.

Elsewhere in the Pacific Northwest, Browman (pers. comm.) used the presence of blackberry and raspberry (*Rubus*) bushes to locate shell middens. He presumed that these plants favored the increased alkalinity promoted by the shells.

Grabert (pers. comm.) has also described plant indicators of shell middens in the same general area in the Pacific Northwest:

> Typical vegetation on a coastal habitation site, often based on shell midden accumulations of varying sizes, consists of the following: wild crabapple (*Pyrus furca*), several varities of wild rose (*Rosa nutkana, R. pisocarpa, R. gymnocarpa*), wild raspberry (*Rubus idaeus*), blackcap berry (*Rosa leucodema*), and thimbleberry (*Rubus parviflora*).

> Thistles (mainly *Cirsium brevistylum*), the cow parsnip (*Heracleum lanatum,* and the Oregon grape (*Berberis aquifolium*) are other examples of plants growing over shell midden sites. Sites lacking large shell accumulations or none, will not have the entire plant assemblage, or may be hard to distinguish from the surrounding wild cover. Where the soil moisture remains fairly constant, there may also be the skunk cabbage (*Lysichiton americanum*), *Equisetum*, bracken fern, and others.

The worldwide distribution of characteristic vegetation above shell middens is well established. Even in Australia these structures have been identified and photographed from the air (see Chapter 16).

5.5 DRAINAGE OF WETLANDS

Brief mention will be made of drainage of wetlands as an anthropogenic modification of soils. The link between this human activity and the location of abandoned settlements is somewhat tenuous. The effect of the exploitation of wetlands for agriculture has been to diminish the areal extent of the distribution of certain plant types, particularly cryptogams (mosses and lichens). An example of this is the areal reduction of the Lobarion Alliance (Arnold, 1864; Barkmann, 1958) dominated by such lichen species as *Lobaria pulmonaria, L. scrobiculata, Nephroma bellum, N. resupinatum, Menegazzia pertusa, Sticta fuliginosa* and *S. sylvatica.* All of these have been eliminated from much of their former habitat in southwestern Germany by the drainage of wetlands. Evidence for their presence before drainage is provided by old records or herbarium collections. However, since these only date back at the most to the end of the 18th century, we are dealing with anthropogenic modifications of fairly recent age.

5.6 CHAPTER SUMMARY

This chapter describes phytoarchaeological indicators of ancient anthropogenic modification of soils. These modifications result from: clearance of forests; increase of phosphate, nitrate, and other plant nutrients in the soils; establishment of mine tips and slags; disturbance of soils leading to growth of weeds; increase in the calcium status of the soils from buried foundations of walls and buildings; drainage of wetlands.

Case histories involving elevated phosphate levels in soils and their effect on vegetation include a study of the Fürstenstand barrow in Lower Franconia (West Germany), and several sites in Jamaica and Ghana (e.g., at Bagho) where abandoned and ruined settlements are delineated by a ring of luxuriant vegetation thriving on ancient human waste.

Much work in Germany has been centered around the luxuriant vegetation resulting from elevated nitrate levels in the soils around abandoned settlements.

A particularly striking example of the effect of buried structures upon the calcium status of the soils is afforded by the Rätischer Limes in Württemberg, West Germany. The Rätischer Limes is an old Roman boundary wall which has now weathered to ground level in most of its parts. It is colonized by a calciphile plant community dominated by a *Vicia dumetorum-Quercus-Fagus* woodland with abundant *Mercurialis perennis* in the herb layer.

Shell middens throughout the world are characterized by a calciphile plant community and have been described from Australia to the Pacific Northwest.

REFERENCES

Arnold, F. 1864. Die Lichenen des frankischen Jura. *Denkschr. Königl. Bayer. Bot. Ges. (Regensburg)* 5: 1–61.

Barkmann, J. J. 1958. *Physiology and Ecology of Cryptogamic Epiphytes.* Assen, Netherlands.

Brooks, R. R. 1983. *Biological Methods of Prospecting for Minerals.* Wiley, New York.

Fischer-Benzon, R. von 1894. *Altdeutsche Gartenflora.* Lipius and Tischer, Kiel and Leipzig.

Jäger, E. J. 1977. Veränderungen des Artenbestandes von Floren unter dem Einfluss des Menschen. *Biol. Rundsch.* 15: 287–300.

Jacob, H. 1952. Über Ursachen anomaler Phophatanreicherung auf Grabhügeln. *Die Kunde N.F.* 3, 2/4: 37–40.

Lohmeyer, W. 1954. Über die Herkunft einiger nitrophiler Unkrauter Mitteleuropas. *Vegetatio* 5/6: 63–65.

Lorch, W. 1951. Die Entnahme von Bodenproben und ihre Einsendung zur Untersuchung mittels der siedlungsgeschichtlichen Phosphatmethode. *Die Kunde N.F.* 2, 2/3, 21–23.

Malek, J. 1966. Vyvoj vegetace na uzemi osad zaniklich v 15. a 16. stoleti v oblasti jihozapadni Moravy. *Cas. Morav. Mus. (Brno)* 51.

Margl, H. 1971. Zur Ortung von Siedlungswüstungen unter Wald. *Inform. Blätt. Nachbarwiss. Ur.- Frühgeschichte Botanik* 4: 1–4.

Rodi, D. 1974. *Vegetation and Boden Zeigen im Grubenholz den Rätischen Limes an.* Ostalb/Einhorn, Schwäbisch Gmünd 2: 156–159.

Sawbridge, D. F., and Bell, M. A. M. 1972. Vegetation and soils of shell middens on the coast of British Columbia. *Ecology* 53: 840–849.

Wilmanns, O. 1965/66. Anthropogener Wandel der Kryptogamen-Vegetation in Südwestdeutschland. *Ber. Geobot. Inst. ETH. Stiftg. Rübel* 37: 74–87.

Chapter 6
PRESENT-DAY SURVIVAL OF ANCIENT CROPS

6.1 INTRODUCTION

Early settlements throughout the world can often be identified by economic plants introduced by colonists. Such plants were used for a variety of purposes including medicinal, nutritional, and ceremonial, and even for fuel for domestic heating or metallurgy. More often than not, settlements were established close to existing natural plant resources rather than on good agricultural land where these resources could be grown.

We must distinguish between negative and positive vegetational indicators of early settlements and archaeological sites. Negative indications are expressed by local disappearance of certain economic plant species due to their overutilization by primitive communities. This topic will be addressed first in this chapter and will be followed by the much more important subject of positive indications, with particular reference to Africa, Australia and North America. Positive indications include the presence of plants brought to, or raised at specific sites for express purposes, usually nutritional or ceremonial.

6.2 NEGATIVE VEGETATIONAL INDICATORS OF EARLY SETTLEMENTS

6.2.1 Metallurgical Sites

One of the best studies of negative indicators of early settlements is that of Plaen (1987). He has studied some of the indigenous cultures of central Africa dating from the 14th century, including the Kabambian culture of what is now Shaba Province, Zaïre (see also Chapters 2 and 3). This culture was involved in metallurgical exploitation of the enormous copper deposits of that region. The timber chosen by native artisans for their smelters (see Plate 2.1) was not subject to attack from termites and left only a small ash residue. It has been calculated by Plaen (1987) that, near Likasi alone (see Fig. 2.1), some 4400–9000 cubic meters of timber were used each season. This required the employment of 1500–2000 workers who annually produced 154 tonnes of finished copper ingots. The smelterers used the larger branches of certain trees and then cut them to a suitable size for the furnaces. A list of trees used for this purpose is given in Table 6.1.

TABLE 6.1 Timber trees used as fuel for copper smelting and refining by indigenous precolonial African tribes in Zaïre from the 14th century onwards.

Albizia antunesiana	Burkea africana	Cordyla africana
Coula edulis	Dialium englerianum	Diphlorrhynchus condylocarpon
Entada abyssinica	Erythrophloeum africanum	Julbernardia globiflora
J. paniculata	Panda oleasa	Pericopsis angolensis
Pterocarpus angolensis	P. tinctorius	Swartzia madagascariensis
Syzgium guineense	Tessmannia africana	Uapaca sp.

Source: Plaen (1987).

The removal of certain trees for smelting purposes in the vicinity of native furnaces resulted in the destruction of some local vegetation elements. The degree of destruction was related to the importance and duration of exploitation of the site. Despite metal enrichment in the soil by the toxic copper ore brought there for smelting, there has been some degree of natural reforestation, particularly over the older and more important sites. These are thereby no longer recognizable. However, sites dating from the 18th century or later are still recognizable from these negative indicators.

6.2.2 Agricultural Activities

Plaen's 1987 study also considered agricultural settlements. In central Africa, a distinction must be made between ancient cultures (dating back to 1000 A.D.) in which agriculture was based on bananas and other naturally-occurring food crops, and the later period in which food crops were based on cereals and manioc. The former did not involve deforestation, whereas the latter required a "slash and burn" technique in which areas were cultivated and then abandoned after about 20 years because of soil impoverishment. The result of this was a rapid savannization of the natural climax dry forest, particularly in places like the densely-populated Upemba Depression at the southern limit of the equatorial forest belt.

The cessation of agriculture during the dry season allowed for other activities at such times. These included metallurgy when copper tools were manufactured to further assist agriculture, and of course deforestation, during the wet season.

6.3 POSITIVE VEGETATIONAL INDICATORS OF EARLY SETTLEMENTS

6.3.1 Africa

An important work by Nooten (1972) discusses positive vegetational indicators of early indigenous settlement in central Africa (See Fig. 6.1 for a map of tribal boundaries).

In Ruanda, and elsewhere in central Africa, ceremonial trees were often planted to indi-

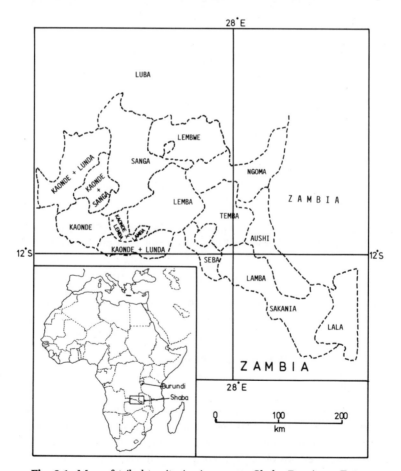

Fig. 6.1 Map of tribal territories in or near Shaba Province, Zaïre.

cate the position of a specific important site such as a village or royal tomb (Nooten, 1972). Species selected for tombs were figs (*Ficus* spp.) or *Erythrina* spp. These markers are extremely useful in pinpointing tombs. The use of fig was probably linked to the common trend among early cultures to provide the dead with sustenance for the long journey to paradise, and even within it. The trenches within the royal tombs were often lined with fig branches and the body was usually enclosed in a small hut made also of the same material. Ceremonial trees dating back to the 18th century are still in evidence today, and although those of earlier sites have died, their progeny sometimes survive as somewhat less precise markers.

The Luba tribe marked two grave sites between Kalumbu and Kimona by wild olive (*Pecholobus pubescens*) trees (*mpafu*) planted by Chief Kongolo to indicate the location of graves of two of his children (Womersley, 1984). The enclosure of the first capital of this chief, situated near Mwibele, was planted with *Lannea antiscorbutica* and *Pterocarpus angolensis*. This enclosure dates from the 15th and 16th Centuries and some of these trees or their descendants still remain there (Reefe, 1977). The Lunda tribe, as well as the Lubas, used to plant a *Lannaea* tree after the establishment of a village and these trees or their descendants are also still present.

Borassu (*Borassus aethiopium*) trees have been observed near abandoned smelter sites in central Africa. Their fruit is favored by the local natives. It is suggested that they brought the fruit to the smelting sites, discarding the inedible nuts which later produced full-sized trees. Near Lubudi, draggonia (*Dracaena reflexa*) trees served a religious purpose. They are present at such sites as the Kiantapo Grotto indicating a human agency for their occurrence.

In the Lamba and Lala tribal regions southeast of Lubumbashi (Shaba, Zaïre), fortified village sites can still be located from the presence of trees derived from stakes planted in the palisades surrounding the villages. The trees have a persistent viability even after being cut down, and readily root again during the rainy season.

Unfortunately, though phytoarchaeological indicators are very useful in central Africa, the sites carry few indications of human remains because of destruction of the bones by the acid soil. However, human artifacts such as pottery and copper implements and ornaments, are abundant.

6.3.2 Australia

The indigenous aborigine people of Australia were hunter-gatherers who made little or no attempt at cultivation of crops. Though they were essentially nomadic, the aborigines did have settlements of some permanence, particularly around natural sources of food such as tuberous plants and berries, or near the sea which provided them with fish and shellfish.

The essential difference between the Australian aborigines and the more advanced tribes of Africa was that the former located semipermanent settlements near static food sources, whereas the latter positioned their settlements over land suitable for agriculture. Traces of both native cultures can be distinguished today by survivors of ancient crops in the African environment, and by the persistence of foci of naturally-rich food sources in Australia. In both cases, localization of these plant sources can lead to locating abandoned settlements and archaeological artifacts.

According to Hallam (1987), the source of most of the material in this subsection of our book, European settlers in Australia in the 1830s recorded aboriginal occupation and usage of areas of concentrated plant resources around lakes and swamps of the river alluvium on the west coast plain in what is now the state of Western Australia. These sites appear to be extremely old and date back as far as 38 000 B.P. (before present, where "present" is taken as 1950).

The famous explorer George Grey (Grey, 1841) observed that the local aborigines had built huts which ". . . differed from those in the southern districts, in being much larger, more strongly built, and very nicely plastered over the outside with clay, and clods of turf, so that . . . they were evidently intended for fixed places of residence."

The staple foodstuff of the coastal aborigines of Western Australia was the native yam, *Dioscorea hastifolia* (Erickson, 1974) known by the natives as *woorine,* which later became corrupted to *warran.* The aborigines dug warran pits to collect the succulent tubers, and in doing so appear to have encouraged further dissemination of this species.

Chauncy (1876) described the warran in the following terms.

> I have seen both men and women sinking in loose sandy soil for an edible root called *warran,* one of the Dioscoreae (Dioscoraceae), which generally grows about the thickness of a man's thumb, and to the depth of 4 to 6 or 8 feet. It has a delicate sweetish flavor when roasted in the hot ashes, something like that of a chestnut and is much sought after. It is dangerous to travel on horseback through the country where it grows, on account of the frequency and depth of the holes, which are not much more than eighteen or twenty inches in diameter. I have sometimes . . . suddenly come on a small hole in the scrub, so small that I could not believe a human being could be at the bottom of it in a stooping position, with the knees on each side of the head. In this position the native dexterously throws the sand by a sudden jerk of the hand backwards, under the arm and up behind the shoulder. The only bald natives I ever saw are the *warran* diggers, who are said to wear the hair off the head by pressing it so frequently against the side of these holes.

Unfortunately for the aborigines, European pastoralists recognised that ground suitable for warran was usually very fertile and eminently suitable for farming, and they soon robbed the natives of their birthright. Referring once more to Hallam (1987), she records that another staple root of aboriginal culture was the *yandyett* (*Typha latifolia* or *T. angustifolia*), whose fibrous and farinaceous rhizome could be roasted, powdered, and baked into a type of bread.

Although the rich yam diggings encouraged semipermanent settlement by aborigines, these natives left behind very little trace of their occupancy since they did not manufacture pottery. Historical records date back only to the late 18th century or early 19th century but do confirm the presence of large populations in the western alluvial plains of Australia and along the east in what is now the state of Queensland (Coleman, 1982) (here a different species of yam (*Dioscorea transversa*) was exploited). Further south, in what is now Victoria, the natives used *Typha* as a food source since the yam does not grow much below 32°S.

In Western Australia, aboriginal artifacts have been uncovered in the vicinity of the yam diggings and consist mainly of stone chips and flakes used for cutting purposes and date at 38 000 B.P. Other sites further south date at 28 000 B.P.

In northern Australia, there was a temporary colonization of the shore by the Macassans. They were originally native to Sulawesi (Celebes) and traded throughout the Malay Archipelago in their sea-going *praus.* They landed along the shores of Arnhem Land (now Northern Territory) where they carried out trade (and often warfare) with the local aborigines (Mulvaney, 1975).

The Macassans had an ingenious method of preserving meat known as trepanging. The meat was boiled in large iron cauldrons over a fire usually of mangrove wood and was then recooked in a tan of mangrove bark which colored and flavored the meat. Subsequently the trepang was decalcified by burying it in sand. It was then smoked in prefabricated bamboo frames. The final product would keep for weeks or even months.

The field archaeologist in Arnhem Land has a relatively simple task to locate Macassan trepanging camps since these native colonists brought with them the astringent fruit of *Tamarindus indica* which seeds prolifically. Tamarind trees serve as botanical markers for the camps because their height and rich green foliage contrast with the flat seascape. The area around these tamarind stands is frequently covered with potshards, bottle glass, and stone hearths.

Plate 2.1. Reconstruction of a Kabambian copper smelter, Shaba Province, Zaïre. Source: Plaen et al. (1982). By courtesy of Pergamon Press, Oxford.

Plate 2.2. A sward of *Haumaniastrum katangense* marking the site of a buried 14th century Kabambian copper smelter in Shaba Province, Zaïre. Source: Plaen et al. (1982). By courtesy of Pergamon Press, Oxford.

Plate 2.3. *Thlaspi alpestre* growing over an ancient lead mine in Derbyshire, England. Photo by A. J. M. Baker.

Plate 2.4. *Armeria maritima* var *halleri* (red), and *Minuartia verna* growing over copper-contaminated ground in the eastern Harz. Photo by W. Ernst.

Plate 2.5. *Viola calaminaria* (yellow) and *Armeria maritima* subsp. *calaminaria* growing over zinc deposits near Aachen, West German. Photo by D. Johannes.

Plate 2.6. *Elsholtzia haichowensis* growing over ancient copper mines and slag heaps in the Daye copper province of central China. Photo by courtesy of D. Ager.

Plate 3.1. Ancient copper workings at Seruwila, Sri Lanka.

Plate 4.1. Stand of *Alyssum corsicum* on ultramafic rocks in the outer suburbs of Bastia, Corsica. The colony probably became established after Venetian traders brought the *Alyssum* as weed seeds in grain from Anatolia. Photo by R. D. Reeves.

Plate 5.1. View of the *Rätischer Limes* Roman wall with its characteristic vegetation cover. Photo reproduced by kind permission of D. Rodi and Einhorn Verlag, Schwäbisch Gmünd, West Germany.

Plate 5.2. Thick cover of *Mercurialis Perennis* covering the Rätischer Limes Roman wall Photo reproduced by kind permission of D. Rodi and Einhorn Verlag, Schwäbisch Gmünd, West Germany.

Plate 6.1. *Taro* plant growing over a drain near an abandoned Maori settlement in North Island, New Zealand. The early Polynesian settlers brought the *taro* with them as food. Source: Ell (1985).

Plate 6.2. *Agave* stand over pueblo ruins at Chevelon Creek, near Flagstaff, Arizona. Photo by courtesy of P. E. Minnis.

Plate 8.1. View of Phillip's Garden archaeological site, site, Port au Choix Peninsula, northwestern Newfoundland, Canada. Photo by M. A. P. Renouf.

Plate 8.2. *Iris versicolor* marking the site of house sites in the Phillip's Garden archaeological site, Port au Choix Peninsula, northwestern Newfoundland, Canada. Photo by M. A. P. Renouf.

Plate 8.3. Waxy green plant (*Antennaria* sp.) indicating archaeological sites at Point Riche, Port au Choix Peninsula, northwestern Newfoundland, Canada. Photo by M. A. P. Renouf.

Plate 8.4. Bare patch in the Karroo bushveld, Cape Province, South Africa. This open area is dominated by *Lycium* sp. as with Indian sites in N. America. The paper marks the area of lithic scatters. There is a large ant-bear burrow in the centre of the photo. These open sites are often disturbed by burrowing animals. Photo by courtesy of G. Sampson.

Plate 8.5. A prehistoric Iron Age midden in Botswana revealed by a covering of the indicator grass *Cenchrus ciliata*. Source: Denbow (1979). By courtesy of the editor of the *South African Journal of Science*.

Plate 8.6. The ramon tree (*Brosimum alicastrum*) growing over Maya ruins at Great Plaza, Tikal, Yucatan Peninsula. Photo by courtesy of P. D. Harrison.

Plate 8.7. Seeds of the ramon tree (*Brosimum alicastrum*) a possible subsistence alternative for the Maya civilisation. The plate shows immature, mature, and sliced seeds. Photo by courtesy of N. Hammond.

Plate 10.1. The origin of crop marks revealed by a cut through Burcot Pit near Dorchester. The corn is higher and more luxuriant over the triangular ditch in the left centre of the photograph. By courtesy of the Ashmolean Museum, Oxford.

6.3.3 New Zealand

The early Polynesian settlers arrived in New Zealand nearly 1000 years ago (see also Chapter 16) though the main wave of settlement arrived in the 14th century. The early settlers brought with them their staple items of food such as the taro (*Colocasia antiquorum*) and kumara or sweet potato (*Ipomoea batatas*). The kumara would not grow the whole year round in New Zealand's colder climate, though the early Polynesians did manage to over-winter the tubers in kumara pits, planting them out again in the spring once the danger of frosts had disappeared. Plate 6.1 shows a taro plant growing in a drain near an abandoned Maori village in the north of North Island, New Zealand. It is almost certainly a descendant of the original taro brought to New Zealand so many centuries ago.

In Chapter 16, there is some mention of the karaka (*Corynocarpus laevigatus*.) It has a golden fruit which is edible both for humans and for the native pigeon which is attracted to the tree and can there be more easily snared by humans. Maoris planted karaka near their settlements and these trees can still be found today. Often they are planted in straight lines and can be detected from the air, thus serving as an indication of old Maori settlements.

Much more recently (C. F. W. Higham—pers. comm.) 19th century gold miners planted apple or pear trees near their houses. At Gabriel's Gully in South Island, New Zealand, Higham was led to the foundations of an old miner's home by following fruit trees which had survived for over a century. At Greek Flat near Cromwell Gorge (also in South Island), he identified a settlement of Greek miners from the olive trees which they had left behind them.

6.3.4 North America

Several studies have been carried out on the modification of plant distributions by prehistoric cultures in North America (Gilmore, 1930; Moseley, 1930; Yarnell, 1958, 1965). Jones (1942) has offered four explanations for the distinctive nature of the flora above archaeological sites: 1) enrichment of the soil by former occupants, resulting in a more vigorous vegetation on the site; 2) physical and chemical alteration of the soil resulting in qualitative floristic differences; 3) the concentration of plants on the site by human agency during its occupation and the persistence of these to the present; and 4) disturbance of the indigenous flora and the progress of floristic development by occupation of the site.

The agave *Agave parryi* has played an important role in Indian cultures of North America and appears to be related to archaeological sites. The economic usage of agave has been described by several workers (Castetter et al. 1938; Brugge, 1965; Felger and Moser, 1970). The Hopi Indians for example, used agave in several ways. It was a source of food, the stalk was used as a war lance, the root was used for fire spindles, and the stalk and fiber were used in ceremonial paraphernalia. Castetter et al. (1938) have summarized the uses as follows:

> . . . food, alcoholic and non-alcoholic beverages, syrup, fiber, cordage, nets, bags, basketry, mats, blankets, clothing (particularly aprons), sandals, pottery rests, headrings, braids, and other miscellaneous woven objects, hair brushes, paint brushes, needle and thread, fish stringers, armour, lances, fire hearths, musical instruments, paint, a gum-like caulking material, soap, for smoking medicine, and ceremonial objects.

Minnis and Plog (1976) studied the distribution of *Agave parryi* (Plate 6.2) in an area of Arizona to the north of the species' usual range (Fig. 6.2). The area is characterized by con-siderable archaeological diversity. The sites range from pit house villages dating back to the 8th or 9th Centuries to pueblos such as Pinedale Ruin, Sholow Ruin, and Stott's Ranch ruin of the 13th and 14th Centuries (Haury and Hargrave, 1931). The period of greatest population density was the 12th and 13th Centuries. In the Chevelon Creek drainage, the primary types of site are small pit house villages, artifact scatters, and small one to two-room jacal struc-tures with masonry foundations. None of the sites in this part of the area exceeds 40 rooms

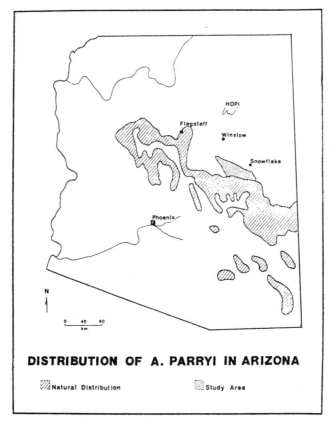

Fig. 6.2 Distribution of *Agave parryi* in Arizona and in the study area where it was associated with Indian archaeological sites. Source: Minnis and Plog (1976). By courtesy of the editor of *The Kiva*.

and 99% have fewer than 20 rooms. In the Phoenix Park and Cottonwood drainages, artifact scatters increase in relative proportion and the average number of rooms on pueblo sites also increases. For example, Pinedale Ruin and Stott's Ranch ruin each exceed 200 rooms.

The study by Minnis and Plog (1976) was carried out over a plateau just north of the Mogollon Rim. They concluded that the distribution of the *Agave parryi* in this region was due to its introduction by prehistoric human communities, basing this conclusion on the following evidence: 1) the only occurrence of agave in the area was on archaeological sites; 2) the agave occurred outside its natural range; 3) agave is not a "weedy" species with a propensity to occupy disturbed habitats; 4) agave is utilized by virtually every Indian group in Arizona; 5) the nature of the intra-site distribution of agave would favor the perpetuation of the species once introduced by man; and 6) the nature of agave reproduction would favor perpetuation as above.

A useful study of the probability of introduction of certain plant species by Pueblo Indians in New Mexico has been carried out by Yarnell (1965). His study site was in the Bandelier National Monument on the Pajarito Plateau near Sandoval and Santa Fe counties.

The Pajarito Plateau is a crescent-shaped, canyon-cut tableland that abuts the Jemez Mts. in the west. The mountains are remnants of a Pleistocene volcanic area that also produced the ash covering the plateau in the form of a rhyolitic tuff that forms sandy soil.

The natural plant communities in the area are the pinyon (*Pinus monophylla*), juniper (*Juniperus communis*), yellow pine associations. Junipers are abundant to the virtual exclusion of pinyon pine at lower elevations. Middle elevations are covered by both pinyon pine and juniper, while higher elevations are covered primarily with yellow pine.

The study area contains at least 200 Pueblo ruins dating back to pre-Spanish days and antedating 1300 A.D. Several cave sites were also visited during the survey.

Occurrences of about 100 species of plants were observed over the Pueblo sites. Of these, 31 were of doubtful significance for locating archaeological remains, 21 were of probable significance (Table 6.2), and the remainder were considered to have no significance. Yarnell (1965) assessed the degree of significance from the following three criteria: 1) degree of confinement to ruins; 2) extent of archaeological and ethnological association with Pueblo Indians; and 3) special considerations such as ecology and range.

TABLE 6.2 Plants considered to have been introduced by Man to early Pueblo settlements on the Pajarito Plateau, New Mexico.

Species	No. sites	Possible usage
Atriplex canescens	25	ritual, food, flavouring
Chamaesaracha conioides	2	food
Cleome serrulata	12	medicine, food, pottery paint
Croton texensis	12	medicine
Cucubita foetidissima	3	medicine, food
Datura meteloides	12	narcotic
Eriogonum cernuum	7	food, medicine
Kallstroemia parviflora	1	medicine
Lithospermum caroliniense	1	dye
Lycium pallidum	7	food
Munroa squarrosa	12	food
Physalis foetens var. neomexicana	15	food
P. hederaefolia var. cordifolia	9	food, condiment
Plantago purshii	5	medicine
Salvia subincisa	4	medicine, food
Sanvitalia abertii	6	food
Solanum elaeagnifolia	9	paint, medicine
S. jamesii	10	food
S. triflorum	3	food, condiment
Thelasperma intermedium	4	beverage
Verbesina encelioides	8	medicine, ritual

After: Yarnell (1965). Reproduced by permission of the American Anthropological Association from *American Anthropology*.

Of the species listed in Table 6.2, those most closely related to Indian cultures appear to be the three *Solanum* species (a staple food of Pueblo Indians—and of course of Europeans today), *Cleome serrulata*, *Lithospermum caroliniense*, and *Salvia subincisa*. The natural altitudinal range of the *Salvia* extends to only about 1700 m. In the Pajarito Plateau, it exceeds this altitude by 300 m and is plentiful thereat. Perhaps the most striking evidence of the association of *Cleome serrulata* with Pueblo Indians has been furnished by Whiting (1939) who observed that:

It is general practice to allow certain weeds to grow unmolested in the otherwise carefully-hoed Hopi fields. While strictly speaking this cannot be called agriculture, it is interesting to note that essentially the same method is used to cultivate the coxcomb (*Amaranthus cruentus*). This introduced plant is allowed to seed itself from year to year in the irrigated gardens. Similarly, plants of the Rocky Mountains beeweed are allowed to mature and to disperse their seeds in Hopi cornfields providing an abundant supply of young plants for the cook pot the following spring. The little wild potato (*Solanum jamesii*) often yields an abundant harvest under similar treatment.

The study by Yarnell (1965) provides a fascinating insight into the way phytoar-chaeology gives us a living record of the culture of ancient indigenous cultures. It is perhaps one of the best illustrations of the persistence to the present day of ancient crop plants.

In the Upper Sonoran life zone of the drier interior of British Columbia (Canada), Washington and Oregon (U.S.A.), the plant communities vary considerably. Plants that frequently mark archaeological sites in this zone include the balsam root sunflower (*Balsamorhiza sagitatta*) and the camas (*Camassia quamash*). Sometimes plants which are normally found in the coastal area, occur on these sites. These include wild currants and occasionally the bitter root (*Lewisia rediviva*). G. F. Grabert (pers. comm) relates how he once accidentally located a winter dwelling site in the Marron Valley near the Okanogan River in British Columbia. He did this by observing the occurrence of three very scrubby but viable Oregon grape bushes that had grown and managed to survive at about 800 m. They were growing over the slight depression of a deep pit dwelling. The fill retained enough moisture during the summer to allow life and propagation but not expansion. Human action had brought the seeds to the site but their survival was a matter of chance.

6.3.5 Central America

Introduction

Perhaps one of the most intriguing and contentious questions concerning plant indi-cators of ancient ruins is that of the role of certain plant species in the Maya culture of the Yucatan Peninsula. Interest in this subject dates back to the late 1920s when Charles Lind-bergh identified plant patterns over Maya ruins by aerial photography shortly after his epic solo flight across the Atlantic Ocean. The debate stems from observation of the presence of certain economic plants over these ruins at an abundance greater than in the background rainforest. Some authorities believe that plant distribution are ecological and influenced by edaphic and physical properties of the soil. Others believe that the plants are descendants of economic crops planted during the Late Classic Maya period. The latter theory will be dis-cussed in this chapter and the ecological model will be presented in Chapter 8.

Plant survivors of the Maya Late Classic period

A study by Folan et al. (1979) was carried out over ruins of the Late Classic Maya period at the city of Coba (see Figs. 6.3 and 15.2) in the Yucatan Peninsula. Coba is located 45 km inland from Quintana Roo, Mexico. It epitomizes the description of similar sites by the 16th century Bishop, Diego de Landa (fide Tozzer, 1941):

> . . . their dwelling place was as follows: in the middle of the town were their temples with beautiful plazas, and all around the temples stood the houses of the lords and the priests, and then those of the most important people. Thus came the houses of the richest and of those who were held in highest estimation nearest to these, and at the outskirts of the town were the houses of the lower class.

Landa further stated that *balche* (*Lonchocarpus longistylus*) trees (used to make ceremonial drinks from the bark) were planted in the improved lands of the lords and that these were located around their residences in the core of the cities.

In their work at Coba (Folan et al., 1979) first identified the houses of the various social strata of Maya society. These were of two main types: 1) platforms supporting high status vaulted structures owned by elite families, and 2) platforms supporting only rectangular unvaulted structures owned by the lower classes. Folan et al. postulated that the balche and other economic plants such as fruit trees (Table 6.3) were to be found near the dwellings of the lords, whereas fewer species and number of individual trees would be found in the poorer quarters. They recorded a total of 3579 tree specimens and matched the survey lines (Fig. 6.3) with the residential units and hence delineated the civic-ceremonial core zone and adjacent high-status residential area. They also recorded the position of the inner and outer suburban zones occupied by the lower classes.

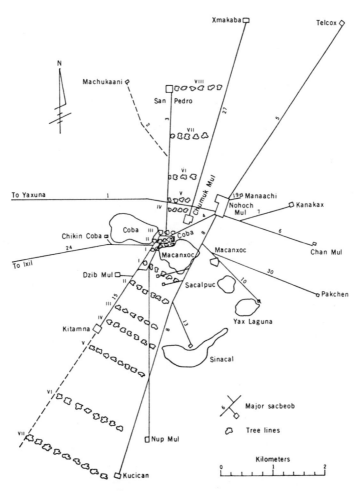

Fig. 6.3. Plan of the Maya city of Coba showing sampling transects. Source: Folan et al. (1979). Copyright 1979 by the American Association for the Advancement of Science.

TABLE 6.3 Economic plant species found over ruins of the Late Classic Maya city of Coba

Purpose	Scientific name	Common name
Fruit	*Achras zapota*	zapote
	Acrocomia mexicana	cocoyol
	Brosimum alicastrum	ramon
	Byrosonima crassifolia	nance
	Cardiospermum corindum	guayas
	Chrysophyllum mexicanum	chiceh
	Enterolobium cyclocarpum	pich
	Sideroxylon gaumeri	subul
	Spondias purpurea	kilim
Fibre	*Ceiba aesculifolia*	piim
Bark	*Lonchocarpus longistylus*	balche
Resin	*Achras zapota*	zapote
	Protium copal	pom or copal

After: Folan et al. (1979). Copyright 1979 by the American Association for the Advancement of Science.

The occurrence and frequency of these ceremonially or economically important trees diminished in the lightly inhabited limits of the survey area. This indicated a direct relation between status and certain species and quantities of trees. The lords and priests of Coba, along with other important people residing in the civic-ceremonial core controlled more fruit (79%), bark (96%), and resin-producing (72%) trees than did other residents at Coba (Folan et al., 1979). It appears they had almost absolute control over trees used to produce ceremonial drinks (e.g. balche) and over the incense-producing *pom* (*Protium copal*).

6.4 CHAPTER SUMMARY

This chapter is concerned with the present-day survival of ancient crops. These crops may indicate abandoned settlements with their associated archaeological artifacts. There is some mention of negative phytoarchaeological indicators such as depletion of sources of fuel or food near such sites located in Africa, and resulting from smelting or agricultural activities.

In central Africa ceremonial trees such as *Ficus* sp. were often planted over important tombs, and they, or their successors can be used to pinpoint the sites. Trees such as *Borassus aethiopum* provided nuts that were a food source for the precolonial copper smelters. Discarded nuts at these sites now provide stands of *Borassus* that can serve as indicators of these early activities.

In Australia, the hunter-gatherer aborigines tended to make temporary camps near food sources such as the native yam (*Dioscorea hastifolia*). These sites have provided artifacts such as stone chips and flakes used for cutting purposes.

In northern Australia, early visitors from southeast Asia left behind seeds of *Tamarindicus indica* from fruit brought with them. These have now formed dense stands of trees which mark out the camping sites of these people.

In New Zealand, the 14th century Polynesian immigrants brought with them their staple food sources such as the taro (*Colocasia antiquorum*) and kumara (*Ipomoea batatas*). The descendants of these species can still be found at selected localities in New Zealand.

Prehistoric cultures in North America have modified plant distributions to a significant degree and have caused a distinctive flora to be established over specific sites. Examples of this include the occurrence of *Agave parryi* over Pueblo Indian sites in Arizona, and of several *Solanum* (potato) species over Pueblo sites in New Mexico and elsewhere in North America.

In Central America, there are several plants associated with Maya ruins. These include the *ramon* (*Brosimum alicastrum*) and *balche* (*Lonchocarpus longistylum*). These may have been planted for nutritional or ceremonial purposes. There is, however, some dispute as to the reasons for their occurrence over ruins (see Chapter 8 for a further discussion of this question).

REFERENCES

Brugge, D. M. 1965. Navajo use of agave. *The Kiva* 26: 159–167.

Castetter, E. F., Bell, W. H., and Grove, A. R. 1938. The early utilization and distribution of agave in the American Southwest. *Univ. of New Mex. Bull.* #335.

Chauncy, P. 1876. Notes and anecdotes of the Aborigines of Australia. In, R. Smythe [ed.] *The Aborigines of Victoria and other parts of Australia and Tasmania* v.2. John Currey O'Neil, Melbourne: 221–284.

Coleman, J. 1982. A new look at the north coast: fish traps and "villages". In, S. Bowdler [ed.] *Coastal Archaeology in Eastern Australia.* Dept. of Prehistory, Aust. Nat. Univ, Canberra: 1–10.

Ell, G. 1985. *Shadows over the Land*. Bush Press, Auckland.

Erickson, R. 1974. *Old Toodyay and Newcastle*. Toodyay Shire Council, New South Wales.

Felger, R., and Moser, M. B. 1970. Seri use of agave (century plant). *The Kiva* 31: 88–98.

Folan, W. J., Fletcher, L. A., and Kintaz, E. R. 1979. Fruit, fiber, and resin: social organization of a Maya urban center. *Science* 204: 697–701.

Gilmore, M. R. 1930. Dispersal by Indians as a factor in the extension of discontinuous distributions of certain species of native plants. *Pap. Mich. Acad. Sci. Arts Lett.* 13: 89–94.

Grey, G. 1841. *Journals of two Expeditions of Discovery in North-West and Western Australia during the Years 1837, 38 and 39*. Boone, London.

Hallam, S. J. 1987. Yams, Alluvium and "Villages" on the West Coastal Plain. In, G. K. Ward [ed.] *Archaeology at A.N.Z.A.A.S. Canberra*. Canberra Archaeological Society, Canberra: 116–132.

Haury, E. W., and Hargrave L. L. 1931. Recently dated pueblo ruins in Arizona. *Smithsonian Misc. Coll.* 82 (11).

Jones, V. H. 1942. The location and delimitation of archaeological sites by means of divergent vegetation. *Soc. Am. Arch. Notebk.* 2: 64–65.

Minnis, P. E., and Plog, S. E. 1976. A study of the site distribution of *Agave Parryi* in east central Arizona. *The Kiva* 41: 299–308.

Moseley, E. L. 1930. Some plants that were probably brought to northern Ohio from the west by Indians. *Pap. Mich. Acad. Sci. Arts. Lett.* 13: 169–172.

Mulvaney, D. J. 1975. *Prehistory of Australia*. Blackburn, Victoria.

Nooten, F. L. van, 1972. Les tombes du roi Cyirima Rujugira et de la reine mère Nyirayuhi Kanjigera. *Ann. Mus. Roy. Afr. Centr.* 77.

Plaen, G. de, 1987. *Les Indices Phytoarchéologiques*. Inst. Mus. Nat., *Lubumbashi (Zaïre)*.

Reefe, T. O. 1977. Traditions of genesis and the Luba diaspora. In, *History in Africa* Vol. 4, 183–205.

Tozzer, A. M. 1941. *Landas Relaciones de las Cosas de Yucatan*. Peabody Museum, Harvard University, Cambridge, Massachusetts.

Whiting, A. F. 1939. Ethnobotany of the Hopi. *Mus. N. Ariz. Bull.* #15.

Womersley, H. 1984. *Legends and History of the Luba*. Crossroads Press, Los Angeles.

Yarnell, R. A. 1958. *Implications of Pueblo Ruins at Plant Habitats*. M.Sc. Thesis, University New Mexico, Albuquerque.

———— 1965. Implication of distinctive flora on Pueblo ruins. *Am. Anthrop.* 67: 662–674.

Chapter 7

PLANT REMAINS USED FOR ARCHAEOLOGICAL CHRONOMETRY AND RECONSTRUCTION OF ANCIENT ENVIRONMENTS AND CLIMATES

7.1 INTRODUCTION

Palynology (pollen analysis) is the science of the investigation of materials by their content of pollen grains or spores. In its widest sense it embraces investigations of honey, of allergies caused by wind-borne pollen, and of the natural classification of flowering plants. In the narrow sense it is mainly concerned with the reconstruction of former vegetation patterns by systematic analysis of the pollen and spore count of geological sediments. Standard works on the subject are by Faegri and Iversen (1964) and by Godwin (1934, 1956).

Pollen is shed in vast amounts from vegetation and is concentrated in soils and consolidated sediments where the walls of the grains resist decay and the pollen can therefore be recovered by suitable mechanical and chemical treatments. Since pollen grains exhibit a wide range of size, shape and wall pattern, and have distinctive numbers and disposition of pores and furrows, it is possible to recognise (under high magnification) the family, genus, and sometimes even the species of plant to which a given grain belongs.

The proportions of different grains in any one sample reflect the composition of the vegetation when the sample was deposited. In northwestern Europe, where the method has been most fully developed, pollen analyzes have revealed a remarkably consistent picture of the vegetational history for the period since the ice sheets began their final retreat over 10 000 years ago. Open park tundra was replaced by birch (*Betula*) woodland and then by pine (*Pinus*) forest and hazel (*Corylus*) scrub. This gave way to mixed oak (*Quercus*) forest. Finally beech (*Fagus*), hornbeam (*Carpinus*), and spruce (*Picea*) expanded their ranges considerably. These changes in composition were climatically controlled and could be measured by studying a system of pollen zones related to the appropriate climatic and time scales.

Pollen analysis of deposits containing archaeological objects allows an approximate dating. The palynological method has been applied with great success to the study of interglacial and even older deposits and to the characterization of the stages of deforestation of Europe by Neolithic and succeeding groups of agriculturalists.

Palynology can also be used for samples millions of years old. For example, vegetational changes at the Cretaceous/Tertiary boundary (Orth et al. 1982) some 65 million years ago have been plotted by palynology in the absence of other methods of dating.

Some workers (e.g. Hofmann, 1984) consider that palynology is overrated and unreliable and have proposed that the use of whole plant remains such as seeds found in archaeological sites is a better guide to a reconstruction of ancient environments and modes of agriculture. This approach has been reviewed by Minnis (1981). A new and promising field has been opened up by the development of plant opal phytolith (POP) analysis as a means of identifying prehistoric vegetation patterns. Although this technique has only recently gained acceptance, it was in the early years of this century that Schellenberg (1908) recognised phytoliths as useful components of archaeological sites. POP analysis is superficially comparable to pollen analysis; both deal with large populations of biogenic particles of microscopic size. Collecting and handling of soil samples in the field for pollen or POP analysis is essentially identical, so soils collected for one purpose may be used for the other.

Pollen and phytoliths are, however, different. Pollen is normally produced in a single repetitive form and is completely organic. Phytoliths are composed of silica originally deposited in plant structures and can have a vastly different morphology even within the same plant specimen. Recent use of POP research in archaeology shows that it is capable of producing significant data, both by itself and in conjunction with other analytical methods.

7.2 PALYNOLOGY IN ARCHAEOLOGY

7.2.1 The British Isles

The Dolfrwynog Copper Bog

There has already been a brief mention (Chapter 2) of the work of Ernst (1969) on pollen of the peats of the Dolfrwynog Copper Bog of North Wales. This bog and the surrounding rocks were a source of copper and gold as early as pre-Roman times, though few artifacts have been discovered at the site, due to extensive mining activities in the late Middle Ages. The pollen analysis involved counting at least 200 grains for each tree species and for the two herbaceous metallophytes *Armeria maritima* and *Minuartia verna*. All other species (mainly shrubs and herbs) were listed as "various." The pollen diagram is shown in Fig. 7.1.

The basic findings of Ernst's 1969 study were as follows:

1) An intensive period of pastoral activity (sheep and cattle) began in the 12th century A.D. (corresponding to 35 cm in the diagram) as evidenced by reduction of numbers of grassy pollen types since the plants were less able to progress to the flowering stage. During the

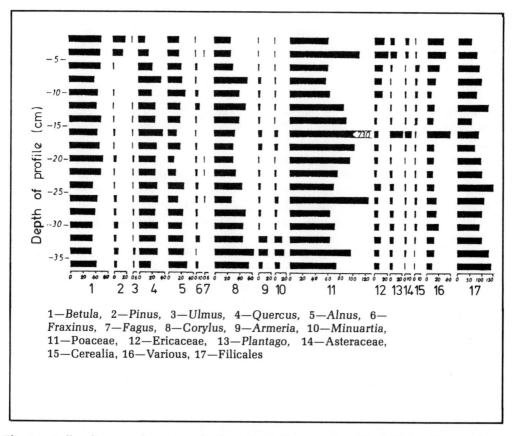

1—*Betula*, 2—*Pinus*, 3—*Ulmus*, 4—*Quercus*, 5—*Alnus*, 6—*Fraxinus*, 7—*Fagus*, 8—*Corylus*, 9—*Armeria*, 10—*Minuartia*, 11—Poaceae, 12—Ericaceae, 13—*Plantago*, 14—Asteraceae, 15—Cerealia, 16—Various, 17—Filicales

Fig. 7.1 Pollen diagram of peat samples from the Dolfrwynog Bog, North Wales. Frequencies are expressed as percentage of the total tree pollen count. Source: Ernst (1969). Courtesy of the editor of *Vegetatio*.

same period, there was a development of heliophile weeds such as *Plantago, Ranunculus,* and various Asteraceae, due to the more open nature of the terrain caused by this pastoral activity.

2) Following a period of extensive utilization of meadowland, the grasses were thereby strengthened for a later period of strong development (34 cm interval). During this period, other heliophile species such as *Corylus avellana* also developed strongly. This was the period when the two copper-indicating metallophytes *Armeria maritima* and *Minuartia verna* reached their maximum abundance and corresponds with the wars with the English (1272–1307 A.D.) when pastoral activity was neglected.

3) Following the end of the Welsh wars there was a further period of extensive agricultural development (Lloyd, 1911) coincident with an increase in cereal growing and a reduction in the ferns (*Athyrium* sp. and *Polypodium* sp.). This was also the time of further opening up of the forests by clear-felling and the development of small-scale agriculture under the tutelage of the monks of the monastery of "Strata Florida."

4) The next grass maximum at 26 cm coincided with a slight increase in the two metallophytes and had the same cause as a similar occurrence in the 16–18 cm level: i.e. conversion of farms to pastureland during the revolts of the 16th century.

5) The development of large-scale agriculture and drainage of peatlands (Howell, 1946) during the period up to the early 19th century (6 cm interval) resulted in the virtual elimination of *Minuartia verna* and *Armeria maritima*, particularly with the burning of the cupriferous peat in the early 1800s to produce copper ore (Henwood, 1857). This period can be dated by the appearance of conifers during a period of afforestation in the middle of the 18th century (Thomas, 1965).

It is clear from these above study that the expansion and decline of the two metallophytes were determined by, and correlated with, anthropogenic factors. It is amazing how such a complete picture of the local environment over a time span of 700 years can be obtained from a few humble pollen grains.

Ancient Celtic Heather Ale

An extraordinary case of how palynology was able to reconstruct a long lost recipe for ancient Celtic "home brew", based on Scottish heather (*Calluna* spp.) and produced on the Island of Rhum (Inner Hebrides), has been reported by The Times (1987).

The recipe for Celtic heather ale was said to have been lost forever during the "Dark Ages." It was a favorite drink during the Bronze and Iron Ages and according to local legend the last two holders of the secret recipe chose death rather than reveal the secret to inquisitive settlers and raiders. The legends say that an old Pict told his torturers: ". . . kill my son and I'll tell you the recipe." When they did so, he taunted them: "You should have killed me first because I shall never tell you the secret."

Since then, pale imitations of the ancient Celtic brew have been made by country people. They used heather, bog myrtle (*Vaccinium myrtillus*), honey and herbs but somehow nothing quite matched the divine ale of the traditional tales.

The cunning Pict, however, reckoned without 20th century archaeologists and the latest biochemical techniques. A leading Scottish distillery has been sufficiently inspired by palynological evidence to sponsor a series of stringent laboratory tests.

In 1985, archaeologists C. Wickham-Jones and D. Pollock discovered on the island of Rhum, not only one of the earliest known human settlements in Scotland (8500 B.P.), but also a later farming community from about 4000 B.P. It was the latter which left behind an insignificant piece of broken pottery containing pollen grains unrelated to those in the surrounding soil.

Dr. B. Moffat, an Edinburgh palynologist, found that the pottery fragment contained heather as its major constituent, followed by a high content of royal fern (*Osmunda* sp.) spores, a lesser amount of meadowsweet (*Filipendula* sp.) and pollen of grains and other herbs (Fig. 7.2). It was not possible for such a mixture to have been derived from natural sources without man's agency, and the mixture appeared to have been fermented. Moffat collected the herbs in the right proportion and made a few bottles of the brew which he described as: "A very drinkable alcohol, comparing quite favorably with beers available in various Edinburgh hostelries . . . a bit savage perhaps, for modern palates."

Three more pottery shards with the same constituents have now been unearthed at the same site in Rhum.

The royal fern continued to puzzle Dr. Moffat until he heard from a biochemist at Osaka University, Japan, that the fern contains athiaminase, an enzyme that destroys vitamin B1, a major constituent of the cell walls of the yeast. It could have been used to stop the fermentation process.

Now a series of experimental brews is to be made by a Scottish distiller at a distillery at Girvan in Ayrshire, because although Dr. Moffatt is convinced that he has the right ingredients, he is unsure about their correct proportion.

The archaeologists hope that the ale becomes commercially viable because royalties would contribute towards the funding of further excavations.

Fig. 7.2 A representation of the ingredients of ancient Celtic heather ale. Source: The Times (1987).

Bronze Age Mead

Another interesting recreation of the composition of an ancient beverage has been reported by Dickson (1978). The discovery was made at a Bronze Age burial site at Ashgrove, Scotland (Fig. 7.3) dated at 3046 B.P. The grave contained a skeleton, various artifacts such as weaponry, and five pottery beakers, the contents of which appeared to have been spilt over the body. Pollen analysis of the spilled material showed that 53.7% of the grains were from the small-leaved lime (*Tilia cordata*), 15.1% were of meadowsweet (*Filipendula* sp.), 7.7% were of heather (*Calluna* sp.) and the rest were from numerous other plant species. The high *Tilia* pollen count was unusual as this species is not indigenous to Scotland and even today is rarely found north of the England-Scotland border (see Fig. 7.3). A contamination source for the pollen can be ruled out. It is noteworthy that the nectar of the *Tilia* and *Filipendula* are favorite foods of bees and their pollen is frequently found in modern honey. Honey was the only source of sugar in prehistoric times and could easily have been transported over long distances. Mead (fermented honey) was a popular prehistoric beverage and

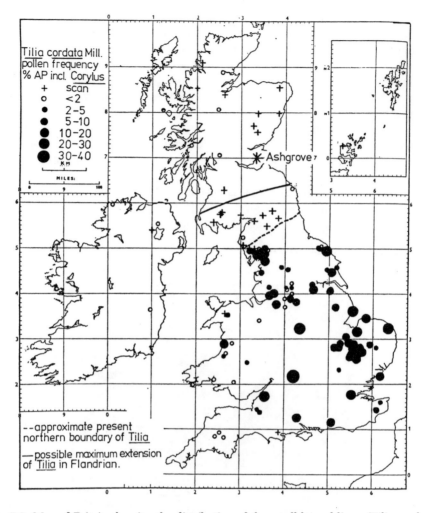

Fig. 7.3 Map of Britain showing the distribution of the small-leaved limes (*Tilia cordata*). Source: Dickson (1978). By courtesy of the editor of *Antiquity*.

is frequently found in Bronze Age burial sites. Meadowsweet was commonly used for flavoring alcoholic drinks in that period.

Dickson (1978) analyzed the residues of the five beakers found at the Ashgrove site and found once again a high percentage of *Tilia* pollen in the residues. This discovery represents the earliest record of a honey/mead discovery in Britain, and once again demonstrates the usefulness of palynology for identifying ancient recipes of alcoholic beverages.

7.2.2 Germany

Late Paleolithic Sites at the Schussenquelle, Baden-Württemberg, South Germany

There are many Late Paleolithic sites in Europe. Those of Spain and southern France are perhaps the most famous because of their cave drawings. There are also several such sites in central Europe including those at the Schussenquelle spring in South Germany (Fig. 7.4) on the watershed of the Danube and Rhine rivers. Pollen grains were examined in three soil profiles of consecutive depths (Lang, 1962). The profiles were taken to correspond with known discoveries of animal remains and human artifacts.

The pollen diagram is shown in Fig. 7.5 and the time frames are explained in Table 7.1.

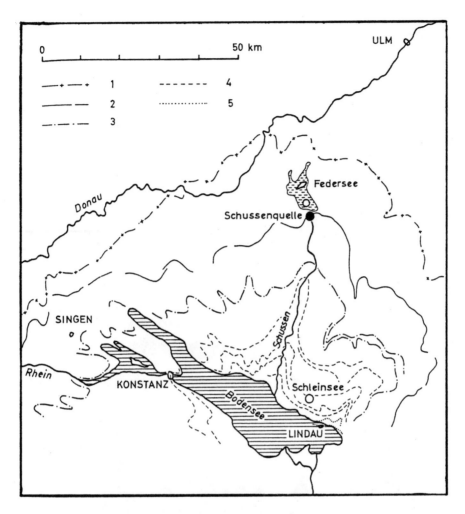

Fig. 7.4 A location map of the Late Paleolithic site at the Schussenquelle, Baden-Württemberg, South Germany. 1) Riss Moraine terminus, 2–5) various stages of the Wurm Moraine. Source: Lang (1962). By courtesy of the Geobotanisches Institut, Zürich.

TABLE 7.1 Divisions of the late glacial period in southern Germany.

Time interval		Vegetation phase	Early paleolithic culture
B.C.	Climatic period		
>8000	IV Pre warm	Fir-birch	
8000–8800	III Younger *Dryas**	Younger fir with sparse forest cover	
8800–10 000	II *Alleröd* oscill.	Younger fir	
10 000–10 300	Ic Older *Dryas*	Birch	
10 300–11 200	Ib *Bölling* oscill.	Older fir	
11 200–13 500	Ia Oldest *Dryas*	Dwarf birch	Late Magdalenian
13 500–14 500	Ia Oldest *Dryas*	Pioneer dwarf birch	Late Magdalenian

*—named after *Dryas octopetala,* a plant of Arctic regions, high mountains, and tundra.
After: Lang (1962). Courtesy of the Geobotanisches Institut, Zürich.

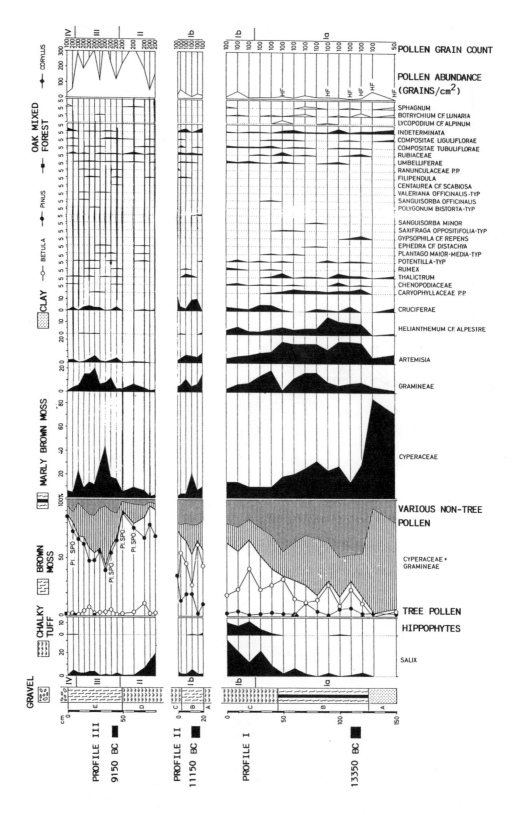

Fig. 7.5 A pollen diagram of sediment profiles of consecutive depth taken at the Schussenquelle Late Paleolithic site. Source: Lang (1962). By courtesy of the Geobotanisches Institut, Zürich.

From these data, together with those from whole plant remains, the following conclusions about the site were made:

1) The main location of the period of independent hunters (lower peat moss) coincides with the dwarf birch (*Betula nana*) phase of the earliest *Dryas* climatic period (Ia in profile I—see also Table 7.1). This according to carbon-14 dating has a median age of 13 350 B.C. The dwarf birch phase lasted for about 2000 years from the 14th millenium B.C. to the beginning of the reforestation phase and is a distinct climatic unit.

2) Carbon-14 dating of the later birch phase gave an age of 11 150 B.C. (profile II). This expansion of forests coincides with the beginning of the *Bölling* climatic period (Ib—see also Table 7.1) or at least is not younger than it.

3) A carbon-14 determination of the beginning of the second vegetative stage (the later fir tree phase) named after *Picea abies*), caused by a decline of forests (profile III) dated it at 9150 B.C. The association of the later fir tree phase (see also Table 7.1) with the *Alleröd* (II) and *Later Dryas* periods was clearly established.

4) From individual discoveries of artifacts in datable layers above the main site, it was established that Late Paleolithic independent hunters visited the Schussenquelle at least up to the *Alleröd* period (II).

5) The following are the most important species identified by palynological studies and whole plant discoveries: *Betula nana, Luzula sudetica, Potentilla aurea, Arabis alpina, Carduus defloratus, Ephedra distachya, Sanguisorba minor, Centaurea scabiosa, Taraxacum officinale* and *Polygonum aviculare*.

An Ancient Settlement at Jemgum an der Ems, Lower Saxony, Northwest Germany

A Bronze-Iron Age settlement at Jemgum an der Ems in northwest Germany has been dated at about the 6th or 7th Centuries B.C. (Haarnagel, 1957). A palynological study was carried out by Grohne (1957) on a section of peat sedge some 1 km distant from an abandoned settlement. This work led to the following conclusions:

1) The Jemgum inhabitants of the 6th and 7th Centuries B.C. raised cereals on the fenland.

2) Human settlement at this period was more widely distributed than was indicated by the settlements so far unearthed.

3) Reduced human activity before and after the period was evidenced from pollen counts below and above the house horizon.

4) The countryside at this time was much more forested than today.

5) Plants of damp meadows and watercourses indicated a pure freshwater vegetation.

6) Up to the time of settlement, there was a detectable tidal influence on the vegetation and the River Ems brought slightly brackish water to the site.

7) The presence of microfossils in the marsh clay showed that the land surface had been periodically inundated.

Palynology and Bog Corpses at Lake Dümmer, Hanover, North Germany

Perfectly preserved corpses (often victims of sacrifice, accident, murder, or punishment) are not uncommon at various peaty sites in Germany, The Netherlands, Denmark, and Ireland (about 40 have already been discovered in Lower Saxony). An important find of two corpses buried in a peat bog at Hunteburg near Hanover (West Germany) has been described by Schneider (1955). Figure 7.6 gives a schematic representation of the profile in which the corpses were found. The results of pollen analysis are given in Fig. 7.7. The bodies were found in a strongly disintegrated black peat horizon at a depth of 101–115 cm. They lay just above the boundary between younger and older peat, which in this area is dated at 600 B.C.

From the curves in Fig. 7.7, it was concluded that the bodies lying at a depth of 100 cm could be correlated with a depth of 90 cm elsewhere, indicating a shallow burial of these corpses.

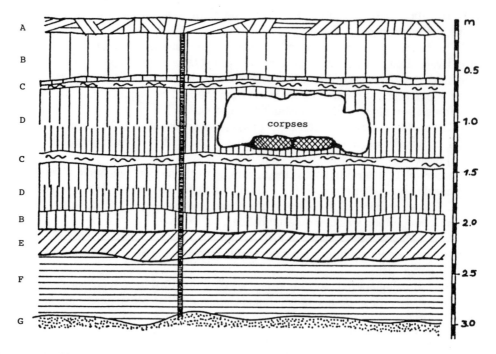

Fig. 7.6 Profile of the grave of two bog corpses uncovered near Lake Dümmer near Hanover, Lower Saxony, Germany. A) superficial layer, B) sphagnum peat, C) wool-grass peat, D) dark mossy peat, E) sedge peat, F) fractured forest peat, G) humus-rich sand. Source: Schneider (1955).

Between each body and the peat cover there was a small sprig of heather with flowers and lightly-swollen fruits. This indicated that the bodies had been buried in late summer.

There was some problem in dating the peat horizon in which the bodies had been laid. However, there was a fortuitous discovery of a Roman coin of 252–268 A.D. in a nearby site . The coin was found immediately beneath an ancient boardwalk dated therefore at about 300 A.D. Pollen analysis confirmed that this level corresponded to a depth of 60 cm below the surface covering the bog corpses. A further fix point is the beginning of the beech (*Fagus*) curve in the pollen diagram which was established by Pfaffenberg (1947) as corresponding to 2000 B.C. Assuming a constant rate of peat deposition between the fixed points of 2000 B.C. and 300 A.D., it was established that the bodies had been buried in 750 B.C.

Other bog corpses dated by palynology have given ages ranging from 500 B.C. to the the middle of last millenium A.D. and indicate a time span of about 2000 years.

This study showed to a remarkable degree how palynology can be used to shed light not only on the age of ancient finds but also on the nature of the climate and environment with which they were associated.

7.3 SEEDS AND WHOLE PLANT REMAINS IN ARCHAEOLOGY

7.3.1 Introduction

In contrast to palynology which can give only indirect (and in some cases unreliable) information about the environment of prehistory, the study of macroplant remains found in tombs and settlements affords direct and reliable evidence about the environment of the site, local agriculture, and the nature of the wild vegetation.

The vegetation found at archaeological sites often consists of cultivated plants. These

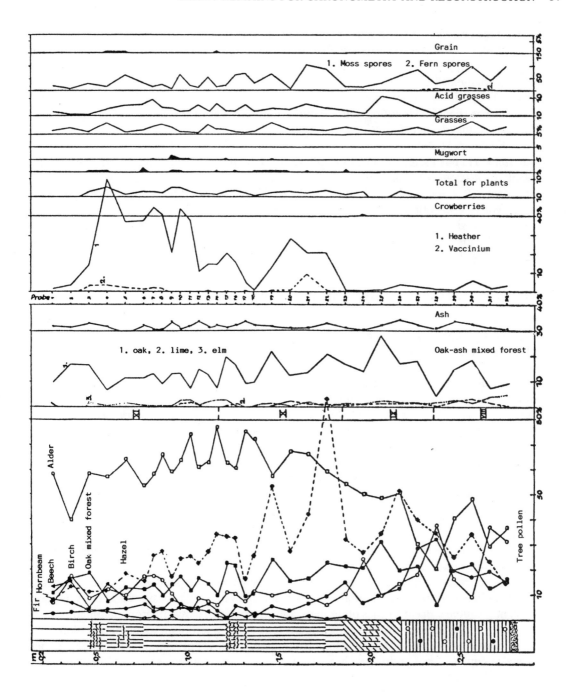

Fig. 7.7 Pollen diagram of peat samples taken from around the horizons in which two bog corpses were found near Lake Dümmer, near Hanover, Lower Saxony, Germany. Source: Schneider (1955).

are either carbonized or non-carbonized. Carbonized plant remains are found in dry sites where there has been free access of air, or where fires may have been in the vicinity. Conditions of preservation vary greatly and the material is usually extremely brittle and difficult to handle. Non-carbonized plant remains are found under damp anoxic conditions (Willerding, 1969) and usually involve preservation only of the hard sclerenchymatic material, though other parts are sometimes preserved.

An exception to the poor preservation of non-carbonized plant remains is the ubiquitous presence of weed seeds in stores of grain that may have been dried by some form of heating process. Weed seeds are also preserved in the chaff after threshing.

The wild plants or weeds at the site of an ancient abandoned settlement give an insight into the then-existing natural environment on the one hand, and into human influence on the other. They afford sharply-defined evidence about their environment with regard to such variables as, light/shade ratios, temperature, humidity, pH of the soil, and the calcium and nutrient status of the soil.

Ellenberg (1978) has classified certain plants as indicators of one or more of the these variables. He has assigned indicator indices to each species so that the presence of several plants in a given area can define the physical and chemical nature of the environment. Hofmann (1984) has applied this principle to establish local conditions at four archaeological sites near Regensburg in Bavaria, south Germany. His work affords a valuable insight into the ways in which analysis of the species composition of whole-plant remains (mainly seeds) can shed light on environmental conditions in the distant past. Case histories of these four sites will be discussed later.

7.3.2 Sources of Seeds Recovered from Archaeological Sites.

Modern Sources

This section is based on a useful review by Minnis (1981) who has shown that sources of seeds removed from archaeological sites (Fig. 7.8) are of both modern and prehistoric origin.

Seeds can be produced in enormous quantities. For example (Quick, 1961), the common tumbleweed (*Amaranthus graecizans*) can produce up to 6 million seeds from a single plant. Asch et al. (1972) report three modern seeds recorded for each prehistoric seed when the flotation process is used for recovery. Because of the magnitude of modern seed rain (deposition), Kaplan and Maina (1977) have suggested that samples be taken from nearby non-archaeological sites in order to provide a control. Keepax (1977) has given four main sources for the presence of modern contamination of the seed at archaeological sites: careless flotation, cross contamination in flotation apparatus, aerial contamination of exposed samples, and presence of modern seeds in the soil before excavation.

Prehistoric Sources

There are three main sources of prehistoric seeds: direct resource utilization, indirect resource utilization, and prehistoric seed rain.

Direct resource utilization is the most widely considered source of prehistoric seed. Many archaeological artifacts are the direct result of collecting processes and consumption of plant resources. Because uses other than consumption can leave macroplant remains, care must be applied in drawing sweeping conclusions from macroplant assemblages alone.

Indirect resource utilization results from many causes. For example, the large number of maize cupules from prehistoric hearths in the American southwest probably results from the use of cobs for fuel.

Another source of seeds in archaeological sites is the prehistoric seed rain which may have blown onto hearths or may have been charred on incinerated middens. A significant source of seed rain is the prehistoric weed growth which would have occurred once a site had been abandoned until the climax vegetation was re-established.

Minnis (1981) studied the problem of post-occupational seed rain by cleaning out a three-room field hut in New Mexico. The structure was cleaned out and abandoned for one year. Resampling by the flotation process showed that the rooms contained, respectively, 63, 87, and 534 seeds.

Differentiation of Seed Sources

One of the most important problems of seed collection over archaeological sites is dif-

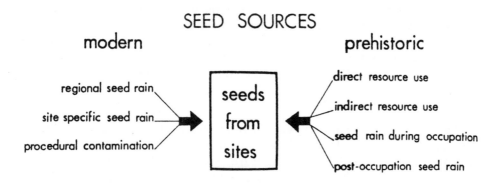

Fig. 7.8 Sources of seeds recovered from archaeological sites. Source: Minnis (1981). By courtesy of the Society for American Archaeology, Washington, D.C.

ferentiation of the different sources. Keepax (1977) lists five criteria for differentiation of modern seed from prehistoric seed: radiocarbon dating, species composition as compared with nearby non-archaeological sites, size and morphology of cultivated grains compared with related wild grasses, unusually high concentrations of seeds, and the nature of the preservation of the remains. This author has suggested rejecting all uncharred seeds as being modern in origin, and retaining only charred specimens as genuine. The main point is that usually only charred seeds can be preserved until modern times. There are few natural processes (except extreme dryness as in Egyptian tombs) which can allow seeds to escape natural decomposition, and few seeds can last for more than a century (Quick, 1961).

The problem of plant preservation has been examined by Hally (1981) who studied phytoarchaeological samples from three domestic structures in northwest Georgia dating to 1550–1700 A.D. Consideration of the frequency of individual plant species in the samples and of the ethnohistorical evidence for aboriginal plant processing, led to the conclusion that most variability could be attributed to whether or not structures burned, and when during the year burning occurred. The analysis demonstrated that the manner in which plant parts became carbonized had a major impact on the accuracy with which phytoarchaeological remains reflected actual plant utilization.

Once modern seed has been separated from prehistoric seed, it is important to differentiate the seeds resulting from different prehistoric processes. Perhaps the best clue is the distribution of seed types within the assemblages. Some distributions may be quite clear in origin, e.g. seeds stored in containers. Similarly, dense concentrations of a particular seed may indicate human agency in its collection.

7.3.3 Some Case Histories of the Use of Plant Remains in Archaeology

Regensburg, Bavaria, South Germany

In the neighborhood of the Celtic settlement of Radasbona (Ratisbona), the Roman fortress *Castra Regina* (Queen's Fort) was, after 150 A.D., the center of their power along the Upper Danube.

In 1964, a section of the wall encircling the old Roman city, along with associated graves, was uncovered. According to Hofmann (1984), soil samples taken from low-lying graves contained seeds of the following species: *Ceratophyllum submersum, Polygonum persicaria, Sambucus ebulus, Rubus idaeus, Chenopodium album,* and *C. hybridum.* The archaeological artifacts did not provide dating any more precise than from the time of the Roman Emperors to the early Middle Ages.

It was clear that the plant remains were derived from the local environment rather than having been gathered for a specific purpose. From the presence of aquatic plants such as *C. submersum,* it was evident that the graves had remained open for some time and that water had been allowed to flow through them. The aquatic plants are found only in warm, shallow, base-rich or eutrophic waters. The other plants are terrestrial. Their high light demand indicates that at the time of sedimentation the environment was deforested and exposed to the sun.

Sengkofen

A Late Neolithic find has been reported from Sengkofen in the parish of Mintrachting near Regensburg (Hofmann, 1984). A bowl containing several liters of carbonized grain was found in one of the graves. Among grains of barley and wheat were seeds of the following weeds: *Bromus arvensis, Brachypodium* sp., *Setaria viridis, Galium aparine, Polygonum aviculare, Solanum nigrum,* and *Chenopodium* sp. It is clear that these weed seeds had been collected along with the grain crop.

From the nature of the weeds, it was possible to make a fairly precise assessment of the fields of the Late Neolithic period. Humidity indicators suggested a dryish soil and acidity indicators pointed to a neutral to slightly basic limy soil. Nitrogen indicators showed a fertile soil. The *Setaria* indicated a sandy soil and the other plants a sandy loam.

Hienheim

The linearband ceramic Neolithic settlement of Hienheim (Bakels, 1978) is situated near the town of Kelheim, also in Bavaria. Erosion has removed the top 60 cm of cover so that the upper soil horizons are completely absent. However, post holes and graves still remain and 22 species of wild plants were identified in soils taken from within them.

The plant samples all seemed to have originated from cornfields and correlated with an agrarian economy. The indicator indices of the plants suggested a slightly moist, neutral to slightly acid nitrogen-rich soil. The calcium deficiency of the soil was revealed by the presence of *Rumex acetosella, Bromus arvensis,* and *Polygonum convolvulus.* It is clear that erosion at the time of settlement had already removed the topsoil and had decalcified the remaining soil, leaving a rather infertile basis for agriculture.

Straubing

The final case history of Hofmann (1984) concerns the cellar of Roman barracks at Straubing (also not far from Regensburg). From the discovery of coins, the site was dated at the 3rd century A.D. Samples taken from a store of barley grains contained 16 species of weed seeds, all typical of cornfields. The indicator indices of certain species showed that the crop had been grown in a loamy soil. The humidity index indicated a well-watered, though not water-saturated, soil. This was also indicated by presence of *Polygonum lapathifolium* and *Rumex crispus.* The nitrogen indices of several of the weeds suggested a nitrogen-rich soil.

The large number of weed species indicated long-term agriculture at the site with evidence of neglect shown by the presence of *Silene cucubalus* (= *S. vulgaris*), a plant often found in poorly-tended fields.

It was concluded that in the 3rd century A.D., the climate was more moist than it is today. This has been confirmed by dendrological studies on sub-fossil oaks of the region (Becker, 1982).

These case histories show some of the potential of a technique, sometimes known as paleoethnobotany, which should reinforce and complement the more common palynological procedure.

7.4 PLANT OPAL PHYTOLITHS IN PHYTOARCHAEOLOGY

7.4.1 Introduction

Rovner (1983) has written an excellent review on the use of plant opal phytoliths (POP) in archaeology. Opal phytoliths are created from hydrated silica dissolved in groundwater that is absorbed through a plant's roots and carried through the vascular system. The silica is precipitated anywhere that significant amounts of water are used or lost. Although produced in living plants, the resulting particles contain no carbon but are comprised primarily of amorphous opal (Jones and Segnit, 1971) with trace minerals in varying amounts.

The fundamental aim of POP analysis is to identify, and if possible, quantify, the original flora that produced the soil POP assemblage. This is accomplished in two ways: 1) use of gross production differences occurring in broad plant groups, and 2) investigation of particle morphology and variation to establish diagnostic type categories and type assemblages. Gross production differences may be used at very broad levels, as in distinguishing forest from grassland. The production of POP by grasses is very much greater than by trees.

Taxonomic study of POP based on particle morphology and classification, gives much more precise levels of parent-plant identification in archaeological contexts. For example the monocotyledons are highly siliceous and produce large quantities of morphologically-distinct particles. Fig. 7.9 shows distinctive grass opal phytoliths. A corresponding representation of POP for non-grasses is given in Fig. 7.10.

Plant opal phytoliths may be removed from soils by various techniques. One of these involves shaking the soil with an organic solvent having a specific gravity of 2.3 (such as bromoform mixed with a lighter organic solvent). The POP float to the surface and leave most other soil components at the bottom of the container. The reader is referred to Rovner (1983) for a fuller description of separation methods for POP.

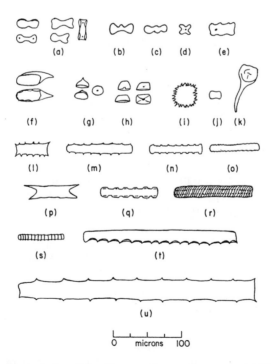

Fig. 7.9 Distinctive grass opal phytoliths. Types a–d, p, and s are panicoid. Types l–o, q, r, and t–u are festucoid of the elongate class. Source: Rovner (1983). By courtesy of the editor of *Advances in Archaeological Method and Theory.*

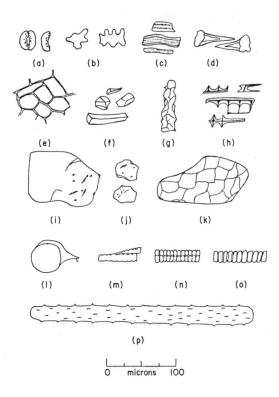

Fig. 7.10 Distinctive non-grass opal phytoliths: (a–e) deciduous trees, (f–h) coniferous trees, (i–k) dicotyledonous herbs, (l–p) monocotyledonous herbs. Source: Rovner (1983). By courtesy of the editor of *Advances in Archaeological Method and Theory.*

7.4.2 Some Examples of the Use of Plant Opal Phytoliths in Archaeology

The Palaeoecology of Archaeological Sites

Rovner (1983) has shown how POP can be used for studying the palaeoecology of archaeological sites. For example in a study of plant succession in north central Wyoming (U.S.A.), MacDonald (1974) studied phytolith assemblages from two archaeological sites, the Worland Mammoth Site (11 000 B.P.) and the Medicine Lodge Creek, a stratified site dating from 7000 B.P. to the present. Festucoid phytoliths were common in all samples, but the presence of panicoid and chloridoid phytoliths in some samples suggested different climatic episodes in the past. High levels of panicoid phytolith forms at the Worland Mammoth site indicate a warmer climate than exists today. At the Medicine Lodge Creek site, the phytolith assemblage from the lower 7000 B.P. level showed a similar rise in panicoids indicating a warmer climatic episode.

A phytolith study at the Fifty Site in the Middle Shenandoah Valley of Virginia (Carbone, 1977) indicated a drier period from the end of the Middle Archaic through to the Late Archaic period. This was not confirmed by the pollen data, and Rovner (1983) emphasizes that although palynology has a longer history than POP analysis, this does not a *priori* endow the former with greater reliability.

Phytolith Studies on Prehistoric Agriculture

Rovner (1983) details several cases where POP analysis has been used to study prehistoric agricultural patterns. Among these are several interesting programs from Central America. For example, an epidermal maize fragment containing articulated phytoliths at the Early Preclassic site of Cuello, Belize, provided the first direct evidence that maize was part of the Early Maya lowland farming inventory (Hammond et al. 1979). This was later confirmed by the discovery of carbonized maize itself (Hammond and Miksicek, 1981).

Phytolith analysis has also been used in the Maya Lowlands to provide information on the agricultural technology of the Late Preclassic and Classic periods. In a study of hydraulic channels and raised fields at Pulltrouser Swamp, Belize, Turner and Harrison (1981) reported water lily (*Nymphaea*) phytoliths in raised field soils. Water lilies which grow in open water may have been transported to the raised fields for use as mulch or fertilizer.

Phytoliths and Prehistoric Plant Use

One of the first uses of POP analysis by Schellenberg (1908) in Turkestan revealed plant remains in mud brick prehistoric dwellings and showed that plant material had been used to bind the mud bricks. More recently, a study of ash deposits at Tel Yin'am in Israel (Liebowitz and Folk, 1980) revealed the presence of wheat straw and confirmed Pliny's reference to the use of straw in iron smelting at this site.

In an account of Amazonian aboriginal groups, Linne (1965) noted the use of siliceous bark as temper in pottery production. Use of plant with a high silica content may have been to cause the plants to act like a grit or sand temper.

Soil samples collected from Bronze Age Troy (Collins, 1979) showed that wheat (*Triticum durum*) was present throughout the samples as well as kalamia (*Arundo donax*) (used for canes, thatching and baskets). The wheat was a food source and provided straw for bedding, mud brick manufacture, and fuel.

POP analysis is still in its infancy and much remains to be done, particularly in the field of systematics, but it seems likely that the technique will prove to be a useful adjunct to the more commonly accepted technique of palynology.

7.5 CHAPTER SUMMARY

The use of plant remains such as pollen (palynology), whole plant material, and plant opal phytoliths (POP), in phytoarchaeology is reviewed in this chapter. Plant opal phytoliths are siliceous remnants of plant parts that appear after the original plant material has decayed away.

Palynology can be used for dating purposes and to recreate the original floristic and climatic environments of archaeological remains. Case histories are presented from Wales, Scotland, and north and south Germany. A novel example of the use of palynology concerns the recreation of the recipe of an ancient Celtic heather ale from pollen found in a very old Celtic barrow on the island of Rhum. Bronze Age mead has also been recreated from pollen found at a burial site at Ashgrove, Scotland.

Pollen remains from a Late Paleolithic site in south Germany have enabled scientists to recreate the entire climatic record for a period of 7000 years. Palynology has also been used to date neolithic corpses preserved in peat bogs in Lower Saxony.

Several examples have been reported of the use of charred macroplant residues such as seeds in order to recreate agricultural environments and food sources of the Roman period in south Germany.

The field of POP analysis is reviewed and case histories given from North and Central America. These show that the technique can be used to study the paleoecology of these sites.

REFERENCES

Asch, N. B., Ford, R. I., and Asch, D. L. 1972. Paleoethnobotany of the Koster site: the archaic horizons. *Rep. Invest. Ill. State. Mus.* #24.

Bakels, C. C. 1978. Four linear band ceramic settlements and their environment. *Analecta Praehist. Leidensia* 11: 22–30.

Becker, B. 1982. Dendrochronologie und Paläoökologie subfossiler Baumstämme und Flussablagerungen. Ein Beitrag zur nacheiszeitlichen Auenentwicklung im südlichen Mitteleuropa. *Mitt. Komm. Quartärforsch. Österr. Akad. Wiss.* 5: 46.

Carbone, V. A. 1977. Phytoliths as paleoecological indicators. *Ann. N.Y. Acad. Sci.* 228: 194–205.

Collins, S. M. 1979. *Phytoliths as Indicators of Plant Use in Ancient Troy.* M.Sc. Thesis, University Minnesota, Duluth.

Dickson, J. H. 1978. Bronze age mead. *Antiquity* 52: 108–113.

Ellenberg, H. 1978. Zeigerwerte der Gefässpflanzen Mitteleuropas. *Scripta. Geobot.* 9: 1–122.

Ernst, W. 1969. Pollenanalytischer Nachweis eines Schwermetallrasens in Wales. *Vegetatio* 18: 393–400.

Faegri, K., and Iversen, J. 1964. *Textbook of Pollen Analysis.* Munkgaard, Copenhagen.

Godwin, H. 1934. Pollen analysis: an outline of the problems and potentialities of the method. *New Phytol.* 33: 278–305.

———— 1956. *The History of the British Flora.* Cambridge Univ. Press, Cambridge.

Grohne, U. 1957. Botanische Untersuchung der vorgeschichtlichen Siedlung Jemgum a.d. Ems. *Die Kunde, N.F.* 8½: 44–52.

Haarnagel, W. 1957. Die spätbronze-früheisenzeitliche Gehöftsiedlung Jemgum bei Leer auf dem linken Ufer der Ems. *Die Kunde, N.F.* 8 ½: 2–44.

Hally, D. J. 1981. Plant preservation and the content of paleobotanical samples: a case study. *Amer. Antiquity* 46: 723–742.

Hammond, N., and Miksicek, C. H. 1981. Ecology and economy of a formative Maya site at Cuello, Belize. *J. Fd. Archaeol.* 8: 259–269.

Hammond, N. Pring, D. Wilk, R. Donaghey, S. Saul, F. P. Wing, E. S. Miller, A., and Feldman, L. H. 1979. The earliest lowland Maya: definition of the Swasey phase. *Amer. Antiquity* 44: 92–110.

Henwood, W. J. 1857. Notice of copper turf of Merioneth. *Edinb. New Philosoph. J.* 5: 61–63.

Hofmann, R. 1984. Archäologische Pflanzenreste als Indikatoren fur vorzeitliche Siedlungsverhältnisse. In, S. Rieckhoff-Pauli and W. Torbrugge [eds.] *Führer zu Archäologischen Denkmälern in Deutschland,* Vol. 5. Konrad Theiss Verlag, Stuttgart 174–181.

Howell, E. J. 1946. Cardiganshire. In D. Stamp [ed.] *The Land of Britain.* London.

Jones, J. B., and Segnit, E. R. 1971. The nature of opal I. Nomenclature and constituent phases. *J. Geol. Soc. Australia* 118: 57–69.

Kaplan, L., and Maina, S. L. 1977. Archaeological botany of the Apple Creek site, Illinois. *J. Seed. Technol.* 2: 40–53.

Keepax, C. 1977. Contamination of archaeological deposits by seeds of modern origin with particular reference to the use of flotation. *J. Archaeol. Sci.* 4: 221–229.

Lang, G. 1962. Vegetationsgeschichtliche Untersuchungen der Magdalenien-Station an der Schussenquelle. *Veröff. Geobot. Inst. ETH, Stiftg. Rübel.* 37: 129–154.

Liebowitz, H., and Folk, R. L. 1980. Archaeological geology of Tel Yin'am, Galilee, Israel. *J. Fd. Archaeol.* 7: 23–42.

Linne, S. 1965. The ethnologist and the American Indian potter. In F. R. Matson [ed.] *Ceramics and Man.* Viking Press, New York.

Lloyd, J. E. 1911. *A History of Wales.* Longmans, London.

MacDonald, L. L. 1974. *Opal Phytoliths as Indicators of Plant Succession in North Central Wyoming.* M.Sc. Thesis, Univ. Wyoming, Laramie.

Minnis, P. E. 1981. Seeds in archaeological sites: sources and some interpretive problems. *Amer. Antiquity* 46: 143–152.

Orth, C. J. Gilmore, J. S. Knight, J. D. Pillmore, C. L. Tschudy, R. H., and Fassett, J. E. 1982. Iridium abundance measurements across the Cretaceous/Tertiary boundary in the San Juan and Raton Basins of northern New Mexico. *Geol. Soc. Am. Spec. Pap.* 190: 423–433.

Pfaffenberg, K. 1947. Getreide- und Samenfunde aus der Kulturschicht des Steinzeitdorfes am Dümmer. *Jb. Naturhist. Ges. Hannover* 1947: 94–98.

Quick, C. R. 1961. How long can a seed remain alive. In, A. Stefferud [ed.] *Seeds, the Yearbook of Agriculture.* U.S. Govt. Print. Off. Washington, D.C.

Rovner, I. 1983. Plant opal phytolith analysis. *Advances in Archaeological Methods and Theory (Academic Press)* 6: 225–266.

Schellenberg, H. C. 1908. The remains of plants from the North Kurgan, Anau. In, R. Pumpelly [ed.] *Explorations in Turkestan.* Carnegie Institute, Washington, D.C.

Schneider, S. 1955. Botanisch-geologische Untersuchung der Fundstelle der Moorleichen im Grossen Moor am Dümmer. *Die Kunde, N.F.* 6, ¾: 40–49.

Thomas, K. 1965. The stratigraphic and pollen analysis of a raised peat bog at Llanllwch near Carmarthen. *New Phytol.* 63: 73–90.

Times 1987. Search for a drop of the ancient stuff. *The Times,* London.

Turner, B. L., and Harrison, P. D. 1981. Prehistoric raised-field agriculture in the Maya lowlands. *Science* 213: 399–405.

Willerding, U. 1969. Vor- und frühgeschichtliche Kulturpflanzenfunde in Mitteleuropa. *Neue Ausgr. Funde Niedersachs.* 5: 287.

Chapter 8

VEGETATION CHANGES OVER SPECIFIC ARCHAEOLOGICAL SITES

8.1 INTRODUCTION

Vegetation changes over archaeological sites have already been documented in Chapter 6 insofar as these changes relate to *advertent* human collection of economic plants for food, medicinal, and ceremonial purposes. This chapter will be concerned with specific examples of the *inadvertent* presence of plants over archaeological sites.

Yarnell (1965) has described the occurrence of specific plants and plant assemblages over ancient Indian archaeological sites in North America. He has proposed three main ways in which such plant distributions can occur: 1) presence of favorable soil (Bank, 1953; Dall, 1877; Meigs, 1938; Zeiner, 1946); 2) introduction by non-human forces (Brown, 1936; Small, 1927); 3) introduction by man (Bank, 1953; Hrdlicka, 1937; Jepson, 1909; Lundell, 1939; Meigs, 1938; Mosely, 1931). In a further discussion of the subject, Yarnell (1965) has pointed out that certain species are genetically suited to disturbed locations as proposed by Anderson (1953) who stated that:

> . . . habitat preferences are inherited in substantially the same fashion as any other character.

According to Yarnell (1965):

> As long as an area remains undisturbed, it exists as a closed habitat, i.e. one in which each ecological niche is filled by well-adjusted species. Few aliens can become established in such an environment, not having evolved the specific genetic requirements. When human or other activities result in the creation of open habitats, weedy aliens can compete and, because of their more generalized habitat requirements, maintain an advantage over many native species until the habitat returns to its former condition. If disturbances were continuous, a hardy alien could become well established in open habitats in a region and come to occupy a much extended range. Any plant growing in an open habitat could have been introduced to that locality by man or some natural means of distribution. However, when the plant is one with a close relationship to man and the habitat is one which has been opened by human activities, there is a likelihood that the introduction was influenced by some human agency. Many plants, in fact, are known as *camp followers*. They can travel with man because he creates open habitats wherever he goes, and he transports their seeds unwittingly perhaps, in most cases.

Examples of vegetation changes over archaeological sites will now be described.

8.2 NORTH AMERICA

8.2.1 Walnut Canyon, Flagstaff, Arizona

Site Characteristics

The archaeological remains in Walnut Canyon National Monument (Fig. 8.1) are those of the Sinagua Indian culture, a local variant of the Pueblo agricultural people of the southwest. The sites date back to 1000–1300 A.D. and are predominantly cliff dwellings.

The general environment of the archaeological sites is the pinyon-juniper zone of

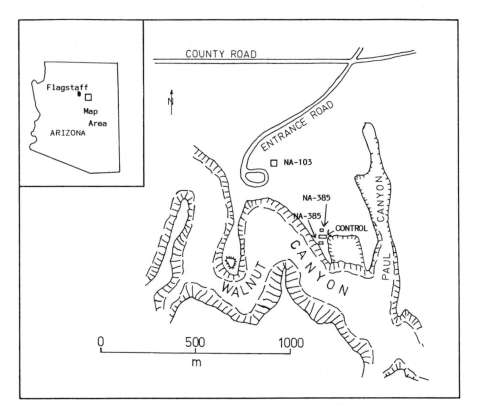

Fig. 8.1 Map of Walnut Canyon National Monument, Flagstaff, Arizona, showing location of four archaeological sites. Source: Clark (1968).

approximately 2100 m elevation, but there is a wide range of vegetation types along the steep canyon walls, ranging from douglas fir (*Pseudotsuga menziesii*) to yucca (*Yucca baccata*) and prickly pear cactus (*Opuntia engelmannii*).

Findings of the Study

The vegetation distribution over three of the sites (NA103, NA385 and NA386, see Fig. 8.1) was analyzed by Clark (1968). Sample plots were selected to include visible boundaries of the building foundation outlines. The plots averaged 12 x 20 m and were traversed by 20 m lines at 1.5 m intervals. Each line was divided into 3 m sections for a total of 63 sections.

The plant cover was sampled by the line intercept method (Canfield, 1941, see also Chapter 9). The plant mapping produced data on the relative frequency (number of times that a specific plant species occurs in a given line segment, i.e., total number of appearances divided by the number of segments), and relative cover (total cover for a given species divided by length of line). Where total frequency and cover were normalized to 100, the relative percentage frequencies and cover were established.

The species composition of the three test plots was compared with that of a control plot of similar ecology but not situated over archaeological remains.

The main findings of the survey were, that of 31 species of vascular plants (excluding grasses) examined on the test plots, only 11 appeared in the control. Each test plot contained species that were unique to it.

Of the 21 plant species deemed by Yarnell (1965) to have been used by Pueblo Indians for economic purposes (see Chapter 6), only one, *Lycium pallidum,* was found over the Walnut Canyon sites. This species had a relative frequency of 11.2% and relative cover of 9.4%.

Clark (1968) considered that the presence of certain plants unique to the sites was not due to human agency but to favorable soil structure and other non-human interrelating forces. These forces were considered to include better catchment of wind-borne seeds, presence of seed-carrying animals, and poor growing conditions for competing grasses.

8.2.2 Port au Choix National Historical Park, Newfoundland

Site Characteristics and History

Phillip's Garden (Fig. 8.2) is a site in northern Newfoundland known to span the Maritime Archaic Indian (4200–3200 B.P.) and Dorset Palaeoeskimo (1900–1300 B.P.) occupation. The site has been extensively investigated by Renouf (1985) and Harp (1976). To quote the former:

> It is located on the north coast of the Point Riche Peninsula, in a large grassy field which in summer is a garden of iris and other wildflowers. In area the site exceeds 20,000 m² and at least 48 shallow house depressions are spread over the upper two of three raised terraces. Harp's excavations exposed the remains of two house forms which he interpreted as a winter and summer variant, and consequently he considered the site to be a more or less sedentary base from which forays could be made, for various purposes such as caribou hunting inland or salmon fishing along the coast. The bone preservation was exceptionally good; over 25,000 bones were recovered from just one house feature. According to Harp (1976), over 98% of these were from harp seal (*Phoca groenlandica*), which today migrates into the area in early spring. Harp collected nearly 23,000 artifacts from a complete or partial excavation of 20 house depressions including harpoon blades, scrapers, and miscellaneous items of ground slate, soapstone, bone and ivory.

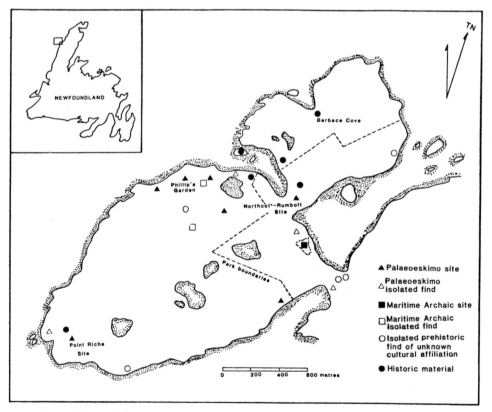

Fig. 8.2 Map of Point Riche and Phillip's Garden archaeological sites in the Port au Choix Peninsula, northwestern Newfoundland, Canada. Source: Renouf (1985). By courtesy of the editor of *Polar Record*.

Plant Indicators at the Phillip's Garden Site

Renouf and Hall (1985) mapped the vegetation over the Phillip's Garden site using 10 m² quadrats. A photograph of the site is shown in Plate 8.1. Mapping was carried out in June when the spring vegetation was in its early stage of growth, enhancing rather than obscuring elevational and vegetational differences. Many house site features were readily observable as their depressions created abnormally wet conditions which favored the growth of marsh plants such as *Iris versicolor* (Plate 8.2). Two other house depressions became visible in late July.

Plant Indicators of Archaeological Sites at Point Riche

Renouf (1986) and Renouf and Hall (1985), in the course of their investigations at the Point Riche archaeological site (Fig. 8.2) (believed to be of the same age as the settlement at Phillip's Garden), noticed the prominent association of the site with a waxy, dark green plant (Plate 8.3). This seemed to grow only in areas where there was cultural material and was used to delineate the site boundaries (Fig. 8.3). The plant has been provisionally identified as a species of *Antennaria*. It covers an area of approximately 2000 m², which may be taken as the minimum site area and includes 14 house depressions within it. Numerous artifacts have so far been recovered from the site.

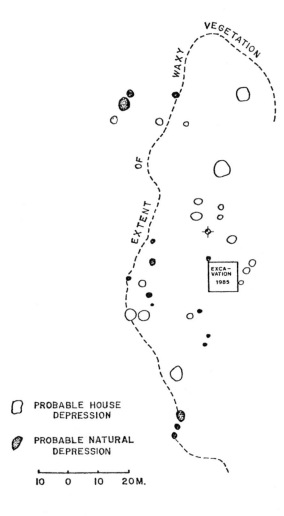

Fig. 8.3 Site boundaries of the Point Riche archaeological site delineated by the presence of waxy green vegetation. Source: Renouf (1986).

8.2.3 Angel Mounds, Indiana

Angel Mounds in Indiana, is a large Late Prehistoric (Middle Mississippian) settlement of about 50 ha consisting largely of house patterns and habitation refuse (Black, 1944). There are several large earth mounds including those with a typically truncate pyramidal form. The 1000 m southern edge of the village is bounded by the Ohio River while the east, north and west sides were enclosed from bank to bank of the river by a bastioned stockade.

In the course of a proton magnetometric survey of the site, Johnston (1964) observed that the stockade was visible from aerial photographs because of the variability of soil pH above the wall site and the consequent vegetational differences that have been studied by Zeiner (1946). It was particularly evident that *Aster pilosus* was never found growing over the more acid palisade line though it was abundant immediately adjacent to the structure. Zeiner concluded that:

> . . . it is apparent that there is a correlation between pH, elevation (remnants of the stockade), and floral distributions of certain indicator species. When the pH falls to 5.0 and below, *Aster pilosus* is stunted in growth or absent, depending on the degree of acidity. *Plantago lanceolata* is also intolerant of the more acid regions. *Plantago aristata*, *Rumex acetosella*, and *Danthonia spicata* on the other hand, grow well with the pH below 5.0 and are not tolerant of more alkaline soils.

8.2.4 Alaska and Northern Canada

It is appropriate to add a few more observations (largely anecdotal) concerning the relationship between vegetation and archaeological sites in Alaska and northern Canada. 1) H. T. Shacklette (pers. comm.) has made a number of observations in the course of biogeochemical and geobotanical prospecting in Alaska and northern Canada

> In 1959 I collected mosses at Point Barrow (then considered the northernmost place on the North American Continent, later the most northerly point was found to be in Canada) which for many centuries was used by the Eskimos (who now prefer to be called "Inuit", which in their language means "The People") as a place to prepare and store seal, bear, walrus and fish meat. After preparation, the meat was stored in trenches dug through the peat surface to the permafrost layer. Then the trenches were covered first with large whale bones, then with sod to form a roof. The areas near the storage trenches are densely carpeted with nitrophilic mosses (species in the Splachnaceae Family in the genera *Splachnum* and *Tetraplodon*). These mosses are found only on nitrate-rich soils, usually the dung of herbivorous mammals, and are, in general, rather rare. They are very conspicuous by their being very bright green, in contrast to the dull green or brown surrounding vegetation, and I am quite sure they could be seen when *en masse* by color photography used for remote sensing. The sites where the meat was prepared for storage, often at a distance from the storage trenches, could be found by observing the bright green almost continuous carpets of these nitrogenous mosses.
>
> In 1958, while working on Yakobi Island in the Pacific Coast just off southeastern Alaska, I found a striking example of a pattern formed on the floor of a dense forest by a nitrophile moss *Tetraplodon mnioides*. A deer had died and decomposed, even the bones had disappeared, but an exact pattern of the deer's body was formed by the carpet of moss. Soils in northern regions are usually very deficient in nitrogen, and the effect of nitrogen added to the soil as reflected by plant growth doubtless remains visible after many years, perhaps centuries.

2) Another Shacklette anecdote concerns the Brooks Range:

> . . . of mountains which extending east and west separates the taiga, which is sparsely forested, from the Arctic tundra to the north which forms a vast plain covered with bogs and lakes extending to the Arctic Ocean. Near the center of

this range is a pass through the mountains, which perhaps from the Late Pleistocene period has been a migration route for enormous herds of caribou (the North American reindeer) and the Inuit people who followed the herds from summer to winter pastures. This pass has long been noted by botanists and others for the profusion and vigour of the vegetation growing therein. This pass was named "Anaktuvuk" by ancient Inuit people, and this name is still used on our present maps. I have flown in a light airplane through this pass, and the vegetation in the pass and on trails leading to the pass, is conspicuously luxuriant. Perhaps most people who have noted this profuse vegetation do not know that the name "Anaktuvuk" means in the Inuit language "The place of defecation."

3) the final Shacklette anecdote is in the form of a quotation from Wiggins and Thomas (1962):

> The Eskimo populations along the sea coast of arctic Alaska have maintained reasonably permanent villages for centuries, but there has been much minor shifting, particularly of summer hunting camps. Occasional major moves have been necessitated by failure of a water supply, contamination of freshwater lakes from which they drew their drinking water, or by depopulation of a village by an epidemic, coupled with the superstition that the diseases were in some way connected with a particular location. Many of these abandoned sites are conspicuously marked by a more luxuriant growth of the vegetation than on the adjacent tundra only a short distance away. Soil near ancient houses contains a much higher percentage of nitrogenous material than that of the open tundra. Several species of mosses and liverworts and a few vascular plants are either confined to such areas or are far more plentiful there than on unfertilized soil. For example, swathes in the vicinity of ruined houses and meat cellars at the old village of Nuwuk are closely carpeted with dense stands of *Splachnum*, a moss that is never found on sterile soil, but which occurs in small patches on caribou droppings or on other organic waste. *Marchantia polymorpha*, a ubiquitous liverwort, is found on the Arctic slope on the sides of mounds formed by crumbling earthen houses or on remnants of old meat cellars. Vascular plants that grow more frequently and more luxuriantly on abandoned houses and village sites include: *Papaver radicatum*, *Stellaria laeta*, *S. humifusa*, *Dupontia fisheri*, *Phippsia algida*, and *Poa arctica*. *Saxifraga hirculus* grows far more densely and produces a more brilliant carpet of yellow blossoms in swales immediately adjacent to old villages than on undisturbed and unfertilized tundra flats. *Saxifraga cespitosa* often is more robust around old villages than elsewhere, particularly if the site was originally a gravelly or sandy one. *Chrysosplenium* is frequent about such sites, and *Cochlearia ranker* is more closely crowded here than on mineral soils.

8.3 SOUTHERN AFRICA

8.3.1 Sea Cow Valley, Cape Province, South Africa

Introduction and History

The Sea Cow (Zeekoe) Valley Archaeological Project, Cape Province, South Africa, began in 1979 with an archaeological survey of the central and upper Sea Cow Valley in the Upper Karroo (Fig. 8.4). It has an archaeological area of 5000 km² and with its 16 000 surface sites (i.e., stone artifacts etc) reflecting various activities of prehistoric hunter-gatherer populations, is one of the largest archaeological sites anywhere on earth. At least 8 consecutive occupation events have been documented (Sampson, 1972). The first occupation was of Mid-Pleistocene age and the last (The Smithfield Industry), dates back to 1200 A.D. This was still the prevailing artifact tradition at the time of the first contact of the San hunter-gatherers at the time of European contact in the late 1700s.

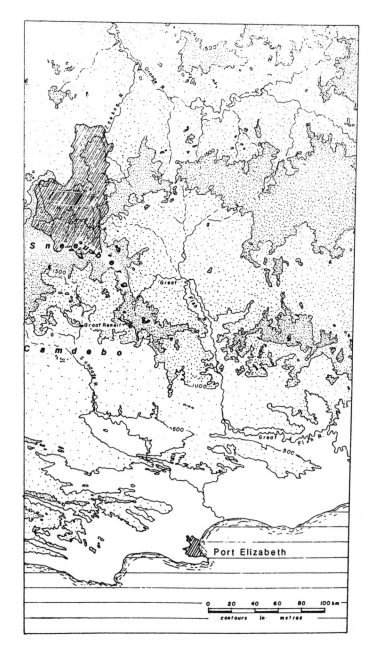

Fig. 8.4 Map of the Seacow Valley archaeological region, Cape Province, South Africa. Source: Sampson (1986). By courtesy of the editor of *The Naturalist*.

According to Sampson (1986):

The San were obviously highly mobile on the landscape, as are modern Kalahari San, whose mobility patterns serve as valuable analogues. A band would settle near one spring until the surrounding food plants and/or firewood ran out, and/or the game drifted away. They would then move to another waterhole, having carefully assessed its resources, and considered how long its catchment had been rested since the last visit. On arrival, they seldom occupied the same camping spot used on their previous visit as this would not yet be free of waste, feces and vermin. If it was last used at a different time of year, it might have been prudent to shelter from some other wind direction. If the prevailing wind shifted during this visit, it would be no great task to move camp to one of several other sheltered spots on the same ridge. Thus it came about that Smithfield camps are clustered in the vicinity of certain spring eyes, and surrounded by smaller workstations up to 4–5 km from the camping area.

Vegetation Studies

Sampson (1986) has studied the effect on vegetation of 453 San camps in the Sea Cow Valley region. He observed the omnipresence of *Lycium* sp. (Plate 8.4) which serves as an indicator not only of the camps, but of flint flakes and other cutting tools of the San people. This observation is particularly interesting in view of the known association of *Lycium pallidum* with ancient Indian archaeological sites in North America (Yarnell, 1965—see also earlier in this chapter).

Dense scatters of lithic flakes were found in sites dominated by such species as *Tribulus terrestris, Arctotheca calendula, Salvia verbenaca, Oxalis depressa,* and *Ifloga paronychoides.* These species have all proved to be useful as guides to spotting the whereabouts of camps from afar. All of them are typical weeds of cleared areas, and there are reasons for supposing that the camp surfaces were originally stripped of their natural bush cover by the occupants. So far, 972 San camps have been recorded in the Sea Cow Valley region and form a total area of 1.2 km² in the entire 2065 km² of the valley.

There is a potential for estimating the date of last occupation of a Smithfield camp by examining the level of plant recovery on the camp surface. This presents the possibility of determining ages by botanical methods alone and at a fraction of the cost of radiocarbon assays.

The discovery of visible veld damage, associated with traces of prehistoric activity, serves to highlight the extreme vulnerability of the Karroo ecosystem.

8.3.2 Iron Age Middens in Botswana

An extraordinary correlation between Iron Age middens in Botswana and stands of the grass *Cenchrus ciliaris* (African foxtail or buffalo grass) has been observed by Denbow (1979). This work will also be referred to in Part II of this book since it has obvious implications for aerial photography.

To quote Denbow (1979):

> During an archaeological reconnaissance of the Serowe-Palapye area of eastern Botswana, an initial correlation was noted on the ground between occurrences of dense, monospecific stands of the grass *Cenchrus ciliaris* and the midden deposits of Iron Age sites (Plate 8.5). Although *C. ciliaris* occurs sporadically in the bushveld of eastern Botswana, it seemed to form the dominant vegetation of the first middens observed. These middens were all open, grassy areas covered with *Cenchrus* and surrounded by denser woodlands dominated by *Colophospermum mopane* and *Terminalia* and *Acacia* species
>
> Aerial reconnaissance showed that the midden sites occurred as bald spots. Over 100 such "spots" were discovered by aerial photography and the sites were then examined on the ground to decide whether or not they had archaeological significance. All 100 sites were found to be actual archaeological sites and in the area of each, were other middens not identified by aerial photography. The sites of some of these middens are shown in Fig. 8.5. . . . the correlation of *C. ciliaris* with cultural deposits is not restricted solely to prehistoric sites, nor confined to mopane woodlands. During the archaeological reconnaissance this grass was found to be one of the first invaders of recently-abandoned kraals (stockaded villages often containing cattle enclosures). It has also been found on 19th century Tswana middens and other Iron Age sites near Molepolole and Gaborone in southern Botswana where the surrounding vegetation is dominated by *Acacia-Terminalia* scrub savanna . . .

. . . Since *Cenchrus* has been observed to be one of the first perennials to colonise recently-abandoned kraal deposits, it is possible that this species has a greater tolerance than other locally-occurring plants for the very high concentrations of nitrates and phosphates initially found in kraal sites. Once established on a midden or kraal deposit, its dense rhizomatous growth, combined with other edaphic factors, seems to have inhibited subsequent invasion of other trees and shrubs unless the cover of *Cenchrus* is later thinned or destroyed by overgrazing or some other means.

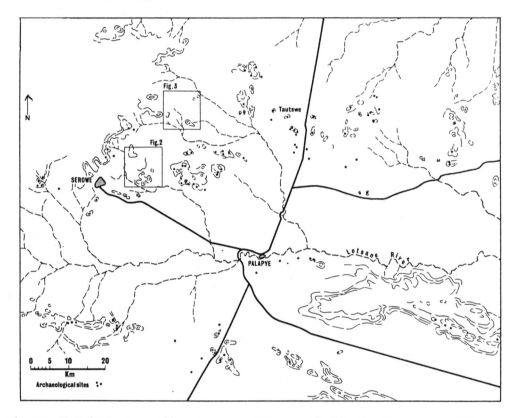

Fig. 8.5 Site of Iron Age middens in eastern Botswana identified by the presence of the grass *Cenchrus ciliaris*. Source: Denbow (1979). By courtesy of the editor of *The South African Journal of Science*.

8.4 GREAT BRITAIN

8.4.1 Vegetation over Archaeological Sites in the Brenig Valley, Wales

Introduction

A very thorough investigation of vegetation covering archaeological sites in Britain has been carried out by Palmer (1974) who studied the plant cover of five Bronze Age monuments in the Brenig Valley, Denbighshire, Wales. Because the plant mapping procedure and statistical treatment are described more fully in Chapter 9, only the barest details of the work will be presented here. A map of the area is shown in Fig. 8.6.

Site V is typical of these large Bronze Age platform cairns. It is composed entirely of stone, having a stone kerb of large boulders. This and other monuments in the area have been extensively disturbed.

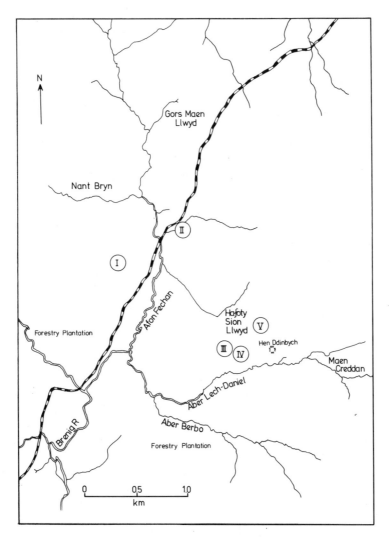

Fig. 8.6 Sites of Bronze Age monuments in the Brenig Valley, Denbighshire, Wales. Source: Palmer (1974). By courtesy of the author.

Methodology

   The vegetation of the valley was surveyed by plotting various vegetation zones on a 6 inch to one mile Ordnance Survey map from vantage points on both sides of the valley and then verifying the zones by walking on them. Four main types of vegetation were recognized and were categorized as follows: heathland moorland (zone H), marshland (zones C, J and M), improved grassland (zone Gi), and natural grassland (zones Gd, Ga, E, EH, N, NH, FN and Mo).

   Five monuments were selected for detailed survey of the vegetation, one in zone H, three in zone Gi, and one in zone J. Belt transects (see Chapter 9) composed of contiguous 30 x 30 cm quadrats were laid across each monument and its surroundings and the presence or absence of each of 25 different species were recorded. Over site V, a grid of one meter square quadrats was also used and some 50 species were counted within it. The data were tested by normal association analysis and reciprocal averaging (see Chapter 9).

Conclusions of the Survey

   The statistical data led to the conclusion that there was a difference between the monuments and their surroundings in the degree of "heathiness" or "grassiness" of the vegetation. On all sites the pH and soil remained virtually constant and no differences could be attributed to these two variables.

There were two reasons for the differences. The first of these was related to the direct influence of the structure of the monuments on the degree of drainage and soil type. The second difference was related to the monuments causing the surface vegetation to have different management from the surroundings: e.g. preventing the monument vegetation from being burnt, and preventing ploughing. In the latter case, the vegetation on the monuments was always more healthy than on the surroundings and was almost certainly a relic of the heather moorland which covered the land before ploughing.

Although differences in vegetation had nothing to do with the fact that the monuments were archaeological, Palmer (1974) concluded that the mapping procedure used by him would always serve to indicate whether or not there was a stony structure below the soil. Such structures discovered by vegetation mapping would then have to be studied by other methods to determine whether or not they were archaeological.

8.5 CENTRAL AMERICA

8.5.1 Plant Indicators of Maya Ruins

Introduction

There has already been some discussion in Chapter 6 about the relationship between specific vegetation and Maya ruins in the Yucatan Peninsula. This chapter included a discussion of the survival of crops from ancient cultures. Among the plants associated with Maya ruins is the *ramon* (*Brosimum alicastrum;* Plate 8.6). There has been intense discussion in recent years as to whether the occurrence of this species is related to survival of an ancient crop or whether there are ecological reasons for its present distribution. The core reference for this association is an unpublished MA thesis by Puleston (1968). He proposed that the distribution of this species is linked to its dietary use and hence to control by the lords of the Maya empire. There is, however, a sufficient body of opinion linking the distribution of the ramon to ecological factors, to justify reporting the evidence in this present chapter rather than in Chapter 6. Lambert and Arnason (1982) have linked the occurrence of the *ramon* with edaphic and physical properties of the soil produced by Maya ruins in the substrate. Puleston (1968) proposed that ramon was a subsistence alternative (see Plate 8.7 for picture of seeds) for the Classic Maya of the southern lowlands of the Yucatan Peninsula, and that its occurrence in the ceremonial precincts and housemounds at Tikal, Guatemala (see Fig.15.2) was evidence of its cultivation in residential areas. This proposal has been accepted by other Mayanists such as Culbert (1974), but others (e.g. Sanders, 1973) doubt that the Maya would have depended entirely on such a resource. Folan et al. (1979) suggested that the Maya aristocracy maintained and controlled the distribution of economically important fruit, fiber, bark and resin trees in the city centers (see Chapter 6) and contended that the present trees are descendants of those planted by the ancient Maya and that their present distribution corresponds to that of Classic times.

Evidence for an Ecological Relationship between Ramon and Maya Ruins

The work of Lambert and Arnason (1982) presents some of the best evidence that the relationship between ramon and Maya ruins may be ecological rather than economic. Their work was carried out at Lamanai, Belize. They made plant measurements over 12 transects each of which included ruins and highbush forest. They found several plant species that were associated with high structures among the ruins. These were: *Brosimum alicastrum* (ramon), *Protium copal* (copal), *Bursera simaruba* (chacha), *Pimenta dioica* (naba kook), *Talisia oliviformis* (kinep), and *Allophyllus campostachys* (bikhach). Four species were more common on the low structures and throughout the highbush forest: *Spondias mombin* (hu hu), *Chrysophila argentea* (akuum), *Guazuma ulmifolia* (pixoy), and *Stemmadenia donnelsmithii* (chalkin).

The density of the ramon trees was greatest on the steep sides of the high structures where the soil rarely exceeded 15 cm in depth and covered limestone ruins. The soil was exceptionally well drained and had a high exchangeable calcium content (24 500 ppm) as well as having a high pH (7.5). Below the surrounding forest the soil was much deeper and had a lower pH (6.1) so that decline of the ramon could be linked to increasing competition from other species over the more stable and more fertile substrate.

Numerous housemounds occur throughout the region and could easily be distinguished by the presence of the *naba kook* tree with its peeling yellowish bark. The mound soils are also well drained and have a high exchangeable calcium content. Other species on the mounds include *copal (Protium copal), kinep,* and an occasional ramon.

Lambert and Arnason (1982) compared the density of ramon at Lamanai with that at Tikal and Coba (Table 8.1). Though Lamanai is much smaller in area than either of the other sites, the density of ramon on high structures is greater than at Tikal or Coba. This in itself seems to lend little credence to an ecological *raison d'être* for the ramon, but the authors have pointed out that if *all* trees growing at Tikal and Coba are counted, the relative importance of ramon diminishes. If trees had been planted at the ceremonial centers it might have been expected that tree roots would have penetrated the hill of buried structures. Lambert and Arnason (1982) however, found no evidence of this. These authors also doubt whether existing specimens of ramon could have been survivors of former plantings since competition from wild plants would have rapidly changed the character of the plantations. They believe that what is now seen at Tikal, Coba and Lamanai is not a replication of planting patterns of 1000 years B.P. but rather the ecological end result of species competition and selection.

The debate continues, and like most great debates will probably never be solved to the satisfaction of all concerned.

TABLE 8.1   Comparison of distribution and dominance of *Brosimum alicastrum* **(ramon) at three Maya ceremonial centers.**

Sampling site	Area sampled (ha)	Ramon per ha.
TIKAL		
0–0.5 km from city center	5	63
0.5–1.0 km from city center	5	49
2.5–3.0 km from city center	5	4
4.5–5.0 km from city center	5	71
COBA (refer to Fig. 6.3)		
A—0.25–0.75 km N of lake	19	56
B—0.75–1.25 km N of lake	26	13
E—2.25–2.80 km N of lake	49	1.3
H—0–0.5 km S of lake	45	6
I—0.5–1.0 km S of lake	50	8
K—1.5–2.0 km S of lake	51	4
LAMANAI		
High structures	15	106
Outcrops	20	33
Low structures	25	17
Highbush forest	30	12

After: Lambert and Arnason (1982). Copyright 1982 by the American Association for the Advancement of Science.

8.6 CHAPTER SUMMARY

This chapter is concerned with vegetational changes over specific archaeological sites. In North America, case histories include aboriginal sites at Walnut Canyon National Park in Arizona; Angel Mounds, Indiana; Alaska; northern Canada; and Newfoundland.

In Newfoundland at Port aux Choix National Historical Park, there is a close association between a species of *Antennaria* and Dorset (1900–1300 B.P.) paleo-Eskimo building sites containing rich archaeological remains. *Iris versicolor* is another good indicator of these Eskimo sites. In Alaska, there are numerous examples of vegetation associated with specific archaeological sites.

In southern Africa, temporary settlements of the San bushman tribe are delineated by open areas in the veld, dominated by *Lycium pallidum,* the same species associated with Pueblo Indian sites in North America. Another vegetational indicator of archaeological sites in southern Africa is provided by stands of the buffalo grass (*Cenchrus ciliaris*) which occurs over Iron Age middens in Botswana. These can even be recognized from the air.

In Britain, a study in the Brenig Valley, Wales, has revealed a specific vegetation community over Bronze Age platform cairns.

In Central America, the vegetation over Maya ruins has been further studied and it is proposed that the *ramon (Brosimum alicastrum)* (see also Chapter 6), grows over Maya ruins only because of edaphic and physical characteristics of the substrate, instead of having been planted deliberately by the Maya for nutritional or ceremonial purposes.

REFERENCES

Anderson, E. 1953. *Introgressive Hybridization.* Wiley, New York.

Bank, T. P. II 1953. Ecology of Prehistoric Aleutian village sites. *Ecology* 34: 246–264.

Black, G. A. 1944. *Angel Site, Vanderburgh County, Indiana.* Indiana Historical Society, Indianapolis.

Brown, C. A. 1936. The vegetation of the Indian mounds, middens, and marshes in Plaquemines and St. Bernard Parishes. *Louis. Dept. Conserv. Bull.* 8: 423–440.

Canfield, R. H. 1941. Application of the line interception method in sampling range vegetation. *J. Forest.* 39: 388–394.

Clark, A. B. 1968. Vegetation on archaeological sites compared with non-site locations at Walnut Canyon, Flagstaff, Arizona. *Plateau* 40: 77–90.

Culbert, T. P. 1974. *The Lost Civilization: The Story of the Classic Maya.* Harper Row, New York.

Dall, W. H. 1877. On succession in shell-heaps of the Aleutian Islands. *Contr. N. Amer. Ethnol.* 1: 41–91.

Denbow, J. R. 1979. *Cenchrus ciliaris:* an ecological indicator of Iron Age middens using aerial photography in eastern Botswana. *S. Afr. J. Sci.* 75: 405–408.

Folan, W. J. Fletcher, L. A., and Kintz, E. R. 1979. Fruit, fiber, bark, and resin: social organization of a Maya urban center. *Science* 204: 697–701.

Harp, E. 1976. Dorset settlement patterns in Newfoundland and southeastern Hudson Bay. In, M. Maxwell [ed.] *Eastern Arctic Prehistory: Palaeoeskimo problems. Mem. Soc. Amer. Archaeol.* 31: 119–138.

Hrdlicka, A. 1937. Man and plants in Alaska. *Science* 86: 559–560.

Jepson, W. L. 1909. *The Trees of California.* Cunningham, Curtis and Welch, San Francisco.

Johnston, R. B. 1964. Proton magnetometry and its application to archaeology. *Prehist. Res. Ser. Indiana Hist. Soc.* 4: 56–62.

Lambert, J. D. H., and Arnason, J. T. 1982. Ramon and Maya ruins: an ecological, not an economic, relation. *Science* 216: 298–299.

Lundell, C. L. 1939. Plants probably utilized by the Old Empire Maya of Peten and adjacent lowlands. *Pap. Mich. Acad. Sci. Arts Lett.* 24: 37–56.

Meigs. P. III. 1938. Vegetation on shell mounds, Lower California. *Science* 87: 346.

Mosely. E. L. 1931. Some plants that were probably brought to Northern Ohio from the West by the Indians. *Pap. Mich. Acad. Sci. Arts Lett.* 13: 169–172.

Palmer, J. P. 1974. *An Investigation of the Vegetation of the Brenig Valley with Special Reference to the Vegetation of some Archaeological Monuments in the Valley.* M.Sc. Thesis, University of Wales.

Puleston, D. 1968. M.A. Thesis, University of Pennsylvania.

Renouf, M. A. P. 1985. Archaeological research in the Port au Choix National Historic Park, northwest Newfoundland. *Polar Rec.* 22: 693–697.

———— 1986. Archaeological investigations at Phillip's Garden and Point Riche, Port au Choix National Historic Park. *Report of 1985 Field Activities. Memorial University, St. Johns.*

Renouf, M. A. P., and Hall, C. 1985. Archaeology of the Port au Choix National Historic Park. *Report of 1984 Field Activities. Memorial University, St. Johns.*

Sampson, C. G. 1972. The Stone Age industries of the Orange River Scheme and South Africa. *Mem. Nat. Mus. Bloemfontein* 6: 1–288.

———— 1986. Veld damage in the Karoo caused by its pre-trekboer inhabitants: preliminary observations in the Seacow Valley. *The Naturalist* 30: 37–42.

Sanders, W. T. 1973. In, T. P. Culbert [ed.] *The Classic Maya Collapse.* Univ. New Mexico Press, Albuquerque.

Small, J. K. 1927. Among floral aborigines. *J. N.Y. Bot. Gdn.* 28: 1–20.

Wiggins, I. L., and Thomas, J. H. 1962. *A Flora of the Alaskan Arctic Slope.* Arctic Institute of North America Spec. Pub. #4, Toronto.

Yarnell, R. A. 1965. Implications of distinctive flora on Pueblo ruins. *Amer. Anthropologist* 67: 662–674.

Zeiner, H. M. 1946. Botanical survey of the Angel Mounds site, Evansville, Indiana. *Am. J. Bot.* 33: 83–90.

Chapter 9

PLANT MAPPING AND STATISTICAL TREATMENT OF DATA

9.1 INTRODUCTION

Unless the vegetation cover over an archaeological site is markedly different from that of its surroundings, purely visual inspection will not be sufficient, and recourse will have to be made to plant mapping.

Plant mapping techniques vary widely from the simple to the complicated and we must differentiate between field operations and the later statistical treatment of the data. With the advent of the computer, a number of sophisticated statistical procedures can be applied.

Ideally plant mapping should be carried out by a skilled botanist or ecologist since the amateur might not be able to distinguish closely-related plants from each other. This is not to say that such work is beyond the capabilities of an intelligent amateur. The cardinal requirement is an ability to recognize and rerecognize a given plant species even if it cannot be named immediately. In the field, each plant can be placed in a press or photograph album, given an appropriate code number, and named correctly once a botanist has had a chance to examine the reference collection. The basic principles of plant mapping (Brooks, 1983) follow.

9.2 MAPPING TECHNIQUES IN PHYTOARCHAEOLOGY

9.2.1 Selection of Quadrats

Plant mapping involves the selection of a number of sample plots known as quadrats. There is no general agreement on the best method of selection of these quadrats. Some workers believe that they should be selected in a random manner, whereas others believe that they should be chosen subjectively. This latter procedure, though frequently used, is open to criticism insofar as it makes the assumption that the vegetation associations are already known.

If the subjective approach is to be used, the following procedure should be adopted. Every plot should have the utmost uniformity that it is possible to find in the area concerned; not only with regard to plant species, but also with consideration of such factors as aspect, slope, drainage, relief and altitude. Particular care must be taken that the quadrats do not include two or more different plant Associations as may occur with plots of non-uniform slope.

The size of the quadrat now has to be established. As a general rule, the size should be the minimum needed to include most of the plants of the Association and will obviously be related to the homogeneity of the community. In assessing the size of the minimal area, the law of diminishing returns will obviously apply: i.e. successive increases in size of the sample area will give successively smaller amounts of additional information. The concept of minimal area has been reviewed by Goodall (1952). A species-area plot at first rises sharply and then becomes flatter, although never completely horizontal because the whole area would have to be included in the quadrat to be sure of including every single species in the area. Greig-Smith (1964) has discussed the problem of minimal area at some length, and there appears to be no general agreement on a universal criterion to determine this area. As a general rule however, the following procedure may be adopted in the field.

Begin with a small quadrat of perhaps 5 m², note the species within it and then increase the size of the plot progressively (10, 50, 100 m^2 etc.) noting at each stage additional species encountered. When there is an appreciable drop in the rate of increase of new species found, the optimum quadrat size will have been found.

When the size and position of the test plots have been established, the next procedure will involve an evaluation of the *density* of individual species and their *spacing* (reciprocal of density). In determining density, direct counting or a scale of numbers may be used. The scale is somewhat arbitrary but can give good results in the hands of a competent field worker. The system is as follows: 1) very rare, 2) rare, 3) infrequent, 4) abundant, 5) very abundant. One disadvantage of this system is that the data are heavily dependent on the personal assessment of one individual and are not always comparable with data collected by other workers. The use of this scale is nevertheless justified on the grounds of speed and practicality. It is also a useful system when the vegetation cover is so dense that counting of absolute numbers of individuals would be impracticable. A phytoarchaeological map of an area need contain nothing more than the density or spacing data enumerated above, but if other parameters are added a more meaningful map can be compiled.

The space demand of a species introduces another concept, that of *cover*. It is assumed that the entire shoot system of a plant is projected on the ground and that this area (equal to the area of shade if the sun were directly overhead), represents the cover. Cover is usually expressed as a percentage. The total of all species will often exceed 100% due to overlap.

A quick method of assessing cover involves measuring the total length of interception by plants on line transects. The proportion of the total length of the transect intercepted by a given species is a measure of its cover (see Greig-Smith, 1964 for further details of these and other means of measurement).

Some mention should also be made of the concept of layering. The vegetation may be considered not only laterally but also vertically. In the vertical concept, a number of distinct layers are recognized. These are the tree layer, shrub layer, herb layer and moss layer. Clearly, the denser the upper tree layer, the greater will have to be the tolerance towards reduced amount of light by the lower members of the community. Mosses, as might be expected, will tolerate the lowest light intensity.

There are several other criteria of plant communities which can be employed in phytoarchaeological plant mapping. These are are based on the European school of phytosociology (see Chapter 2) and are unfortunately not taught to any extent in British and American centers of learning. They do however feature prominently in European scientific literature and are mentioned briefly below.

Sociability expresses the space relationship of individual plants and can be expressed in terms of a simple scale (Braun-Blanquet, 1932) as follows: soc.1) growing in one place singly; soc.2) grouped or tufted; soc.3) in troops small patches or cushions; soc.4) in small colonies in extensive patches or forming carpets; soc.5) in great crowds.

Vitality is a measure of how a plant prospers in the community and can be expressed by a number of conventional symbols (Braun-Blanquet, 1932) as follows: ●) well developed and regularly completing life cycle; ◎) strong and increasing but usually not completing life cycle; ⊙) feeble but spreading and never completing life cycle; ○) occasionally germinating but not increasing.

Periodicity is a measure of the regularity or absence of rhythmic phenomena in plants, such as flowering, fruiting etc. A study of this criterion involves continuous and systematic research and is outside the scope of this book.

If mean values for density, spacing, cover and other parameters are determined for each species and averaged over several quadrats (preferably chosen randomly), it will be possible to characterize the plant Associations in the test area and to attempt to correlate this with the archaeological environment. The study of plant Associations (phytosociology) is of some importance in phytoarchaeology and has already been mentioned in Chapter 2.

9.2.2 Transects

Although the use of quadrats is the most usual approach in phytoarchaeological mapping, a different approach will be needed for plants growing over narrow archaeological sites. In such cases, the use of line transects or belt transects is recommended. Line transects consist of parallel straight lines run through an area with the aid of tape measures and compasses, whereas belt transects consist of lines of continuous quadrats running across the profile of the area. Fig.9.1 shows data for a belt transect undertaken in Western Australia. The purpose of this particular study was the identification of minerals rather than archaeological sites. Nevertheless the same principles of plant mapping and data presentation apply and the figure gives a useful model of what can and should be done.

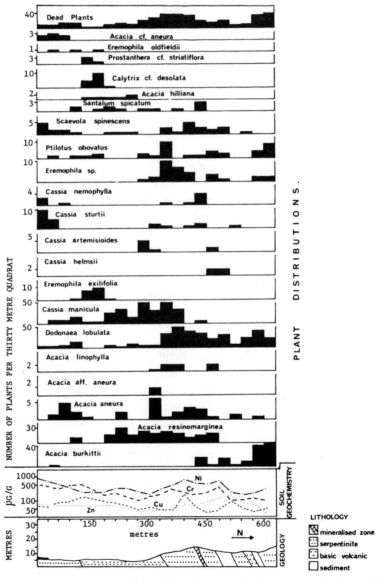

Fig. 9.1 Belt transect across various geological rock types in Western Australia. Although specifically designed for geological evaluation, this form of plant mapping is equally applicable to phytoarchaeology. Source: Severne 1972.

Representation of plant densities in each quadrat can be made in various ways. A simple method is to record the number of individuals in each 30 × 30 m (a common dimension) quadrat or else to record each species as a percentage of the total number of individuals of all species in each quadrat.

It is much easier to carry out plant mapping in arid areas than in thick bush. In the latter environment, the line transect is usually more appropriate. If a multi-storey vegetation assemblage is involved, it is hard to evaluate the extent to which each plant or plant grouping intersects the line. In such cases an alternative method consists of laying a tape measure through the community and recording every individual of a specified size (e.g. trunk diameter) within a predetermined distance of the tape. There are of course many variants of this procedure which can be adapted to specific conditions.

9.3 SOME STATISTICAL METHODS OF HANDLING PLANT MAPPING DATA

9.3.1 Introduction

In the course of a book covering such a wide field, it is not to be expected that a single chapter will be able to provide an in depth discussion of the complicated field of statistics. The purpose of this chapter will be to present the bare outlines of selected statistical procedures that can be applied to phytoarchaeological mapping data, so that the phytoarchaeologist may understand the significance of the statistical data, even if he is not used to doing the operations himself. As far as possible the discussion will be illustrated by specific practical examples.

Since plant mapping applied to archaeological prospecting has only recently begun to be applied, there is as yet, no solid base of previously-exploited statistical procedures applied to specific problems. However, the principles of the subject are exactly the same as for the much more widely applied field of indicator geobotany (Brooks, 1983, see also Chapter 2). The purpose of the latter is to identify rock types or mineralization in the substrate below the vegetation cover. If the natural geological substrate is replaced by an artificial one governed by anthropogenic modification of existing soils or rocks caused by the presence of building foundations, cultural relics, remnants of ancient agriculture, or mining and metallurgical traces, the parallel between geobotany and phytoarchaeological mapping becomes very obvious.

9.3.2 Vegetation Dominance Types

One of the simplest semi-quantitative methods of analysis of phytoarchaeological mapping data is one which does not require the use of a computer. It is based on recognition of dominant species and the classification of the quadrats according to these *Vegetation Dominance Types* (VDT).

An example of the uses of VDT is provided by the work of Sawbridge and Bell (1972, see also Chapter 5) who studied the vegetation over shell middens in British Columbia. Thirty-two plots were established in stands of apparently homogeneous vegetation. Plots varied in size and shape because many middens were small and plant communities were often patchy. Vegetation was analyzed by the Braun-Blanquet (1932) cover/abundance scale for each species in the tree, shrub, herb and moss layers.

Stands were grouped together on the basis of dominant species. Initially, a synthesis table was constructed containing only the dominants (defined as species with a percentage cover exceeding 50) from each plot. Plots were then rearranged into groups of similar stands. Subsequently, non-dominant species were sought which occurred consistently in some VDTs and not in others. These were included in the final table (Table 9.1).

Four vegetation types (*Alnus, Thuja, Tsuga* and *Pseudotsuga*) and three sub-types (*Mnium, Rubus spectabilis,* and *Picea*) in the *Alnus* VDT were found on the 23 middens

TABLE 9.1 Occurrence, according to vegetation dominance type, of dominant species and five species of restricted distribution from 32 midden sites from British Columbia, Canada.

Species	Alnus-Mnium	Alnus-Rubus spectabilis	Alnus-Picea	Thuja	Tsuga	Pseudotsuga
Alnus rubra	XXX	XXX	XX	XX	XX	
Acer macrophyllum	XX	XX			X	
Polystichum munitum	XX	XX	XX	X	XX	XX
Mnium insigne	XXX		XX	X		
Urtica dioica	XX					
Tellima grandiflora	XX					X
Poa trivialis	XX					
Galium triflorum	XX					X
Carex deweyana	XX					
Eurhyncium praelongum	X	X				
Rubus spectabilis	X	XXX	X	X	X	
Dryopteris austriaca		XX	X			
Picea sitchensis	X		XXX	XX	X	X
Thuja plicata	X	X	X	XXX	XX	XX
Tsuga heterophylla		X	XX	XX	XXX	XX
Gaultheria shallon		X		X	XX	
Plagiothecium undulatum					X	
Pseudotsuga menziesii				XX	XX	XXX

XXX—commonly dominant, XX—occasionally dominant, X—not dominant.
Source: Sawbridge and Bell (1972). By courtesy of the Ecological Society of America.

investigated. Although this study did not result in the identification of a specific vegetation type indicative of shell middens, the principles of the work were sound and can serve as a model for others wishing to apply a simple and effective method to their phytoarchaeological mapping.

9.3.3 Discriminant Analysis

Introduction

Before beginning the theoretical treatment of *discriminant analysis,* there must be some understanding of the terms dependent and independent variables. An independent variable is one which is not subject to change, whereas a dependent variable is one which depends on another. As an analogy we could consider that the physical state of the substrate below vegetation growing at an archaeological site is the independent variable, whereas the species composition of the vegetation is a dependent variable: i.e. it depends on the physical state of the substrate and not vice versa.

In many cases it is appropriate to attempt to express a dependent variable y in terms of more than one independent variable $x_1, x_2, \ldots, x_n$. One general model frequently used is that in which data are fitted to an equation of the form:

$$y = a_1 x_1 + a_2 x_2 + a_3 x_3 + \ldots a_n x_n + C.$$

An estimate of a coefficient a in the regression model can be found from the rate of change of the dependent variable with respect to variable x, with all other variables being held constant. These estimates, the sample partial regression coefficients, are generally different from the simple regression coefficients of y on x. The multiple regression can be expected to account for more of the variation in y than any simple regression does. It should be noted that, because the variance of only one variable (y) is subjected to analysis, multiple regression is multivariate only in the sense that several variables are measured on each sample.

As in the two-variable case, the method of least squares can be used to provide the best estimates of the parameters a_1, a_2, a_3, . . . , a_n, and C. By minimizing the sum of the squared deviations of the observed values of y from the line, a set of m + 1 simultaneous equations is obtained.

Computational procedures for dealing with situations where m is large, are discussed in several works on statistics (Davis, 1973; Efroymson, 1960). One such procedure is described as stepwise regression (Efroymson, 1960). At each stage of the computation, this procedure selects the independent variable that increases by the most significant amount the variance of y that is explained by the regression equation. If, and only if, this amount is more significant than a predetermined probability level, this independent variable is inserted into the regression equation. Following the insertion of a variable into the regression equation, the other variables already in the equation are rechecked to find if they are still significant at the predetermined level of significance. If not, they are removed from the equation. On completion of the analysis, the percentage of the variance in the dependent variable which has been explained by the regression equation, is computed.

The Mahalanobis D^2 Statistic

One way in which multiple regression equations can be used to provide discrimination of data is the so-called *Mahalanobis D^2 statistic* (Mahalanobis, 1936). This statistic is calculated from the means, variances and covariances of the variables measured in replicate samples from the various groups. It is in effect a measure of the "distance" between the groups. The larger the value of D^2, the greater the degree of discrimination.

It is appropriate at this stage to give an actual case history originally applied to a geobotanical study. However, since geobotanical and phytoarchaeological mapping demand exactly the same statistical treatment, the plant data can be assumed to apply to the vegetation on and off an archaeological site.

Let us suppose that plant mapping was carried out over 43 quadrats measuring 30 × 15 m. Twenty-six of these quadrats (A) were over the foundations of ancient ruins, 11 (B) were away from the ruins and 7 (A/B) were transitional quadrats encompassing both archaeological sites and the surrounding background. It is further supposed that 34 different plant species (numbered 1–34) were sampled. Using discriminant analysis, a numerical score was assigned to each quadrat on the basis of an equation of the form shown above. Where x_1–x_{34} are the number of individual plants of species 1–34 in each quadrat and a_1–a_{34} are coefficients so chosen as to maximise the differences between the scores for the three types of quadrat. These coefficients are chosen by computer calculations. C is a constant.

Using the Mahalanobis D^2 statistic, it was possible to predict the true nature of the substrate, i.e. archaeological site or not, in 26 out of 26 of the "ruins" sites, 10 out of 11 quadrats over background, and 6 of 7 quadrats overlapping both ruins and background (Table 9.2). This degree of discrimination was achieved by use of only 20 of the 33 species observed. It is obvious that computer-assisted programs of this nature will serve to improve the potential of phytoarchaeological mapping to a high degree.

TABLE 9.2 **Characterization of substrates by discriminant analysis (Mahalanobis D^2 statistic) of theoretical phytoarchaeological data.**

Species	D^2	No. of correct predictions		
		A (26 quad.)	B (11 quad.)	A/B (7 quad.)
21	0.5	11	6	0
23	5.7	2	11	1
21,23	6.2	10	6	1
21–23	9.4	15	3	1
6,21,23	7.4	16	7	1
2,21,23	8.3	21	7	1
2,3,21,23	9.1	16	8	1
2,4,21,23	12.1	17	8	1
2,4,14,21,23	21.1	19	9	1
2,4,14,15,21,23	29.1	22	10	1
2,4,14–16,21,23	29.2	22	11	2
2,4,14–16,21,23,25	29.4	20	10	2
2,4,14–16,21,23,27	33.0	21	10	2
2,4,12,14–16,21,23,27	41.3	22	10	3
2,4,12,14–16,21,23,24,27	42.5	22	10	4
1,2,4,12,14–16,21,23,24,27	48.2	23	10	3
1,2,4,5,12,14–16,21,23,24,27	50.4	24	10	3
1,2,4–6,12,14–16,21,23,24,27	51.8	24	10	3
1,2,4,5,8,12,14–16,21,23,24,27	56.6	24	10	4
1,2,4,5,7,8,12,14–16,21,23,24,27	58.7	24	10	4
1,2,4–8,12,14–17,21,23,24,27	67.8	24	10	4
1,2,4–8,12,14–17,19,21,23,24,27	76.2	24	10	5
1,2,4–8,12,14–17,19,21,23,24,27,28	89.8	24	9	4
1,2,4–8,12,14–17,19,21,23,24,27,29	81.3	23	9	5
1,2,4–8,12,14–17,19,21,23,24,27,29	100.3	24	10	6
1,2,4–8,12,14–17,19,21,23,24,27,31	119.4	25	9	6
1–8,12,14–17,19,21,23,24,27,31,32	137.5	25	10	6
1–9,12,14–17,19,21,23,24,27,31,32	138.1	25	10	6
1–8,10,12,14–17,19,21,23,24,27,31,32	138.2	25	10	6
1–8,11,12,14–17,19,21,23,24,27,31,32	140.2	24	10	6
1–8,12–17,19,21,23,24,27,31,32	147.2	25	10	6
1–8,12,14–19,21,23,24,27,31,32	144.3	24	10	6
1–8,12,14–19,21,23,24,26,27,31,32	142.8	24	10	6
1–8,12,14–19,21,23,24,27,30–32	173.9	26	10	5

A—stations over archaeological sites, B—stations away from archaeological sites, A/B stations overlapping both archaeological sites and their surroundings.

9.3.4 Dimensional Analysis

Introduction

The aim of *dimensional analysis* (Lorr, 1983) is essentially that of data reduction in which a whole array of complex variables can be reduced to a smaller number of important factors to explain the processes occurring in the system under study. Dimensional analysis has two main models: Factor Analysis and Principal Components Analysis (PCA).

Factor Analysis

Factor analysis is a technique used for the interpretation of relationships between the variables in a multivariate collection of data. It allows the data to be expressed in terms of a number of factors that is fewer than the number of original variables. The factors created are new variables having the form of linear combinations of the original variables. Each factor extracted, successively accounts for a decreasing proportion of the data variance.

The analysis may be carried out by examining the relationship between the samples (Q mode) or the relationship between the variables (R mode). R-mode factor analysis is particularly useful in clarifying the relationship between variables in a complex array of data. Where the variables are abundances of various plant species over adjacent archaeological and non-archaeological sites, the analysis can lead to explanations of the data variability in terms of anthropogenic modification to the substrate.

Principal Components Analysis

In *Principal Components Analysis* (PCA), the aim is to account for as much of the variance as possible in the successive components. The model may be expressed as:

$Z_j = a_{j1}F_1 + a_{j2}F_2 + \ldots + a_{jn}F_n (j = 1,2,3, \ldots n)$ where Z_j is the observed standard score on test j, the a's represent the component coefficients or loadings, and the F's are the component scores. In other words, the observed score on variable j is expressed as a linear combination of weighted component scores. The principal components are obtained so that:

1) The first component and each successive one, accounts for the maximum variance possible.

2) The second principal component (the linear combination of the observed variables) accounts for as much of the remaining variance as possible, subject to the restriction that it be uncorrelated with the previous component.

The process is repeated until all the variance is accounted for by n components. Since the last few components are very small and statistically unreliable, they are usually discarded.

Once the principal components have been obtained, the data can be ordinated, i.e., presented in graphical form, using a two dimensional plot or three dimensional triangular diagram using the first two or three components. A specific case history will now be considered.

Example of Use of PCA in Phytoarchaeology

There has already been some mention in Chapter 8 of a phytoarchaeological study in the Brenig Valley, Wales (Palmer, 1974). The reader should consult this chapter for background details. However, to summarize briefly: a transect of 131 quadrats (30 × 30 cm) was placed across a Bronze Age monument in the Valley. The presence or absence of each of 25 plant species (Table 9.3) was recorded and PCA applied to the data. The two principal components represented the degree of "heathiness" or "grassiness" of species or quadrats.

TABLE 9.3   List of species used for transect of Bronze Age monument in the Brenig Valley, Wales. Numbers refer to Fig. 9.4.

1. *Trifolium repens*	2. *Rumex acetosella*	3. *Dactylis glomerata*
4. *Poa Pratensis*	5. *Agrostis tenuis*	6. *Polytrichum commune*
7. *Lolium perenne*	8. *Juncus squarrosus*	9. *Galium saxatile*
10. *Calluna vulgaris*	11. *Cerastium fontanum*	12. *Festuca ovina*
13. *Holcus lanatus*	14. *Juncus effusus*	15. *Sagina apetala*
16. *Anthoxanthum odoratum*	17. *Cynosurus cristatus*	18. *Carex echinata*
19. *Vaccinium myrtillus*	20. *Aira praecox*	21. *Carex demissa*
22. *Deschampsia flexuosa*	23. *Nardus stricta*	24. *Veronica serpyllifolia*
25. *Bellis perennis*		

Source: Palmer (1974). By courtesy of the author.

Fig 9.2 shows a graph of quadrat (stand) scores as a function of position across the transect, where quadrat numbers 43–116 are over the monument itself.

The "heathy" quadrats over the monument gave lower scores and are clearly distinguishable from those over the "grassy" surroundings.

When the two main principal components ("grassy" and "heathy") for the quadrats on

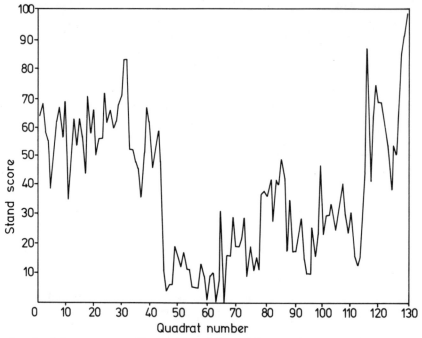

Fig. 9.2 Graph of factor scores (first principal factor) for quadrats as a function of distance across a Bronze Age monument in Wales. Quadrats actually above the monument (45–115) have lower factor scores than those of the surrounding areas. Source: Palmer (1974).

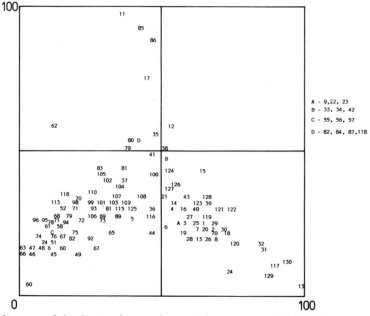

Fig. 9.3 Scatter diagram of the first and second principle components for 131 quadrats across a Bronze Age monument in Wales. The more "heathy" (on-monument) quadrats lie to the left and the more "grassy" (off-monument) ones to the right. Source: Palmer (1974).

and off the monument were plotted on a graph (Fig.9.3), the ordination separated them neatly into two groups with the more "grassy" off-monument quadrats being on the right, and the more "heathy" on the left. It will be remembered from Chapter 8 that the distinctive vegetation over the monument was thought to represent the original heath vegetation of the region before it had been affected off the monument by agriculture.

This application of PCA enabled the researcher to discover which were the main variables affecting the vegetation and at the same time to decide the degree to which they delineated the monument site.

9.3.5 Cluster Analysis

Introduction

Cluster analysis (Lorr, 1983) is a technique for classifying objects into related groups and subgroups (taxonomic classification). The concept of clusters encompasses the duality of homogeneity within clusters and heterogeneity between clusters. Many methods of computation and presentation are available and the data can be correlated by comparing variables (R mode) or samples (Q mode). As with most other multivariate techniques, the method is most practical with a computer.

The simplest way of correlating multi-element data is to generate a matrix that contains the correlations between all possible pairs of elements considered. Such a matrix is however, difficult to interpret and impossible to plot meaningfully upon a map. With use of cluster analysis, however, it is possible to group variables according to their mutual correlations, i.e. to choose mutually-correlated variables that exhibit the greatest within-group correlation relative to the between-group correlations, taking into account all possible combinations of the given elements.

An Example of Cluster Analysis in Phytoarchaeology

A good example of the use of cluster analysis in phytoarchaeology has been given by Palmer (1974) in his study of vegetation over Bronze Age monuments in the Brenig Valley in Wales.

A total of 131 quadrats containing 25 species (Table 9.3) was used for the survey and cluster analysis carried out. The hierarchial classification is shown in Fig.9.4. The first split is on *Aira Praecox* (#20) and more-or-less splits the quadrats into those on and off the monuments. The final classification is of 8 subgroups of which group 8 is present both on and off the monument site. Groups 5, 6, and 7 are present in only off-monument quadrats and groups 1–4 are present only in on-monument quadrats. All the groups contain "heathy" plants but

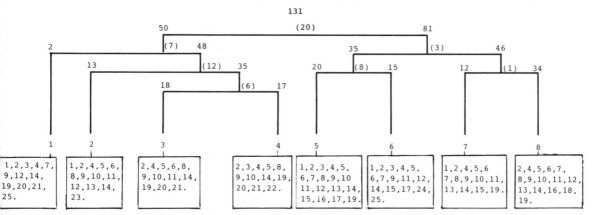

Fig. 9.4 Cluster (hierarchical) classification of quadrats from a transect across a Bronze Age monument in Wales. The number of quadrats is shown as unbracketed numerals. Numbers in brackets refer to the plant species as in Table 9.3. The on-monument plant species are to the left of the dendrogram and are found in groups 1–4. Source: Palmer (1974).

groups 1–4 are the more "heathy". Group 8 is a mixture of both "heathy" and "grassy" quadrats but has few species per quadrat, one of which is usually *Juncus effusus*. The greatest incidence of group 8 on the monument is between quadrats 78–87 and this is where the most serious disturbance had occurred from robbers. Large depressions were left on the surface where pits had been dug.

9.4 CHAPTER SUMMARY

The principles of plant mapping and statistical analysis of phytoarchaeological data are enumerated in this chapter. Plant mapping procedures are explained and related to such phytosociological factors as *density, spacing, cover, sociability, vitality,* and *periodicity*. The concepts of *quadrats, minimal areas,* and *line* or *belt transects,* are also discussed. Statistical procedures described, include: *vegetation dominance types* (VDT), *discriminant analysis, Malanobis D² analysis, principal components analysis* (PCA), *factor analysis,* and *cluster analysis* (CA). The principles of CA and PCA are illustrated by case histories at the Brenig Valley archaeological site in Wales.

REFERENCES

Braun-Blanquet, J. 1932. *Plant Sociology.* McGraw-Hill, New York.

Brooks, R. R. 1983. *Biological Methods of Prospecting for Minerals.* Wiley, New York.

Davis, J. C. 1973. *Statistics and Data Analysis in Geology.* Wiley, New York.

Efroymson, M. A. 1960. Multiple regression analysis. In, *Mathematical Methods for Digital Computers.* Wiley, New York pp. 191–203.

Goodall, D. W. 1952. Quantitative aspects of plant distribution. *Biol. Rev.* 27: 194–245.

Greig-Smith, P. 1964. *Quantitative Plant Ecology, 2nd Ed.* Butterworths, London.

Lorr, M. 1983. *Cluster Analysis for Social Scientists.* Jossey-Bass, San Francisco.

Mahalanobis, P. C. 1936. On the generalized distance in statistics. *Proc. Nat. Inst. Sci. (India)* 12: 49–55.

Palmer, J. P. 1974. *An Investigation of the Vegetation of the Brenig Valley with Special Reference to the Vegetation of some Archaeological Monuments in the Valley.* M.Sc. Thesis, University of Wales.

Sawbridge, D. F., and Bell, M. A. M. 1972. Vegetation and soils of shell middens on the coast of British Columbia. *Ecology* 53: 840–849.

Severne, B. C. 1972. *Botanical Methods of Mineral Exploration in Western Australia.* Ph.D. Thesis, Massey University, Palmerston North, New Zealand.

PART II

AERIAL PHYTOARCHAEOLOGY

Chapter 10
INTRODUCTION TO AERIAL ARCHAEOLOGY

10.1 HISTORICAL INTRODUCTION

Aerial photography, as opposed to the more restricted field of aerial archaeology, had its beginnings in 1858. A pioneer French photographer, Gaspard Felix Tournachon (who affected the odd pseudonym of "Nadar"), photographed Paris from a balloon using cumbersome equipment which even included a makeshift darkroom. His deeds led the well known satirist H. Daumier to portray the event in a famous cartoon (Fig. 10.1) which carried the caption: "Nadar has raised photographer to the highest of all arts."

Fig. 10.1 Cartoon by H. Daumier of Nadar's aerial photography of Paris. Reproduced by permission of the Boston Museum of Fine Arts.

The first aerial photograph of an archaeological site was also taken from a balloon. It was a shot of Stonehenge, southern England taken by Lt. P. H. Sharpe in 1906 (Capper, 1907). It was not, however, until after World War I that the full potential of aerial photography for archaeological purposes was recognized. This potential was both realized and exploited by one man, the great pioneer O. G. S. Crawford, who became the first Archaeological Officer of the British Ordnance Survey. Crawford had been an observer in the Royal Flying Corps during World War I and his first source of information was pictures taken during training flights of the Royal Air Force.

As reported by Deuel (1969), Crawford dated the beginning of aerial archaeology from 1922.

One day Dr Williams-Freeman, who then lived at Weyhill in Hampshire, England, the site of an RAF aerodrome, asked Crawford to come over and look at some photographs that his friend Air-Commodore Clark-Hall suspected contained 'something archaeological'. Thirty-five years later, shortly before his death, Crawford related the incident in a BBC talk:

"I well remember the occasion. Clark-Hall brought out his photographs and showed them to us. They were covered with rectangular white marks which at once recalled to my mind the ones I had started to map nearly ten years before. Here in these few photographs was the answer to the problem, but it was much more than that. The photographs also showed dark lines which were obviously silted-up ditches. They were revealed by the darker growth of corn, which grew better over them and therefore had a darker green color than the rest. There were also some areas of downland that had not been ploughed since the early fields with their lynchets and had been finally abandoned some 1600 years ago. I realized that air-photography was going to be an enormous help to archaeologists in unravelling the marks of all kinds left in the ground and above it by prehistoric man. It was a dramatic revelation, for at that very moment I knew that a new technique had been found, and that I had the means of developing that knowledge and making it available to the world at large . . . It must be remembered that at that time the very existence of those fields was almost unknown though a few countrymen had seen the lynchets and recognized what they were."

Crawford now set out to produce the kind of map he had unsuccessfully struggled with a good many years before. He then made an exhaustive study of the rectangular lynchets, which he called "Celtic Fields" to distinguish them from the Post-Roman Saxon strip system that was brought into England by the Germanic invaders. The result of his investigations was not only a milestone in aerial archaeology but also helped to establish the archaeology of agriculture.

The term "Celtic Fields" is now used throughout Europe, particularly in the Netherlands and Germany, to describe these early agricultural formations. It is particularly appropriate that this description of Crawford's early work was contained in a chapter of Deuel's book entitled "The Ghosts of Wessex," so called because of the ephemeral appearance of these markings.

One of the earliest of Crawford's achievements was the recognition of crop marks (see later in this chapter) in 1921, and their use in tracing the Stonehenge Avenue. Excavation of this site in 1923 proved the existence of buried ditches at places where there was no surface relief. These formation had become apparent due to differences in surface vegetation. In a report to The Observer of 22nd July, 1923, Crawford wrote:

All this is absolutely new and was never before suspected, and there can be no reasonable doubt that it is correct. Personally I feel quite certain that the marks on the air-photographs are those of the Avenue banks, but I do not expect all others to be convinced until trenches have been dug across to prove it. I have just returned from walking, with another archaeologist along the whole length of the Avenue. We could not see the faintest trace on the surface until we got a mile beyond West Amesbury. But here, between the Old and New King Barrows, here is a bank in a field track exactly at the point where Stukeley's measurements placed the Avenue, and where one of the two parallel lines on the air-photograph comes out. Here, about a mile from Stonehenge, I picked up a piece of 'blue' stone. We could see a double line in a field of potatoes quite plainly—apparently the deeper soil of the silted-up flanking ditches promotes better growth . . .

In 1924, Crawford carried out extensive flights over Hampshire, Wiltshire and Dorset. His archaeological findings were published in 1928 in what became the first definitive work in the new field of aerial archaeology (Crawford and Keiller, 1928).

Many of the early aerial photographs were published in Antiquity, a journal founded by Crawford in 1927. In the 1930s, the work was continued by Major G. W. A. Allen over much of England from The Fens to Wessex.

After the hiatus caused by World War II, there was renewed interest in aerial photography with impetus to the field given by such later pioneers as Flt.Lt. D. N. Riley (Riley, 1982), D. R. Wilson (Wilson, 1982), L. Deuel (Deuel, 1969), and J. K. St. Joseph (St. Joseph, 1977). The latter carried out flights on behalf of Cambridge University which extended over the whole of the United Kingdom. Photographs taken by these men formed the basis of what is now one of the greatest specialized collections of air photographs in Britain, under the curatorship of D. R. Wilson of the University of Cambridge Committee for Aerial Photography.

The following quotation from Wilson's book (Wilson, 1982) summarizes the general situation in Britain:

> The first official involvement in archaeological air-photography by a national body came with the establishment in 1965 of an Air Photographs unit within the English National Monuments Record (NMR). This provided for the first time a distinct national archive in which all archaeological air-photographers were invited to deposit prints or negatives . . . The number of local fliers engaged in archaeological reconnaissance of often quite limited areas greatly increased in the 1970s. The NMR unit has played an invaluable liaison role in relation to these, furnishing advice and practical assistance, encouraging the deposit of photographs in the national archive, and providing an annual forum for fliers and users of air-photographs.
>
> In England the responsibility for local archaeological archives, in which the work of plotting from air-photographs is generally done, as well as for much of the local flying, rests with county planning officers and archaeological units or their equivalents, though before the introduction of the unit system in 1973–4, much more of the local archives were in the hands of county museums.

Since the 1970s, the whole science of remote sensing has been revolutionized by the advent of satellite imagery (see Chapter 11). The early LANDSAT series of satellites did not really have sufficient resolution to identify anything other than the largest of archaeological sites. However, the recent launching of satellites with much better resolution should enable a much wider application of remote sensing by satellite imagery for the identification of such sites.

10.2 SURFACE INDICATIONS OF ARCHAEOLOGICAL SITES

10.2.1 Soil Marks

From the pioneer work of O. G. S. Crawford it emerged that it was possible to use aerial photography to distinguish three main criteria for the presence of archaeological sites beneath the surface of the terrain. These are crop marks, soil marks, and shadow marks. There are in addition other less prominent features such as damp marks, frost marks and snow marks (Riley, (1946). In this book only crop marks will be described in any detail, with some mention of soil marks and shadow marks.

Soil marks (Fig. 10.2) are indications on bare earth of contrasts between soil and sub-soil or between ditch fillings and normal soil. Soil marks are also found when the debris of destroyed buildings is encountered. Any upturned soil may reveal a change of coloration. Many prehistoric earthworks (Solecki, 1957) have been revealed where there is no evidence of surface relief. The main enemy of soil marks is not so much weathering as agricultural modification of the terrain. Soil marks are best studied in winter and spring over areas at least temporarily devoid of plant cover, such as cultivated fields.

10.2.2 Shadow Marks

Shadow marks are intaglio or raised images made by prominent earthworks as a result of shadows cast by a low-elevation sun over a feature with some degree of architectural relief such as a bank or ditch (Fig. 10.3). A good example of shadow marks is provided by Plate 16.6 which shows defensive trenches around a Maori *pa* (fort) in Auckland, New Zealand.

10.2.3 Crop Marks

Crop marks are perhaps the most important of the indications of subsurface archaeological sites. According to Riley (1982), their discovery dates back to 1857 when Stephen Stone, an Oxford don, recorded 13 rings in the corn at Standlake, Oxfordshire (Fig. 10.4). These turned out to be ring ditches containing ancient urns.

Crop marks are the visual difference in the growth of vegetation (grass, weeds or planted crops) on an archaeological site compared with its surroundings. They are illustrated

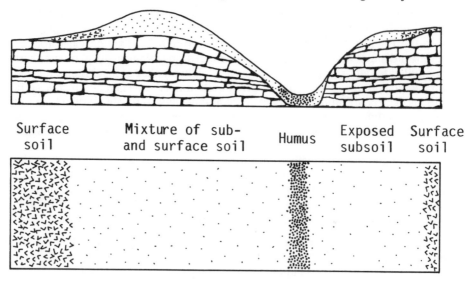

Fig. 10.2 Representation of a soil mark. Source: Deuel (1969).

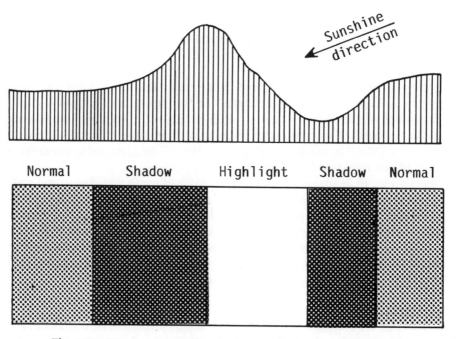

Fig. 10.3 Representation of a shadow mark. Source: Deuel (1969).

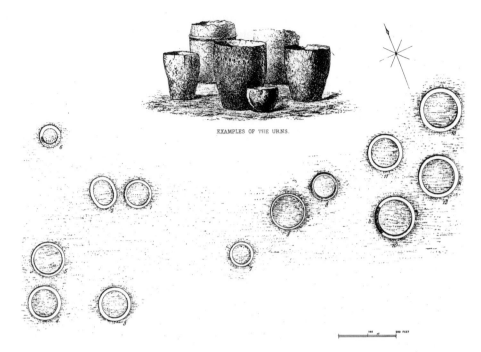

EXAMPLES OF THE URNS.

Fig. 10.4 A group of ring ditches at Standlake Oxfordshire, southern England, planned in 1857 by Stephen Stone. Source: Riley (1982). By courtesy of Shire Publications, Princes Risborough.

in Fig. 10.5, and it will be noted that these are either positive (luxuriant growth) or negative (stunted growth). The use of crop marks to detect archaeological sites is most effective over flat terrain, such as in most of southeastern England. Most crop marks are of the positive variety and are found most often in cereal crops such as wheat, barley or oats.

The months of optimum detection of crop marks vary with the crop and from year to year. However, an approximate indication is provided by Fig. 10.6 (Scollar, 1965); it shows that these marks can appear at any time from late March to the end of September.

Crop marks are usually more evident in times of drought when the crop wilts, except in the fillings of ancient ditches and pits where the deeper soil has more reserves of moisture. Crop marks can also result from differences in germination rates where plants situated above ancient ditches may be more advanced than elsewhere in the area.

When crop marks first appear they are faint and blurred, but as the season advances the marks become more defined. As pointed out by Wilson (1982), the development of crop marks is to some extent dependent on the soil type. Coarse soils have a poorer water retention capacity than have fine clays, and will cause water stress to appear sooner in crops growing upon them. Crop marks can appear in 2–3 days over coarse soils but may take as many weeks to appear over fine clays. In periods of prolonged drought the crop marks may disappear completely as the whole of the field becomes evenly desiccated.

A classical example of a crop·mark was photographed from the ground in 1938 (Plate 10.1). It was produced in a field of corn at Burcot Pit in Dorset and was caused by the ditch of an Iron Age enclosure which had been filled in. This famous picture has appeared in many textbooks.

There are several examples of aerially-photographed crop marks in other chapters of this book. Plate 13.1 shows a Neolithic settlement near Foggia, Italy, revealed by crop marks and Plate 12.4 shows a Roman fort revealed in the same manner at Rhyn in Shropshire, England. An Iron Age settlement at Wonston, England is delineated in Plate 12.3 by crop marks, and Plate 15.2 shows these marks near Amalucan in Mexico where ancient Formative Culture burial sites and canals were revealed quite recently.

The crop marks discussed above all occurred at sites where there was a deficiency of moisture. Similar marks can be produced where water is in excess, so that there is waterlogging and plant stress caused by an impenetrable barrier (such as remains of an ancient wall) just below the surface.

The question of crop marks will not be discussed further and the reader is referred to standard textbooks on the subject (e.g. Wilson, 1982; Riley, 1982; Deuel, 1969).

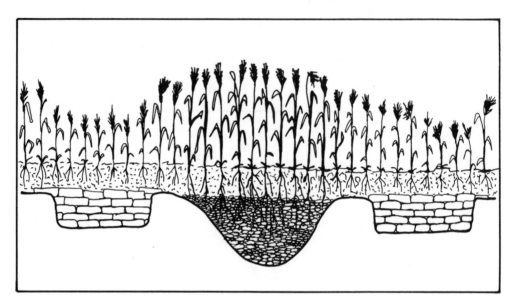

Fig. 10.5 The effect of buried archaeological features on the growth of crops (crop marks). a—positive marks over a ditch, b—negative marks over wall foundations.

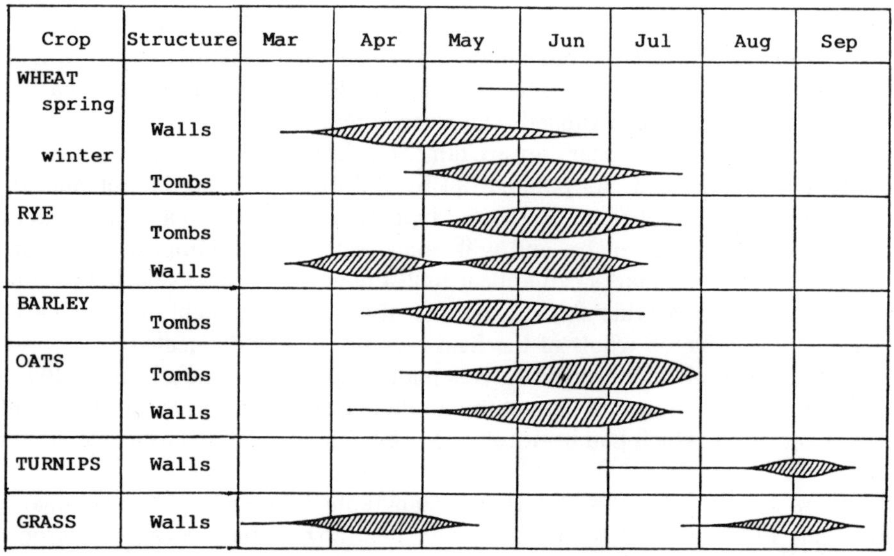

Crop	Structure	Mar	Apr	May	Jun	Jul	Aug	Sep
WHEAT spring								
	Walls							
winter	Tombs							
RYE	Tombs							
	Walls							
BARLEY	Tombs							
OATS	Tombs							
	Walls							
TURNIPS	Walls							
GRASS	Walls							

Fig. 10.6. Optimum seasonal times for detecting crop marks. After: Scollar (1965).

10.3 THE LITERATURE OF AERIAL ARCHAEOLOGY

Since its inception in the 1920s, aerial archaeology has spawned an enormous literature, a literature so great as to preclude a full listing of relevant publications. We have however, been fortunate in receiving from Dr. D. R. Wilson (Curator for Aerial Photography for the Cambridge Committee for Aerial Photography) a selective reference list which will at least serve as a starting point for those interested in further information. This reference list is given in Table 10.1; it is heavily biased in favor of British publications. It does, however, contain some reference to non-British publications.

Useful English-language journals that feature papers on the phytoarchaeological aspect of aerial photography are *Antiquity* and *American Antiquity*. Also of interest is the journal *Aerial Archaeology* which is exclusively devoted to the subject.

TABLE 10.1 A selected bibliography of work on aerial archaeology.

GENERAL

Aerial Archaeology	Bradford (1957)	Dassie (1978)
Maxwell (1983)	Riley (1982)	St. Joseph (1977)
Wilson (1975 1982)		

HISTORY

Crawford (1928 1954)	Daniel (1975)	Deuel (1969)

EUROPE EXCEPTING BRITAIN

Agache (1978)	Agache & Bréard (1975)	Bradford (1957)
Bradford (1956a 1956b)	Brongers (1976)	Christlein & Braasch (1982)
Norman & St. Joseph (1969)	Schoder (1974)	Scollar (1965)

SPECIAL OR REGIONAL WORK IN BRITAIN

Benson (1974)	Beresford & St. Joseph (1979)	Binney & Hills (1979)
Frere and St. Joseph (1983)	Gates (1975)	Knowles & St. Joseph (1952)
Leech (1977)	McCord (1971)	Riley (1980)
St. Joseph (1964–1980)	Webster & Hobley (1964)	

PHOTOGRAPHIC AND CARTOGRAPHIC WORK IN BRITAIN

Hampton (1975)	Hampton & Palmer (1978)	Hogg (1980)
Palmer (1976 1977)	Wilson (1979)	

AFRICA AND THE MIDDLE EAST

Baradez (1949)	Chevallier (1964)	Poidebard (1934)
Poidebard & Mouterde (1945)	Schmidt (1940)	

AUSTRALIA

Connah & Jones (1983)

NORTH AMERICA

Lyons & Avery (1977)	Vogt (1974)

CENTRAL AND SOUTH AMERICA

Adams (1980)	Chohfi (1987)	Johnson & Platt (1930)
Kidder (1929)	Mason (1931)	

10.4 CHAPTER SUMMARY

This introduction to aerial archaeology begins with an extensive historical account of pioneer work carried out in Britain during the early 20th century. Surface indications of buried archaeological remains include *crop marks, soil marks, shadow marks, damp marks, frost marks,* and *snow marks.* Particular attention is paid to crop marks, since these have proven to be the most useful for aerial archaeological purposes. The literature of aerial archaeology is reviewed.

REFERENCES

Adams, R. E. W. 1980. Swamps, canals and the location of ancient Maya cities. *Antiquity* 54: 206–212.

Agache, R. 1978. *La Somme Pré-romaine d'après les Prospections Aeriennes à Basse Altitude.* Société des Antiquaires du Picardie, Amiens.

Agache, R., and Bréard, B. 1975. *Atlas d'Archéologie Aerienne de Picardie.* Société des Antiquaires du Picardie, Amiens.

Baradez, J. 1949. *Fossatum Africae.* Arts et Métiers Graphiques, Paris.

Benson, D. 1974. *The Upper Thames Valley: an Archaeological Survey of the River Gravels.* Trust for Wessex Archaeology, Salisbury.

Beresford, M. W., and St. Joseph J. K. S. 1979. *Mediaeval England: an Aerial Survey.* Cambridge University Press, Cambridge.

Binney, M., and Hills, A. 1979. *Elysian Gardens.* Save Britain Heritage, London.

Bradford, J. S. P. 1956a. Field work and aerial discovery in Attica and Rhodes, Part I. *Antiquaries J.* 36: 57–69.

———— 1956b. Field work and aerial discovery in Attica and Rhodes, Part II. *Antiquaries J.* 36: 172–180.

———— 1957. *Ancient Landscapes: Studies in Field Archaeology.* G. Bell, London.

Brongers, J. A. 1976. *Air Photography and Celtic Field Research in The Netherlands.* Nederlandse Rijksdienst voor het Oudheidkundig Bodemondezoek, Amersfoort.

Capper, J. E. 1907. Photographs of Stonehenge as seen from a war balloon. *Archaeologia* 60: 571.

Chevallier, R. 1964. *L'Avion à la Découverte du Passé.* Arthème Fayard, Paris.

Chohfi, R. E. 1987. Remote sensing of the Machu Picchu region, Peru: an interdisciplinary study. *Proc. 2nd Latin Amer. Rem. Sens. Symp. Bogota,* 35 pp.

Christlein, R., and Braasch, D. 1982. *Das Unterirdische Bayern.* K. Theiss, Stuttgart.

Connah, G., and Jones, A. 1983. Aerial archaeology in Australia. *Aerial Archaeol.* 9: 1–30.

Crawford, O. G. S. 1923. Stonehenge from the air. Course and meaning of "The Avenue". *The Observer* 22nd July, p.13.

———— 1928. History and bibliography of archaeology from the air. In, O. G. S. Crawford and A. Keiller [eds.] *Wessex from the Air.* Clarendon Press, Oxford.

———— 1954. A century of air-photography. *Antiquity* 28: 206–210.

Crawford, O. G. S., and Keiller, A. 1928. *Wessex from the Air.* Clarendon Press, Oxford.

Daniel, G. 1975. *A Hundred and Fifty Years of Archaeology.* Duckworth, London.

Dassie, J. 1978. *Manuel d'Archéologie Aerienne.* Technip, Paris.

Deuel, L. 1969. *Flights into Yesterday: the Story of Aerial Archaeology.* McDonald, London.

Frere, S. S., and St. Joseph, J. K. S. 1983. *Roman Britain from the Air.* Cambridge University Press, Cambridge.

Gates, T. 1975. *The Middle Thames Valley: an Archaeological Survey of the River Gravels.* Trust for Wessex Archaeology, Salisbury.

Hampton, J. N. 1975. An experiment in multispectral air photography for archaeological research. In, E. Harp Jr. [ed.] *Photography in Archaeological Research.* University of New Mexico Press, Albuquerque.

Hampton, J. N., and Palmer, R. 1978. Implications of aerial photography for archaeology. *Archaeol. J.* 134: 157–193.

Hogg, A. H. A. 1980. *Surveying for Archaeologists and Other Fieldworkers*. St. Martins Press, New York.

Johnson, G. R., and Platt, R. R. 1930. Peru from the Air. *Amer. Geogr. Soc. Spec. Pub.* #12.

Kidder, A. V. 1929. Exploration of the Maya country. *Bull. Pan-Amer. Union*: 1200–1205.

Knowles, D., and St. Joseph, J. K. S. 1952. *Monastic Sites from the Air*. Cambridge University Press, Cambridge.

Leech, R. 1977. *The Upper Thames Valley in Gloucestershire and Wiltshire*. Trust for Wessex Archaeology, Salisbury.

Lyons, T. R., and Avery, T. E. 1977. *Remote Sensing: a Handbook for Archeologists*. U.S. Government Printing Office, Washington, D.C.

Mason, J. A. 1931. The air surveys in Central America. *Philad. Mus. Bull.* 2: 73–75, 78–79.

Maxwell, G. (ed.). 1983. *The Impact of Aerial Reconnaissance on Archaeology*. Report #49. Council for British Archaeology Research, London.

McCord, N. 1971. *Durham History from the Air*. Durham County Local History Society, Durham.

Norman, E. R., and St. Joseph, J. K. S. 1969. *The Early Development of Irish Society: The Evidence of Air Photography*. Cambridge University Press, Cambridge.

Palmer, R. 1976. A method of transcribing archaeological sites from oblique aerial photographs. *J. Archaeol. Sci.* 3: 391–394.

_____ 1977. A computer method for transcribing information graphically from oblique aerial photographs to maps. *J. Archaeol. Sci.* 4: 283–290.

Poidebard, A. 1934. *La Trace de Rome dans le Désert de Syrie*. Paul Geuther, Paris.

Poidebard, A., and Mouterde, R. 1945. *Le Limes de Chalcis*. Paul Geuther, Paris.

Riley, D. N. 1946. The technique of aerial photography and archaeology. *Archaeol. J.* 101: 1–16.

_____ 1980. *Early Landscapes from the Air*. University of Sheffield, Sheffield.

_____ 1982. *Aerial Archaeology in Britain*. Shire Publications, Princes Risborough.

Schmidt, E. F. 1940. *Flights of Ancient Cities of Iran*. Chicago Univ. Press, Chicago.

Schoder, R. V. 1974. *Ancient Greece from the Air*. Thames, London.

Scollar, I. 1965. *Archäologie aus der Luft*. Rheinland Verlag, Dusseldorf.

Solecki, R. S. 1957. Practical aerial photography for archaeologists. *American Antiquity* 22: 337–351.

St. Joseph, J. K. S. (ed.). 1977. *The Uses of Air Photography*. A. & C. Black, London.

_____ 1964–1980. Air reconnaissance recent results (a series of 50 notes in *Antiquity* between 1964 and 1980).

Vogt, E. Z. (ed.). 1974. *Aerial Photography in Anthropological Field Research*. Harvard Univ. Press, Cambridge, Massachusetts.

Webster, G., and Hobley, B. 1964. Aerial reconnaissance over the Warwickshire Avon. *Archaeol. J.* 121: 1–22.

Wilson, D. R. (ed.). 1975. *Aerial Reconnaissance for Archaeology*, Report #12. Council for British Archaeology, London.

_____ 1979. Factors affecting the distribution of crop marks in Anglian region. *Aerial Archaeol.* 4: 32–36.

_____ 1982. *Air Photo Interpretation for Archaeologists*. Batsford, London.

Chapter 11

PRINCIPLES OF REMOTE SENSING OF VEGETATION PATTERNS OVER ARCHAEOLOGICAL SITES

11.1 INTRODUCTION

The term "remote sensing" is somewhat arbitrary in meaning and can encompass a wide variety of different techniques operated at various heights above the ground and using different wavelength ranges. The altitudes can range from a few hundred meters to several hundred kilometers.

After the early hand-held cameras operated from small open-cockpit aeroplanes or even balloons, the latest developments in satellite imagery have opened up nearly limitless possibilities in aerial mapping.

Technological progress has also provided greatly improved techniques for remote sensing of natural resources by use of detectors sensitive to the whole of the electromagnetic spectrum from gamma radiation at the one extreme to radar at the other. Fig. 11.1 shows the wavelengths commonly employed in various types of remote sensing and shows their relative absorption by the atmosphere (which, of course, is the limiting factor in their use).

11.2 VISIBLE SYMPTOMS OF STRESS IN PLANTS

Remote sensing of vegetation has the aim of detecting visible (and in some cases invisible) symptoms in vegetation that may be linked to the presence of anomalous features of the soil such as mineralization, excess or deficiency of water, and, of course, the presence of archaeological structures just below the surface. Although the technique has been used in the past mainly for mineral exploration (Brooks, 1983), the same principles may be, and have been, applied to aerial phytoarchaeology.

Remote sensing of vegetation has recently been reviewed by Hodcroft and Moore (1988) who have shown that remote sensing can be used to determine three main characteristics of stressed vegetation: A) the presence of unusual plant assemblages linked to mineralized terrain or to the presence of buried archaeological features. This is illustrated in Fig. 11.2A (in extreme cases the end result can be a complete absence of vegetation); B) Spatial or spectral stress in vegetation (Fig. 11.2B) resulting in gigantism, dwarfism, and, more importantly, discoloration such as chlorosis (Brooks, 1983); C) Temporal stress (Fig. 11.2C) producing early or late growth retardation or premature senescence (Bell et al., 1985).

Modifications in section B above provide the best means of measuring vegetation stress by remote sensing.

11.3 SPECTRAL REFLECTANCE PATTERNS IN VEGETATION

Remote sensing of vegetation depends on measurement of spectral reflectance patterns to measure chlorosis (yellowing of leaves) or other morphological changes due to anthropogenic modification of the substrate, or to recognize differences in plant communities influenced by such modifications. Figure 11.3 shows typical reflectance patterns for various vegetation types. There is a small maximum at 550 nm in the green part of the spectrum as

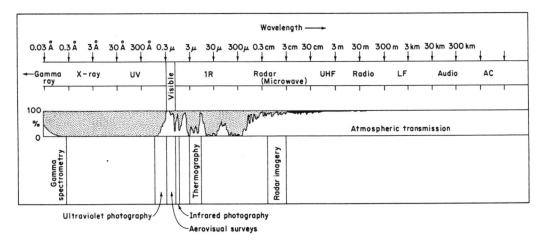

Fig. 11.1 Wavelengths commonly used in various types of remote sensing. Source: Brooks (1983).

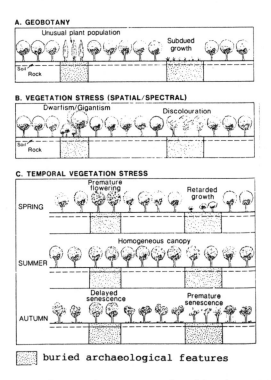

Fig. 11.2 Various symptoms of vegetation stress produced by changes to the substrate such as presence of minerals or archaeological structures. Source: Hodcroft and Moore (1988). By courtesy of the editor of *Mining Magazine*.

well as a much larger one in the near infrared. It has been reported by Brooks (1983) that chlorosis of vegetation due to mineralization or anthropogenic modification results in absorption of the green part of the spectrum by chlorophyll and a concomitant increase in reflectivity at this wavelength. An excellent review by Horler et al. (1981) discusses the reflectance of vegetation at various wavelengths and its application for determining stress in plants. Reflected radiation depends not only on the structure, pigment concentration, and water content of individual leaves that may be affected by stress, but also on such factors as vegetation ground coverage, leaf area, topography and the degree of solar illumination. These variables may complicate or render impractical, stress detection methods using broad band radiation based on physiological factors such as the change in the chlorophyll content of plant tissue. It has been suggested (Horler et al., 1981) that these problems can be largely overcome by techniques utilizing the shape of reflectance spectra rather than radiance values themselves. This approach requires high-resolution spectral measurements and some type of waveform analysis.

To record reflectance spectra (R) of leaves, Horler et al. (1981) employed the first derivative spectra (dR/dλ) using a spectrophotometer. One of the most striking patterns of plant reflectance spectra is the change of R at about 700 nm at the limit of chlorophyll absorption towards the red end of the spectrum. This feature is known as the red edge. The wavelength at the red edge ($λ_R$) changes according to the chlorophyll content of the leaf, as is illustrated in Fig. 11.4 for healthy and chlorotic maize leaves.

A sensitive spectroradiometer has been used to detect minute red edge shifts in the reflectance of a tree canopy in the United States (Collins et al., 1983 Milton et al., 1983). Though specifically applied to geochemical stress caused by mineralization, there is absolutely no reason why this work could not have identified stress in vegetation caused by buried archaeological features such as walls or foundations of buildings.

It will be noted from Fig. 11.3 that reflectance of all types of vegetation is far greater in the near infrared than in the green part of the spectrum. This infrared reflectance is a measure *inter alia,* of the surface area of the canopy. However, stressed plants usually have a smaller leaf area so that the ratio of 550/800 nm is increased in most, though not all cases. The principle of comparing reflectance ratios at two different wavelengths is now well established. The physiological factors that influence the reflectance of vegetation depend entirely on the part of the spectrum which is examined. These factors are summarized in Table 11.1.

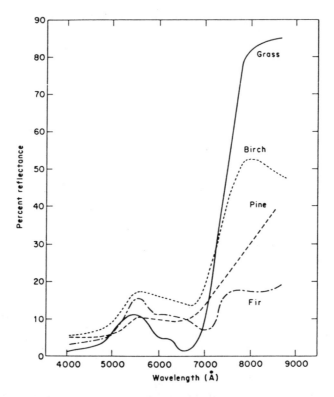

Fig. 11.3 Spectral reflectance curves for various foliage types. Source: Fritz (1967). Reproduced by permission from *Photogrammetric Engineering.* Copyright 1967 by the American Society for Photogrammetry and Remote Sensing.

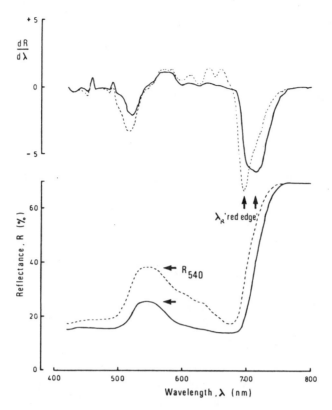

Fig. 11.4 Reflectance spectra for stressed (dotted line) and unstressed (continuous line) maize leaves. The diminution of wavelength in stressed plants at about 700 nm is known as the red shift. Source: Horler et al. (1981).

TABLE 11.1 The main physiological factors influencing remote-sensed radiation from vegetation.

Measurement	Wavelength	Controlling physiological factor
1. Chlorophyll fluorescence	200–400 nm	Chlorophyll content and organization, and inhibition of photosynthesis
2. Visible reflectance	400–800 nm	Pigments, mainly chlorophyll
3. Near-infrared reflectance	800–1200 nm	Leaf and canopy structure
4. Infrared reflectance	1200–2500 nm	Water content
5. Thermal emission	>2500 nm	Plant water status, evapotranspiration

Source: Brooks (1983)

11.4 REMOTE SENSING IN THE ULTRAVIOLET AND VISIBLE RANGE

11.4.1 Introduction

Aerial photography in the ultraviolet and visible parts of the spectrum has been carried out for over a hundred and fifty years (see also Chapter 10). The earliest work of this kind involved hot air balloons, kites and even homing pigeons with miniature cameras attached to their legs. During both world wars, the techniques were used extensively in military reconnaissance.

Since World War II, most developed countries have accumulated a complete range of aerial photographs for the whole of their territory.

11.4.2 Types of Aerial View

A useful guide to simple aerial photography has been provided by Solecki (1957), though his paper is concerned mainly with practical advice to the amateur rather than the expert. If professional rather than amateur assistance is required, there are many sophisticated techniques and flying platforms (aircraft, helicopters, balloons, etc.) which are available. Each country has its experts who can be called upon where necessary.

There are three main types of aerial view: high oblique, low oblique and vertical. High oblique shots include part of the horizon in the frame, and low oblique are at an angle between high oblique and vertical. Some oblique shots often appear upside down in publications because the absence of a horizon makes orientation difficult. Vertical shots are useful for mapping and plotting, but give little indication of relief unless viewed stereoscopically. Because of the speed of the aircraft relative to the ground, the vertical shot is the most likely to be blurred.

It has been recommended by Solecki (1957) that photographs be taken in the most brilliant sunlight possible and preferably between 10 A.M. and 2 P.M. Special shadow effects needed in aerial archaeology may however, dictate an early morning or late afternoon flight.

The choice of camera is an important consideration. Any hand-held camera used on the ground can be used in the air, but care should be taken that the apparatus (and the operator's spectacles !) do not disappear in the slipstream of the aircraft. Preferably two cameras should be used, one loaded with black-and-white film and the other with color or infrared. Use a long-focus lens wherever possible. Otherwise the plane will have to descend to a lower altitude and there will then be the problem of blurring due to the apparently much greater ground speed of the plane. This particular problem is illustrated in the cartoon in Fig. 16.2.

For vertical views, there is a simple relationship between the area covered by the lens and the altitude of the plane.

$$\text{Scale} = \text{focal length of lens in mm}/(1000 \times \text{altitude in m})$$

For example, for a 100 mm lens and an altitude of 300 m, the scale of the negative will be 1:3000. The lower the altitude, the greater must be the shutter speed to compensate for the greater apparent ground speed of the plane. For larger archaeological sites, an altitude of 500–1000 m might be required to encompass the entire site.

11.4.3 Filters and Shutter Speeds

Under normal conditions, a filter will not be necessary for altitudes less than 500 m except in the case of infrared film (see below). A filter is, however, desirable if any part of the horizon is to be included in the shot. The filter eliminates or reduces atmospheric haze. For high oblique or high altitude shots, a red or green filter is generally needed for black-and-white films. A sun shade is also a desirable piece of equipment.

If a 35 mm camera such as a single lens reflex is used, a 90 mm lens should be used for close-up shots of archaeological sites and a 50 mm lens for wider views at altitudes between 150–300 m.

Because of the high speed of aircraft, shutter speeds will need to be faster than for ground work, and a compromise will have to be struck between film speed and graininess of the print. Table 11.2 gives recommended slowest shutter speeds for amateur aerial photographs for vertical or low oblique shots.

One of the major problems encountered by the amateur photographer is that of air turbulence and aircraft vibration. The later is more of a drawback than aircraft speed itself.

TABLE 11.2 Slowest recommended shutter speeds (seconds) for amateur aerial photography.

Altitude (m)	Ground speed (km/h)			
	100	150	250	300
>1200	1/60	1/60	1/125	1/125
1000	1/60	1/125	1/125	1/250
600	1/125	1/125	1/250	1/250
300	1/250	1/250	1/500	1/500
150	1/500	1/500	1/1000	1/100

Source: Kodak (1952). Reprinted by courtesy of Eastman Kodak Company.

The camera should be held away from all structural parts of the plane during photographing. Turbulence can be reduced by flying in the early morning or late afternoon when the problem is at a minimum.

11.4.4 The Targets of Aerial Photography

Archaeological sites differ from the natural environment in that they contain anthropogenic modifications which must be recognized and recorded by the photographer. These modifications can be recognized by crop marks, soil marks and shadow marks (Chapter 10).

Shadow marks should always be photographed with a low sun since the shallow relief must have the sun at a sharp angle to reveal the outline of the structure. In oblique views, the shadow must be facing the photographer but the lens must be shielded because of the full view of the sun. The positioning of the object between the sun and camera is known as counter lighting (Poidebard, 1934).

Crop marks are usually photographed by oblique shots and their appearance is heavily dependent on the time of year and time of day. The reader is referred to one of the standard textbooks such as Wilson (1982) for a full discussion of this important subject.

11.4.5 The Aerial Platform

The balloon used by Lt. Sharpe in 1906 to photograph Stonehenge (Chapter 10) is probably the most stable type of platform that could be obtained. Today, however, there is reliance almost exclusively on helicopters or fixed-wing aircraft. The enormous, one might almost say horrendous, cost of helicopter time virtually precludes the use of these craft for photography by the amateur.

A light airplane with a cruising speed of about 150 km/h is ideal for photography. The choice is usually of a low wing or high-wing machine. The high wing type is ideal for vertical shots (unless there is access to a low wing machine with a hole in the floor) because the wing does not get in the way of the subject to be photographed. Low wing craft are ideal for oblique shots. One of the authors (R.R.B.) however, vividly remembers feeling decidedly "unwell" some years ago in Western Australia when the pilot obligingly banked a low-wing plane to get vertical shots of the ground.

It is not advisable to try to photograph a subject through the plastic window of the aircraft especially when a polarization filter is used. It is usually possible to remove a whole side door of the aircraft taking care that neither the equipment nor the photographer disappears in the slipstream.

It is advisable to fly at a minimum of between 150 and 300 m above the ground, not only because civil law in most countries forbids flying at less than 150 m above populated terrain, but also because of blurring of the shots at low altitude where ground speed appears to be at a maximum.

Finally, the photographer should keep good records of the flight including the altitude, aircraft speed, time of day, date, air conditions, attitude (angle) of the aircraft, type of film, shutter speed, etc.

It is not suggested that aerial photography by the amateur will be as good as that of a professional (who does not need the advice in this chapter anyway), but there is no reason why good photographs should not be taken by a person with lack of experience but with ample common sense.

11.5 REMOTE SENSING IN THE NEAR INFRARED

Just before World War II (Ives, 1939), it was shown that various types of vegetation could be easily distinguished with infrared black-and-white film. A typical film of this kind will have an emulsion which is sensitive to the whole of the visible part of the spectrum and to the near infrared up to 900 nm. Maximum sensitivity will be in the range 770–840 nm. It is customary to use a red filter (such as Wratten 12) with this type of film in order to remove the blue and ultraviolet end of the spectrum. From my own experience in New Zealand and Australia (Brooks, 1972), better results can be achieved with infrared color film.

Infrared color film (CIR) comprises three image layers which are sensitive to green, red and infrared instead of blue, green and red as with normal color film. A yellow filter (e.g. Wratten 12) is used to withhold blue light, towards which the layers are sensitive. Film of this kind has several disadvantages compared to conventional film. The first of these is that the exposure latitude is very limited (½ stop) and unless exposures are exactly correct, disappointing results will ensue. Processing of the film will not normally be undertaken by most commercial interests, and the services of a specialist will have to be sought. Other disadvantages are that the infrared-sensitive layer is somewhat unstable, has a short life, and must be kept cool at all times. Focusing is also a problem for close work because the position for optimum focus differs among the layers so that a compromise has to be obtained.

In spite of these difficulties, good results can be obtained by relatively unskilled operators using conventional cameras operated from a light plane or helicopter. It is advisable to set the camera at a suitable speed (e.g. 1/250 sec) and give trial exposures at several f-stops including the intermediate half stops. This is wasteful of film but film is very much cheaper than aircraft time. When experience has been gained, the photographer will need only one or two exposures for each scene.

The infrared reflectance of vegetation becomes increasingly less detectable at higher altitudes because of absorption of the radiation by water vapor in the atmosphere and also because of Rayleigh scattering which is especially pronounced at the blue end of the spectrum. Although the Wratten 12 filter normally used with CIR film cuts out wavelengths below 520 nm, where scattering is particularly serious, there is still sufficient remaining interference from this source to render infrared photography a problem at high altitudes. For example, at 12 000 m, as much as 90% of the infrared radiation is lost.

Pease and Bowden (1969) discussed this attenuation problem and showed that auxiliary filters with additional minus-blue filtration can greatly enhance the infrared signal from vegetation. For moderate enhancement, filters such as Kodak 82B or CC30B or their equivalents are recommended. For drastic enhancement, use may be made of Kodak filters 80B, 80C, or CC50B (or their equivalent). The use of these auxiliary filters does, however, present additional problems as mentioned above. A shutter speed of at least 1/250 sec is recommended for aerial work. The filter factor for CC50B is 1.5 stops, which involves working near the limits of the aperture range of most lenses. In practice, it is advisable to compromise by reducing the shutter speed to 1/125 sec and suffer some loss of definition. Although the infrared signal is enhanced when auxiliary filters are used, there is less differentiation of vegetation in the image compared with photographs taken at lower altitudes without the use of special filters.

Until the 1970s, much of the work carried out with infrared film was essentially monoband. Perhaps one of the most comprehensive of these surveys was by Paarma et al.(1968) who combined extensive aerial coverage with on-foot determination of the so-called ground truth. Successful results were obtained even with altitudes of up to 9000 m. Although this latter survey was of a geological structure, the same procedure could have been used for an archaeological site.

The modern trend is to use multiband scanners for aerial photography and to use wavelength band ratios rather than single bands. Such multiband (as many as 11) scanners usually include a near-infrared channel.

11.6 THERMOGRAPHIC IMAGERY

Thermography is sometimes confused with near-infrared imagery. In fact it depends on an entirely different system which operates in the range >1200 nm. No photographic film is capable of operating in this wavelength range; instead the thermal signal is detected by some form of optical mechanical scanner (Colwell, 1968) in which the energy is converted into an electrical signal used to generate visible light to produce an image which may be photographed in black-and-white or recorded on tape for further computer processing.

Until recently, thermography has not usually been used for vegetation studies but to measure soil moisture conditions (Press, 1974) or anomalous thermal patterns from ore deposits (Cole, 1977). The only biogenic material previously recognizable by thermography was peat (Talvitie et al, 1981) which is often colder on the surface than the surroundings (except during the day when the surface dries out under solar radiation).

Horler et al. (1981) have shown that thermography may indeed have wider applications to vegetation studies. There are several physiological mechanisms whereby stress may affect the thermal emission from plants and this emission can be measured by some type of radiometer. Such work is only in its infancy, although in the United States Canney et al. (1972) correlated a warmer area in vegetation with the presence of a Cu/Mo soil anomaly, and in France, Lefèvre (1979) linked thermal vegetation anomalies with the subsurface geology.

11.7 RADAR (MICROWAVE) IMAGERY

Remote sensing with radar (1 mm—1 m wavelength) has interesting applications in thickly forested terrain since it is capable of appearing to remove the vegetation completely and of exposing underlying archaeological and geomorphological features. Radar waves of long wavelength (>17 mm) will readily penetrate vegetation and several feet of soil. Shorter wavelengths (11–17 and 24–38 mm) can be used to identify different species of vegetation since these wavelengths respond to varying leaf forms.

Airborne radar systems have been used for regional mapping in Panama, Nigeria and Brazil (Netto, 1979). These and other projects show that multichannel synthetic aperture radar, operating in a range of wavelengths, frequencies, polarities and look directions has a potential for canopy texture imaging. Since even small areas of anomalous vegetation can be detected where stress has reduced leaf area, the potential for aerial phytoarchaeology is obvious.

In radar imagery, a high-frequency signal is generated from the aircraft and strikes the ground beneath. The reflected signal is analyzed by a special type of receiver which, as with thermography, converts the energy into a visual form from which a conventional photograph is obtained.

A good example of the use of radar imagery in archaeology has been provided by Adams (1980) who revealed the presence of patterns of agriculture in the southern Maya lowland in Central America. In this study, a modified form of synthetic aperture radar, designed for scanning the surface of Venus, was provided by the Jet Propulsion Laboratory in Pasadena for an experimental survey of Belize and the Peten area of Guatemala. The radar was side-looking and used a 25 cm band. Flights were made over northern Belize and most of Guatemala with a total coverage of 80 000 km². Radar-detected archaeological data included ancient cities, raised roads, edges of paved zones, and canals (see Chapter 15).

11.8 MULTIBAND SATELLITE IMAGERY

11.8.1 Introduction

No single unichannel sensor will be capable of solving the entire problem of phytoarchaeological surveying. There is the further constraint that several overflights at different times of the year might be advisable to detect subtle changes in vegetation due to stress from archaeological sites. Both of these problems have been overcome by the development of multiband satellite imagery, albeit with some loss of definition because of the great altitudes involved.

The first available satellite imagery was from the Gemini orbiters of the late 1960s (Cole, 1968). Later the four-channel LANDSAT-I was designed specifically for aerial imagery of the earth. This was followed by LANDSAT-II, launched in 1975. The satellites contain a multiband scanner (MSS) with visible bands at 500–600 nm, 600–700 nm, 700–800 nm, and an infrared band at 800–1100 nm. These are known as MSS4, MSS5, MSS6, and MSS7 respectively.

11.8.2 Techniques of Satellite Imagery

Each image of the earth from the LANDSAT satellites is recorded on an on-board tape recorder and later transmitted to a ground receiving station in the United States. NASA processing of the high density computer tapes yields either monochrome photographic images produced on an electronic beam recorder, or digital data stored on a set of computer-compatible tapes (CCT).

Each of the four LANDSAT images for a given scene covers about 48 000 km² and comprises 2340 × 3264 (= 7 637 760) pixels (picture elements). Each pixel corresponds to an area of 79 m × 79 m (about 1 acre) and is established by the scanner assigning a number between 0–255 (thus giving 256 single signatures) which is proportional to the reflectance intensity of that part of the scene.

The availability of imagery data on CCT gives almost limitless opportunity for computer handling of the information. Two types of map can be produced: unsupervised maps classify pixels into groups of similar signatures based only on statistical considerations. Supervised maps subdivide pixels of similar signatures into further groups depending on ground truth determined before or after imagery. Maps can be uniband or they can be obtained by ratioing any pair of the four LANDSAT bands to produce up to 6 different images (Ballew, 1975; Lyon, 1975; Bélanger, 1980). As far as vegetation is concerned, the best pair of channels to choose is MSS5/MSS7. The denser the vegetation, the more it absorbs MSS5, whereas the healthier it is, the more it reflects MSS7. This ratio therefore gives a good estimate of the density and physiological state of the vegetation cover (Bélanger, 1980). Ratioing also eliminates differences of brightness due to uneven solar illumination of the scene. This ratio is also known as the biomass index.

Although satellite imagery has been used mainly for agricultural, ecological, land use, military and mineral prospecting purposes, it is beginning to find favor for archaeological surveys mainly because of the development of new satellites with much better resolution than the old LANDSAT series. These include LANDSAT-D with a resolution of 30 m (compared with 80 m for the older LANDSAT series) and the French SPOT (Système Probatoire d'Observation de la Terre) series with a resolution of only 10 m. In a remarkable display of *glasnost,* the Soviet Union is now offering 5 m resolution photographs from its Cosmos series of satellites.

It is sad to reflect that military satellites with much better resolution have been available for many years. Civilian satellites may at present lack the sophistication of their military counterparts, but it is likely that this imbalance will be redressed to some extent in the future.

Although the old LANDSAT satellites had poor resolution, they could be used for large archaeological sites as has been shown by Stringer and Cook (1974). This work is reported below.

11.8.3 A Case History of the Use of Satellite Imagery in Phytoarchaeology

Stringer and Cook (1974) used LANDSAT satellite imagery to test the feasibility of detecting large Alaskan archaeological village sites. The approach used was to develop digital multispectral signatures of dominant surface categories including vegetation types and known archaeological sites. Imagery scenes were then printed out digitally in a map-like array with a letter reflecting the most appropriate classification representing the pixel.

During the first 6 months, preliminary signatures were developed and tested. It was determined that there was a need to improve archaeological site identification by developing signatures for all naturally-occurring vegetation and surface conditions in the vicinity of the test areas. These signatures were tested by means of comparison of computer signature printouts with aerial photography.

Two large 512 × 512 pixel signature printouts were prepared which, taken together included the entire test area. Archaeological site signatures were tagged. Subjective criteria based on location were applied to the tagged signatures. Unlikely locations were eliminated while the remaining possible sites were compared with known sites identified by field expeditions and aerial photography.

Of 12 known sites along the middle Khotol River, five were identified as sites on the computer printout and several more possible sites were located. However, 7 known sites were not properly identified as such. (a more detailed description of work carried out over one of the more important of these Alaskan sites is given in Chapter 14—section 14.4.2).

It must be remembered that the above study was taken with poor resolution imagery. It is to be expected that satellite imagery will become more effective in discovering archaeological sites now that the new high-resolution satellites (see above) have become available.

11.9 CHAPTER SUMMARY

This chapter is concerned with the principles of remote sensing of vegetation over archaeological sites. The basic principles are enumerated and related to stress in plants caused by archaeological substrates unfavorable for plant growth or which in some cases may promote such growth. Spectral reflectance patterns in plants can be used to determine this stress. These patterns include the so-called *red edge* where reflectance at about 700 nm (red end of visible spectrum) are reduced by 10–30 nm.

Remote sensing in the ultraviolet, visible, and near infrared parts of the spectrum is described, and practical hints are given for amateur photography in this range.

The chapter also includes a description of *thermography* (far infrared) and radar (microwave) imagery, as well as the rapidly-developing use of satellite imagery for aerial phytoarchaeology. Although the 1970s American LANDSAT orbiters have provided data suitable for aerial phytoarchaeology, the images are suitable only for the larger structures because of poor (30 m) resolution. Newer satellites such as the French SPOT series offer much greater promise because of their better resolution (10 m).

REFERENCES

Adams, R. E. W. 1980. Swamps, canals and the location of ancient Maya cities. *Antiquity* 55: 206–214.

Ballew, G. I. 1975. Correlation of Landsat-1 multispectral data with surface geochemistry. *Proc. 10th Int. Symp. Rem. Sens. Environ.* v.2 1045–1049.

Bélanger, J. R. 1980. Landsat and mineral deposits. *Geos* (summer): 10–12.

Bell, R. Labovitz, M. L., and Sullivan, D. P. 1985. Delay in leaf flush associated with heavy metal-enriched soil. *Econ. Geol.* 80: 1407–1414.

Brooks, R. R. 1972. Aerial infrared photography as a guide to geological conditions. *Proc. Australas. Inst. Min. Metall.* #241: 15–19.

_____ 1983. *Biological Methods of Prospecting for Minerals,* Wiley, New York.

Canney, F. C. Hessin, T. D., and Burge, W. G. 1972. Analysis of thermal patterns of geochemically stressed trees at Catheart Mountain, Maine. *4th Ann. Earth Resources Rev.* v.3 (57), NASA, Houston.

Cole. M. M. 1968. Observation of the Earth's resources. *Proc. Roy. Soc. Lond. Sec. A* 308: 173–182.

_____ 1977. Landsat and airborne multi-spectral and thermal imagery used for geological mapping and identification of ore horizons in Lady Annie-Lady Loretta and the Dugald River areas in Queensland, Australia. *Trans. Inst. Min. Metall.* 86: 195–215.

Collins, W. Chang, S. H. Raines, G. Canney, F. C., and Ashley, R. 1983. Airborne biogeophysical mapping of hidden mineral deposits. *Econ. Geol.* 78: 737–749.

Colwell, R. N. 1968. Remote sensing as a means of detecting ecological conditions. *Bioscience* 17: 444 449.

Connah, G., and Jones, A. 1983. Aerial archaeology in Australia. *Aerial Archaeol.* 9: 1–30.

Fritz, N. L. 1967. Optimum conditions for using infrared-sensitive film. *Photogramm. Eng.* 33: 1128–1138.

Hodcroft, A. J. T., and Moore, J. M. 1988. Remote sensing of vegetation—a promising exploration tool. *Min. Mag.* Oct: 274–279.

Horler, D. N. H. Barber, J., and Barringer, A. R. 1981. New concepts for the determination of geochemical stress in plants. In, J. A. Allan and M. Bradshaw [eds.] *Remote Sensing in Geological and Terrain Studies.* Remote Sensing Soc. London, pp. 113–123.

Ives, R. L. 1939. Infra-red photography as an aid in ecological surveys. *Ecology* 20: 433–439.

Kodak 1952. *Pictures from the Air with Your Camera.* Kodak Pub. Rochester.

Lefèvre, M. J. 1979. Detection of a non-outcropping granitic rock by thermal anomaly in the forest cover. *Compt. Rend. Acad. Sci. Paris, Sér. D* 289: 825–827.

Lyon, R. J. P. 1975. Correlation between ground metal analysis, vegetation reflectance, and ERTS brightness over a molybdenum skarn deposit, Pine Nut Mountains, western Nevada. *Proc. 10th Int. Symp. Rem. Sens. Environ.* 1031–1037.

Milton, N. M. Collins, W. Chang, S. H., and Schmidt, R. G. 1983. Remote detection of metal anomalies on Pilot Mountain, Randolph County, North Carolina. *Econ. Geol.* 78: 605–617.

Netto, O. B. 1979. The mapping of natural resources by side-scan radar in Brazil. *Min. Mag.* Oct: 354–359.

Paarma, H. Raevaara, H., and Talvitie, J. 1968. On the interpretation of Ektachrome infrared type 8443 photographs used in mineral reconnaissance and geological surveys. *Photogramm. J. Finl.* 2: 3–22.

Pease, R. W., and Bowden, L. W. 1969. Making color infrared film a more effective high-altitude remote sensor. *Rem. Sens. Environ.* 1: 23–30.

Poidebard, A. 1934. *La Trace de Rome dans le Désert de Syrie.* Paul Geuther, Paris.

Press, N. P. 1974. Remote sensing to detect the toxic effects of metals on vegetation for mineral exploration. *Proc. 9th Int. Symp. Rem. Sens. Environ.:* 2027–2035.

Solecki, R. S. 1957. Practical aerial photography for archaeologists. *Am. Antiquity* 22: 337–351.

Stringer, W. J., and Cook, J. P. 1974. *Feasibility Study for Locating Archaeological Village Sites by Satellite Remote Sensing.* Tech. Rep. Univ. Alaska, Fairbanks.

Talvitie, J. Lehmuspelto, P., and Vuotovesi, T. 1981. Airborne thermal surveying of the ground in Sokli, Finland. *Geol. Surv. Finl. Rep.* #50: 5–13.

Wilson, D. R. 1982. *Air Photo Interpretation for Archaeologists.* Batsford, London.

Chapter 12
AERIAL ARCHAEOLOGY
IN NORTHWEST EUROPE

12.1 INTRODUCTION

Aerial archaeology had its origins in England, as discussed in Chapter 10. A description of aerial archaeology in Europe must therefore, be largely concerned with British work even though numerous investigations have been performed in other countries of western Europe, particularly Germany and Holland. To attempt to cover country-by-country the vast literature on the subject would merely involve a repetition of existing reports in standard works such as Riley (1982) and Wilson (1982). The approach in this chapter will therefore be to discuss the various types of artifact or site investigated, irrespective of geographical boundaries. The *Celtic fields,* will be a good illustration of this approach.

12.2 THE CELTIC FIELDS

12.2.1 Introduction

Celtic fields are sites of Iron Age farms found mainly in Britain, Holland (Brongers, 1976), northern Germany (Brongers, 1973) and Denmark (Fig. 12.1). Paradoxically, their discovery in Holland and northwest Germany was not a result of German efforts, but rather of the aerial reconnaissance flights of the British Royal Air Force in World War II. Although some aerial archaeology had been performed by the Imperial German Air Force in Germany during World War I, the subsequent Treaty of Versailles hindered further work of this nature by strictures on German aerial flights in the first decade after the war.

The term Celtic is somewhat of a misnomer, with little or no ethnological significance. It was coined by Crawford (1923) to denote prehistoric field divisions. In Denmark the sites are known as *oldtidsagre* (ancient fields or farms) whereas in Holland the sites are known as *Heydensche legerplaetsen* (see below).

12.2.2 Celtic Fields in The Netherlands

It is probably in The Netherlands that this research has reached its highest development, due largely to the work of Brongers (1976). The Celtic fields are a system of earthworks surrounding small farmlets or fields. They were described in The Netherlands by the Rev. Johan Picardt in the 17th century (Picardt, 1660). He was very interested in archaeological remains in the province of Drenthe and wrote a book on the subject in which a complete chapter was devoted to: "eenige oude Heydensche legerplaetsen en wallen" (some old heathen settlements and banks). As translated by Brongers (1976), he described the *legerplaetsen* as: "having the shape of a window frame enclosing a square window frame enclosing a square window consisting of 10 m × 10 m leaded panes." The panes: ". . . had banks around them on the circumference which were about two hundred steps in extent." (see Fig. 12.2).

Picardt inferred that the Heydens were in fact Suevens, a wandering Germanic tribe needing temporary shelter during their migrations, and envisaged one family occupying each 10 m × 10 m plot. He suggested that these fields dated back to the reign of Augustus Caesar (about 2000 B.P.), but they appear to have been in constant occupation for a much longer period. Radiocarbon dating shows an occupancy from 3915–1290 B.P., including and extending, well outside the reign of this Roman emperor and the Germanic migrations (375–568 B.C.).

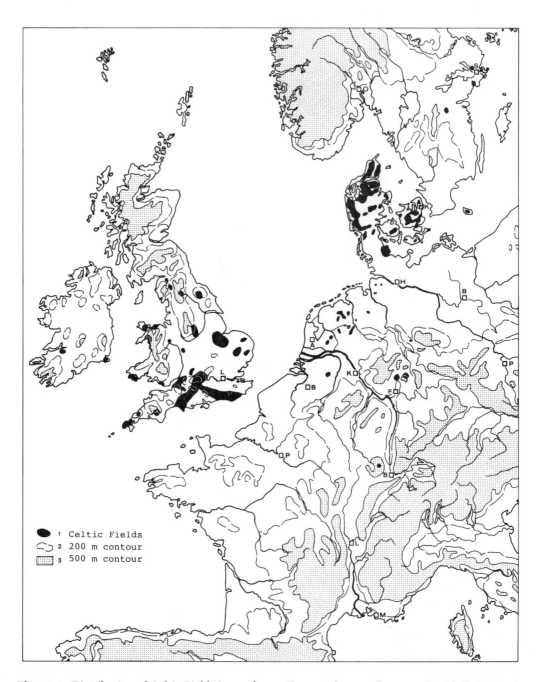

Fig. 12.1 Distribution of Celtic Fields in northwest Europe. Source: Brongers (1976). By courtesy of the author.

Most of the Celtic fields in Holland were discovered by aerial photography, much of it done by the Royal Air Force in World War II. Aerial photography specifically orientated to archaeology is more difficult to carry out in Holland than in Britain because of the much more intensive agriculture in Holland, where the ground has been extensively ploughed and reploughed. Nevertheless, significant finds have been made, particularly in the provinces of Drenthe and Gelderland. Because of the raised bank system around each field, most of the aerial discoveries were made from soil marks or shadow marks (see Chapter 10) rather than

Fig. 12.2. Representation of Celtic Fields in Holland as envisaged by the 17th century archaeologist Johan Picardt. Source: Brongers (1976). By courtesy of the author.

from crop marks, though vegetation patterns can be used in many cases to identify the fields. Plate 12.1 shows the typical quilted pattern of Celtic fields near Wekeromsche Zand in Gelderland. A terrestrial photograph is shown in Plate 12.2 in which the outline of successive banks is visible along the contact with the line of low trees in the background.

At one of the most thoroughly studied of the sites at Vaassen (Gelderland), Brongers (1976) observed a vegetation assemblage of *Molinia* sp. and *Erica* sp. related to intermittent water supply over the fields. The white plumes of the *Erica* were clearly visible in aerial photographs of the fields. This plant community occupied the channels that form the boundaries of the plots.

In his work at Vaassen, Brongers (1976) reported the discovery of several ceramic relics including pottery sherds of the Neolithic (3915 B.P.), Bronze (3560 B.P.), and Iron (2420 B.P.) Ages. The Iron Age relics were the most abundant of all. Very few younger relics were discovered, though there were a few from the Middle Ages. The findings attest to the great age and long period of occupancy of these Celtic fields. For a fuller account of the Dutch work, the reader is referred to the excellent and exceptionally thorough work of Brongers (1976).

12.2.3 Celtic Fields in Britain

The Celtic fields are especially well represented in Wessex, England. Indeed, in their famous book "Wessex from the Air", Crawford and Keiller (1928) devoted one of 6 sections to these remains of ancient agriculture. Among the more remarkable of these sites is the one at Bathampton Down in southwest England. In 1928 Crawford produced his pioneer maps of Celtic fields. As reported by St. Joseph and Wilson (1976), Crawford showed that air photographs could lead to an understanding of the relationship between Celtic fields and other earthworks, as, for example, the hillforts at Bathampton Down and Ogbury (Wiltshire). There has been a dearth of photographs showing Iron Age settlements in relation to the Celtic fields, but Crawford showed several sites of Celtic villages, though with no indication as their plan or other features.

Plate 12.3 is a vertical photograph of a prehistoric, possibly Iron Age, settlement adjacent to a system of Celtic fields at Wonston in Hampshire. In the main enclosure there is a circular structure (center right), and there are several ring marks, perhaps for holding wooden uprights of huts. The Celtic fields approach to within a few meters to the left of the outer ditch of the settlement and the plate shows the close relationship of the two types of archaeological site.

12.2.4 Celtic fields in Germany and Elsewhere in Northwestern Europe

The discovery of Celtic fields in Germany and elsewhere in northwestern Europe by means of aerial photography has been described by Grögel and Wilhelmi (1984, 1983/84) and by Brongers (1973). A training flight of the Bundesluftwaffe was used to obtain aerial photographs in 1982 of a burial ground of Late Bronze or Early Iron Age. This site near Oldenburg, Lower Saxony, West Germany, is linked to Celtic field systems, and is one of the largest in Europe (Fig. 12.3). It consists of 531 mounds revealed by differences in the heath coverage of the site.

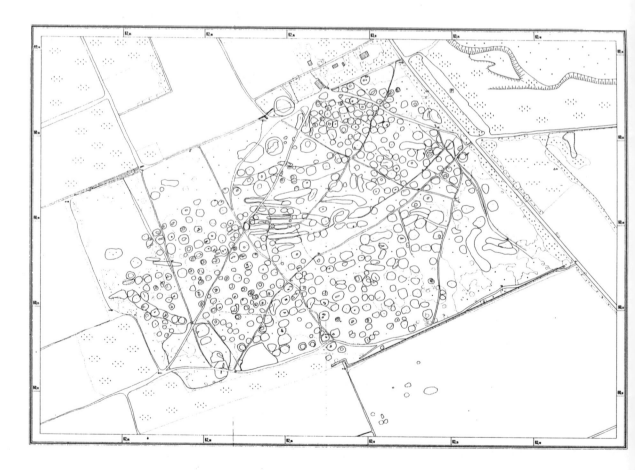

Fig. 12.3 Distribution of Celtic burial sites near Pestrup in the Oldenburg district, Lower Saxony, West Germany. Source: Grögel and Wilhelmi (1983/84) after photos by P. Oertelt and R. Zantopp.

12.3 SITES OF THE ROMAN PERIOD

12.3.1 Introduction

Sites of the Roman period are extremely numerous throughout western, southern and central Europe, particularly in England, Italy and southwest Germany. Pioneering work on the aerial discovery of such sites was again carried out in England (see Chapter 10 for references). One of the best references is the well-known book by Frere and St. Joseph (1983) that contains 142 plates of aerial photographs of Roman military sites, urban sites, roads, forts, villas, temples, and tombs.

12.3.2 Roman Forts

In lowland Britain there are few visible Roman military sites south of the River Thames (St Joseph, 1977). This is because the Roman conquest of Britain was initially a very rapid event as the army swept towards the highland zones of Wales and Scotland. The few lowland forts that were built were occupied only for a short time and were constructed of earth and timber rather than of stone. In many cases, the forts were converted into permanent settlements that submerged the original military sites.

North of the River Thames sites of Roman forts are more common, particularly along lines of military advance such as the famous Watling Street Roman road. The Roman advance was slowed by the Pennine Range in northern England and by the Welsh Marches in the northwest of the country. It is not surprising, therefore, that St. Joseph (1977) was able to report a new discovery of a Roman fort amid the cluster of forts along the northern border with Wales (Fig. 12.4) that attests to the significance the Romans placed on this part of Britain where they were engaged in constant warfare with the Welsh tribes.

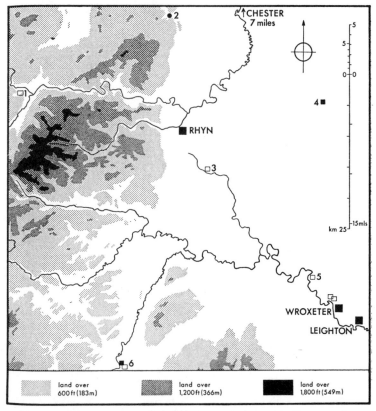

Fig. 12.4 Map of the Northern Marches showing forts built during the Roman advance into Northern Wales. Source: St. Joseph (1977.). 1) Penrhos, 2) Ffirth, 3) Whittington, 4) Whitchurch, 5) Uffington, 6) Forden. By courtesy of the editor of *Antiquity.*

The new hillfort discovered solely by aerial photography (St Joseph, 1977) is situated near Rhyn (Shropshire), and was recognized by crop marks during an aerial flight in 1975. Both vertical and oblique shots were taken at one week intervals just as the marks were beginning to fade with the onset of ripening of the corn. This site (Fig. 12.5 and Plate 12.4) lies on a small plateau between the Ceiriog River and Morlas Brook and is covered mainly with arable fields. The plan of the site (Fig. 12.5) shows two Roman works. The smaller, on the eastern side, is defended by a double ditch system with a gate on the western end. A southern gate is implied by a gap in the inner ditch. At the northwest angle there is a line of pits between the two ditch systems. The area within the ditches is about 6 ha.

The larger enclosure, to the west of the Roman hillfort site at Rhyn, is defined by a larger ditch system and there are four gates. The fort fits into the class of vexillation fortress. The smaller 6 ha fort is presumed to date from 48 A.D. when operations under the governorship of Ostorius Scapula took the Roman army towards this part of Britain.

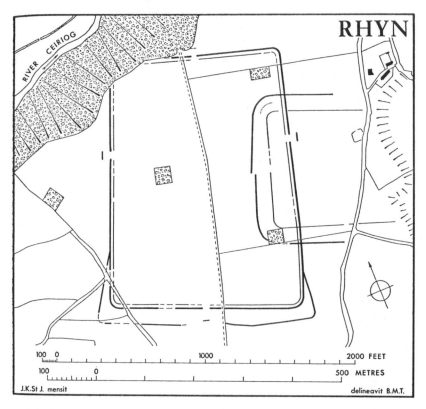

Fig. 12.5 Plan of the Roman fort at Rhyn (Shropshire, England). Source: St. Joseph (1977). By courtesy of the editor of *Antiquity*.

12.3.3 Roman Settlements

England was extensively colonized by Rome after the main invasion by Clàudius Caesar in 43 A.D. The earlier "invasions" by Julius Caesar in 55 and 54 B.C. had merely been raids. The southeast of the country was particularly well colonized since it lay close to the capital (Londinium) and was flat and suitable for agriculture. The East Anglian Fenlands (Fig. 12.6) comprise some 3000 km^2 of flat terrain which is now cultivated on an extensive scale. Beneath this rich farmland is a complicated post-glacial sequence of deposits from marine and freshwater flooding (Godwin, 1978). During the Iron Age the area was covered by the sea, but by 50 A.D. the land had begun to dry out. It was not until the reign of the emperor

Hadrian (120–130 A.D.) that widespread settlement began (Phillips, 1970).

The Stonea area of the Fenlands (Fig. 12.6) is dotted with numerous sites of the Roman period, though many have been destroyed by efficient modern farms of the area. The site at Stonea was uncovered by a very successful combination of aerial photography and subsequent ground surveys as described by Potter and Jackson (1982). Excavations have shown that Stonea was first occupied during the pre-Roman Iron Age and then became, in Roman times, the headquarters of a provincial procurator administering perhaps the whole of the southern Fenlands.

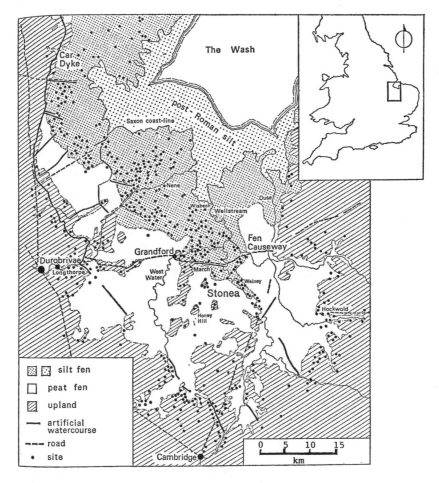

Fig. 12.6 The Roman Fenland in East Anglia showing the Stonea site. Source: Potter and Jackson (1982). By courtesy of the editor of *Antiquity*.

A number of artifacts discovered at Stonea (Fig. 12.7) attests to the general level of prosperity of the region. Potter and Jackson (1982) investigated two of the sites: Stonea Camp, and the remains of a stone-built complex at Stonea Grange Farm (Fig. 12.8). Stonea Camp occupies 3.2 ha and was originally on a promontory protected by now-extinct rivers. The phases of construction were evident, from conversion of a simple enclosure to an extensively defended position. From artifacts found at the site, it appears to date from 40–50 A.D. Potter and Jackson (1982) suggest that the Stonea Camp might have been the site of a battle described by the Roman historian Tacitus (55–117 A.D.). This battle resulted from a rebellion of the Iceni in response to a demand for disarmament. They chose: ". . . a battlefield at a place protected by a rustic earthwork with an approach too narrow to give access to cavalry."

The fort was ultimately overwhelmed despite fierce resistance.

At Stonea Grange are the ruins of a massive stone building. The site may have been part of an administrative center for the Fenland but it was at an inconvenient distance from the main east-west lines of communication. It may therefore have been constructed partly to commemorate the great Roman victory against the Iceni as recorded by Tacitus. It was constructed with masonry brought 40–50 km from quarries in Northamptonshire. From the extent of the foundations it may have been an imposing tower of some two or three storeys. A simplified plan is shown in Fig. 12.9. The presence of heated rooms within the building implies a bath house. Large quantities of glass were found in the area as well as mosaic fragments, tessarae and tiles. The structure was dated to the later period of Hadrian's rule. Abandonment came fairly quickly, probably at the end of the 2nd century A.D. Towards 300 A.D. the site was levelled and a new stone building constructed.

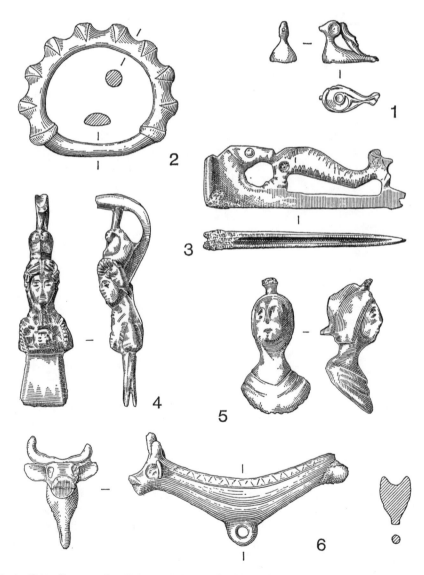

Fig. 12.7 Artifacts discovered at Stonea. 1) Bronze duck attachment: 2) bronze lipped terret: 3) bronze folding knife handle: 4) bronze bust of Minerva: 5) bronze escutcheon: 6) bronze cosmetic grinder. Source: Potter and Jackson (1982). By courtesy of the editor of *Antiquity*.

Plate 12.1. Aerial view of Celtic fields (quiltwork pattern) over Wekeromsche Zand, Gelderland Province, Netherlands. Photo by courtesy of the Nederlandse Topografische Dienst.

Plate 12.2. Ground view of Celtic fields near Vaassen, Gelderland Province, Netherlands. The line of banks can be seen quite clearly against the line of low trees in the background. Source: Brongers (1976). By courtesy of the author.

Plate 12.3. Celtic fields in Wonston (Hampshire, England) showing a nearby settlement. Source: St. Joseph and Wilson (1976). By courtesy of the editor of *Antiquity*.

Plate 12.4. Aerial view of Roman military works at Rhyn (Shropshire, England). Source: St. Joseph (1977). By courtesy of the editor of *Antiquity*.

Plate 13.1. A Neolithic settlement (4500 B.P.) revealed by crop marks south of Foggia, southern Italy. Source:.Bradford (1957). By courtesy of Unwin Hyman Ltd.

Plate 13.2. The ancient Etruscan city of Spina revealed by lighter and darker shades of marsh grass. The white lines are modern drainage channels. Photograph by Professor V. Valvassori.

Plate 13.3. Vertical aerial photograph of ancient terraced fields on the slopes of Mt Hymettos, Attica, Near Athens. A) ancient terracing partly removed by modern ploughing, B) same terraces preserved as modern boundaries, C) negative crop marks showing ancient terrace boundaries. Source: Bradford (1957). By courtesy of Unwin Hyman Ltd.

Plate 13.4. Line of stones (negative vegetation anomaly) showing the edge of ancient terraced field in Attica near Athens. Source: Bradshaw (1957). By courtesy of Unwin Hyman Ltd.

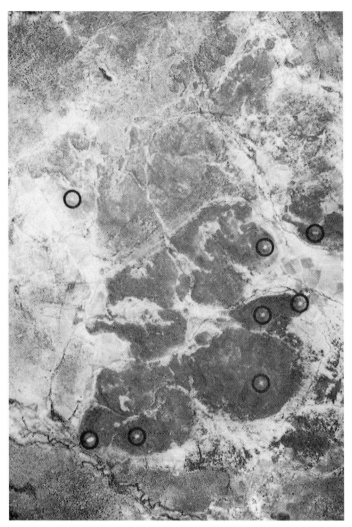

Plate 13.5. Archaeological Iron Age midden sites in Eastern Botswana. The bare patches (ringed) are midden sites covered with the grass *Cenchrus ciliaris*. Source: Denbow (1979). By courtesy of the editor of the *South African Journal of Science*.

Plate 14.1. Obsidian quarry at Glass Butte, Oregon. Note central bare zone surrounded by junipers. Source: Aikens et al. (1980).

Plate 14.2. Oblique view of Coffeepot Flat, Oregon, showing Camps A, B and C. Source: Aikens et al. (1980).

Plate 14.3. Aerial oblique view of Gulf Hazard looking eastward from Hudson Bay, Canada. Source: Harp (1974). Reprinted by permission of Harvard University Press.

Plate 14.4. Aerial photograph and spectral signature plot of the Kaltag area on the Yukon River in Alaska. Source: Stringer and Cook (1974). By courtesy of Professor W. J. Stringer.

Plate 15.1. Aerial view of Maya Classic Period (250–900 AD) canal system near Tikal in the Yucatan Peninsula, Mexico, as revealed by lusher vegetation above the canals. Source: Adams (1980). By courtesy of the editor of *Antiquity*.

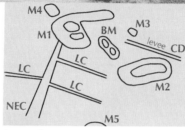

Plate 15.2. Formative Preclassic canal system at Amalucan, Puebla State, Mexico revealed as crop marks in infrared aerial photographs. M1-M4 ceremonial mounds, LC lateral canals, NEC northeast canal, BM buried mound, CD levee of check dam of the northwest diversion canal. Source: Fowler (1987). By courtesy of the editor of *National Geographic Research*.

Plate 15.3. View of Machu Picchu, Peru.

Plate 15.4. Aerial phototraph of the Machu Picchu region. Source: Chohfi (1987a) By courtesy of Servicio Nacional del Peru.

Plate 16.1. Aerial photograph of the Clybucca 3 aboriginal midden site in northern New South Wales. Source: Connah (1978). By courtesy of the editor of *Antiquity*.

Plate 16.2. Aerial photograph of the Stuarts Point aboriginal midden site in northern New South Wales. Source: Connah (1978). By courtesy of the editor of *Antiquity*.

Plate 16.3. Aerial photograph of aboriginal ceremonial stone trackway denuded of vegetation. The site is at Pindera Downs, Tibooburra, Australia. Source: Connah and Jones (1983). Photo by courtesy of G. Connah.

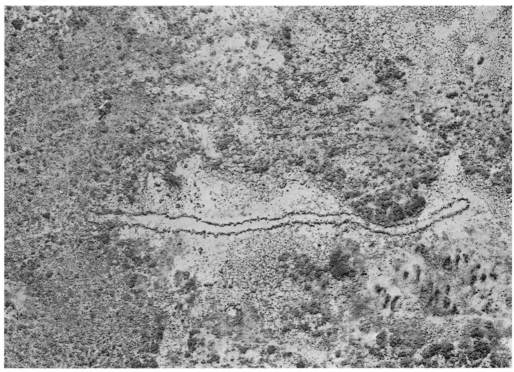

Plate 16.4. Aerial photograph of aboriginal oven mound at Glenhope Mound near Hay, New South Wales. The site is revealed by soil marks after drought had totally stripped the vegetation cover. Source: Connah and Jones (1983). Photo by courtesy of G. Connah.

Plate 16.5. Aerial photograph of aboriginal quarry site at Moondarah, Queensland. Source: Connah and Jones (1983). Photo by courtesy of G. Connah.

Plate 16.6. Aerial photograph of Mount Eden (Maungawhau Pa), a Maori fortress in the center of Auckland, New Zealand. The kumara pits show up clearly as depressions near the summit. Photo by courtesy of White's Aviation Ltd., Auckland.

44

Plate 16.7. Photograph of an ancient Maori kumara pit on Mt. Eden (see Plate 16.6). Source: Ell (1985). By courtesy of the author.

Plate 16.8. Stone walls protecting ancient kumara fields on Great Mercury Island, New Zealand. This is one of the few localities in New Zealand where the kumara could grow year-round without storage in pits. Source: Ell (1985). By courtesy of the author.

Plate 16.9. Karaka plantation near a Maori settlement in New Zealand. The karaka was used for food and its edible fruit attracted native pigeons which could then be easily snared for food. The straight lines of these plantations can be recognised from the air. Source: Ell (1985). By courtesy of the author.

Plate 16.10. Representation of Fijian ring-ditch fort from a painting by J. G. Wilson who visited Fiji in 1856 on board H. M. S. "Herald."

Plate 16.11. Aerial photographs of ring ditch systems in the Navua delta, Fiji, taken at different years and seasons. The upper photo was taken in March 1966 and clearly shows three forts designated by white arrows. In the lower photo taken in January 1973, these structures are no longer visible due to changes in the vegetation. Source: Parry (1984). By courtesy of the editor of the *New Zealand Journal of Archaeology*.

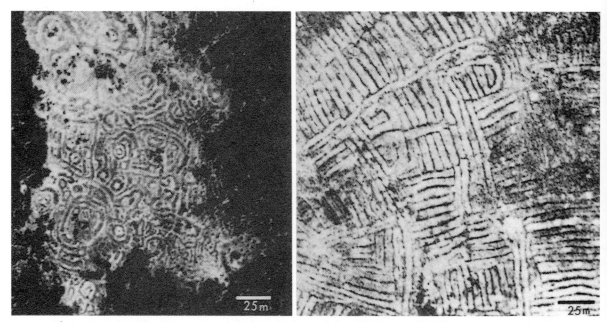

Plate 16.12. Pre-European taro gardens in the Rewa delta, Viti Levu, Fiji. The gardens are clearly visible from the richer (darker) vegetation growing over the surrounding ditches. The left hand photo shows the reticulated maze form, whereas the right photo shows the grid-iron pattern. Source: Parry (1979).

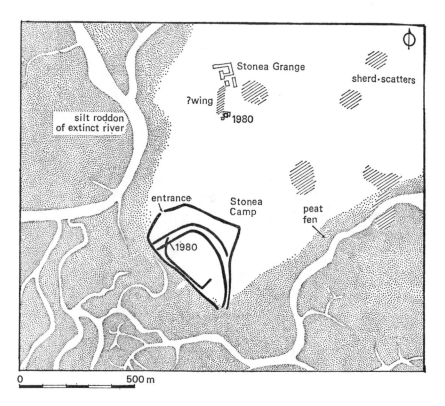

Fig. 12.8 Plan of Stonea camp. Source: Potter and Jackson (1982). By courtesy of the editor of *Antiquity*.

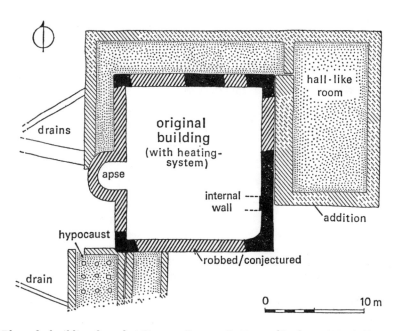

Fig. 12.9 Plan of a building found at Stonea. Source: Potter and Jackson (1982). By courtesy of the editor of *Antiquity*.

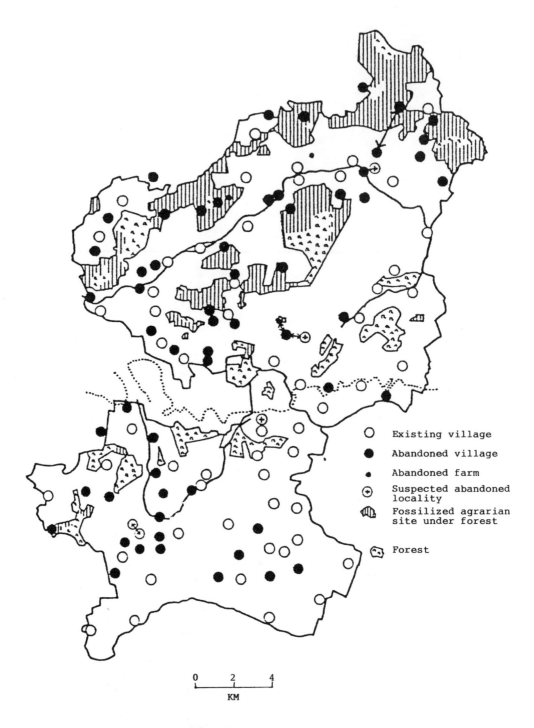

Fig. 12.10 Location of abandoned medieval villages east of Brunswick in Lower Saxony. Open circles, existing villages; large solid circles, abandoned villages; small dots, individual abandoned farms; open circles with dots, putative sites of abandoned villages. The areas with vertical shading represent abandoned medieval fields below forest. Forested areas are shown as a zigzag. Source: Oberbeck (1961). By courtesy of the editor of *Geografiska Annaler*.

12.4 MEDIEVAL SITES

The third type of chronologically distinct site that was revealed partly or wholly by aerial photography concerns medieval sites of Central Europe. In Germany there is a great interest in the so-called *Wüstungsforschung*—a study of abandoned medieval sites (Ortswüstungen). Such sites are common throughout Europe but are less so in Britain than in Germany. In the former, settlement was more concentrated and records better preserved than in Germany, a country continually ravaged by pestilence and war throughout the Middle Ages. The German terrain was also much more heavily forested (even today about one third of West Germany is still covered by forest) so that abandoned settlements were soon reclaimed by the forest and readily disappeared from public knowledge. An example of the great density of Ortswüstungen is given in Fig. 12.10 which shows over 100 such sites in a 200 km^2 area east of Brunswick in Lower Saxony (Oberbeck, 1961). A useful review of the subject has been given by Scharlau (1957).

As with the older Celtic fields and Roman settlements, the wealth of information on abandoned settlements is great. We will restrict our discussion to a single example, one of the more spectacular aerial discoveries of medieval sites. This site is at Düna, near Osterode in the western Harz Mountains of the Federal Republic of Germany. The discovery has been documented by Grögel and Wilhelmi (1983/84, 1984). Aerial photography was carried out by private plane because the site is close to the border with East Germany so that the German Federal government was unwilling to use an Air Force plane. The site, an early medieval mansion, was not visible in enlargements of official aerial photographs but was delineated by vegetational differences shown by low-altitude shots.

The excavation of the early medieval mansion at Düna has been described by Klappauf (1982). The structure lay directly along the early medieval road from Leinetal to Saxony and Thuringia. The ruins lie on a 20 m diameter hill on a peninsula-like tongue of land between two streams. A plan of the site at various stages is shown in Fig. 12.11. Following the original aerial discovery, the site was investigated by several other techniques including geophysics, phosphate analysis, and drilling.

It appears that there were four settlement periods at Düna, the youngest of which dates back to the 14th century when the settlement was abandoned. The oldest appears to be 7th century in origin. The earliest building appeared to have been of timber and its presence is indicated only by post holes.

In the third stage of settlement, the foundations of the mansion were strengthened and the upper part of the building was probably constructed of timber. The stream was diverted by a channel. This settlement has been dated back to the 11th or 12th Centuries.

In the fourth stage, the stream was diverted further to the west and another structure was erected over the old stream bed. This building is dated to the early 14th century. The discovery of an old kettle hook, and other culinary artifacts, leads to the conclusion that the annex was used as a kitchen.

Of particular interest is the discovery of ores and slags at the Düna site. These date to the 3rd–4th and 5th–7th Centuries A.D. respectively, as determined from pottery remains. A large part of the ores originated from the Rammelsberg near Goslar (see Chapter 2), showing that mining must have commenced in the Harz as early as the 3rd Century A.D. (Brockner and Kolb, 1986).

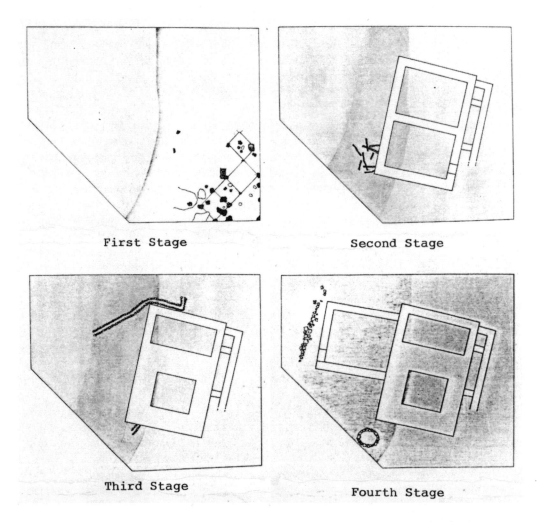

First Stage

Second Stage

Third Stage

Fourth Stage

Fig. 12.11 Plan of the Düna mansion at various time periods. Source: Klappauf (1982).

12.5 CONCLUSION

The future for the discovery of fresh archaeological sites in Europe by use of aerial photography does not appear bright. It is true that modern methods of remote sensing are becoming increasingly sophisticated. On the other hand evidence indicated primarily by crop marks is gradually becoming erased by deeper ploughing and the increasing tempo of agriculture in Europe, which for the first time is becoming a net exporter of grain.

The situation can only be remedied by public awareness of the fragility of European archaeological sites just beneath the surface and by a public desire to preserve such sites. The existence in England of the Cambridge Committee for Aerial Archaeology, and in Germany of such Federal State (Bundesland) institutions such as the Bayerisches Landesamt fur Denkmalpflege and the Baden-Württembergisches Landesdenkmalamt will do much to encourage public interest in site preservation.

We have come a long way since the *Ghosts of Wessex* were first recognized and it is to be hoped that the plough and urban encroachment will not cause these ephemeral indicators of the past to vanish for ever from our environment.

12.6 CHAPTER SUMMARY

This chapter is concerned with aerial archaeology in northwest Europe. The *Celtic fields* are distributed throughout the region and aerial archaeology has revealed their presence mainly by crop marks. Several case histories from England, Germany and Holland are presented.

Sites of the Roman period have also been uncovered by aerial photography. Specific examples from England are described and include a Roman fort in Shropshire and the Stonea Mansion site in East Anglia.

Medieval sites have also been discovered by aerial photography. A description is given of one of these, at Düna in West Germany.

REFERENCES

Brockner, W., and Kolb, H. E. 1986. Archäometrische Untersuchungen an Erz—und Schlackenfunden der Grabung Düna. *Arbheft. Denkmalpfl. Niedersachs.* 6: 74–77.

Brongers, J. A. 1973. "Celtic Fields" in Niedersachsen. *Archäol. Korrespondenzbl.* 3: 129–131.

_____ 1976. *Air Photography and Celtic Field Research in the Netherlands.* Rijksdienst voor het Oudheidkundig Bodemonderzoek, Amersfoort.

Crawford, O. G. S. 1923. Air survey and archaeology. *Geogr. J.* 61: 342–366.

_____ 1928. The Andover District. *Ordnance Survey Prof. Pap.* No.7.

Crawford, O. G. S., and Keiller, A. 1928. *Wessex from the Air.* Clarendon Press, Oxford.

Frere, S. S., and St. Joseph, J. K. S. 1983. *Roman Britain from the Air.* Cambridge Univ. Press, Cambridge.

Godwin, H. 1978. *Fenland: Its Ancient Past and Uncertain Future.* Cambridge Univ. Press, Cambridge.

Grögel, A., and Wilhelmi, K. 1983/84. Luftbildarchäologie und Vermessung in Niedersachsen. Methoden—Probleme. *Die Kunde,* NF, 34/35: 1–12.

_____ 1984. Luftbildarchäologie in Niedersachsen. *Ber. Denkmalpfl. Niedersachs.* 1: 16–24.

Klappauf, L. 1982. Die Ausgrabung eines frühmittelalterlichen Herrensitzes in Düna/Österode. *Ber. Denkmalpfl. Niedersachs.* 2: 135–138.

Oberbeck, G. 1961. Das Problem der spätmittelalterlichen Kulturlandschaft erläutert an Beispielen aus Niedersachsen. *Geogr. Ann.* 43: 236–242.

Phillips, C. W. 1970. The Fenland in Roman Times. *Roy. Geogr. Soc. Res. Ser.* No. 5.

Picardt, J. 1660. Korte Beschryvinge van eenige Vergetene en Verborgene Antiquiteten der Provintien en Landen Gelegen tussen de Noord-Zee de Yssel, Emse en Lippe. Amsterdam.

Potter, T. W., and Jackson, R. P. J. 1982. The Roman site of Stonea, Cambridgeshire. *Antiquity* 61: 111–121.

Riley, D. N. 1982. *Aerial Archaeology in Britain.* Shire Publishers Ltd. Princes Risborough.

Scharlau, K. 1957. Ergebnisse und Ausblicke der heutigen Wüstungsforschung. *Blatt. Dt. Landesgesch.* 93: 43–101.

St. Joseph, J. K. 1977. Air reconnaissance: recent results, 42. *Antiquity* 51: 55–60.

St. Joseph, J. K., and Wilson, D. R. 1976. Air reconnaissance: recent results, 41. *Antiquity* 50: 237–239.

Wilson, D. R. 1982. *Air Photo Interpretation for Archaeologists.* Batsford, London.

Chapter 13

AERIAL ARCHAEOLOGY IN AFRICA, SOUTHERN EUROPE AND THE MIDDLE EAST

13.1 INTRODUCTION

The geographical distribution of aerial archaeology throughout the world is very uneven. Some areas, particularly northwest Europe (see Chapter 12) have been covered extremely well and there is an extensive literature on the subject. In the rest of the world there has been some concentration of effort in Australasia, North America, and Central America, whereas Asia and Africa have remained relatively untouched.

In southern Europe and in the Middle East, several important finds were made between the two World Wars and in the years immediately following World War II. These findings have an historical rather than contemporary framework, and the present chapter will emphasize this historical background, since relatively little follow-up work seems to have emerged. Figure 13.1 shows the locations of the sites discussed in this chapter.

A useful source of information about early aerial archaeology in southern Europe and the Middle East has been provided by Deuel (1969) whose work is the source for much of the material in this chapter.

13.2 AERIAL ARCHAEOLOGY IN THE MIDDLE EAST

Following the pioneering work of Crawford in England (Crawford and Keiller, 1928—see also Chapter 12), several other researchers and aviators attempted to follow in his foot-

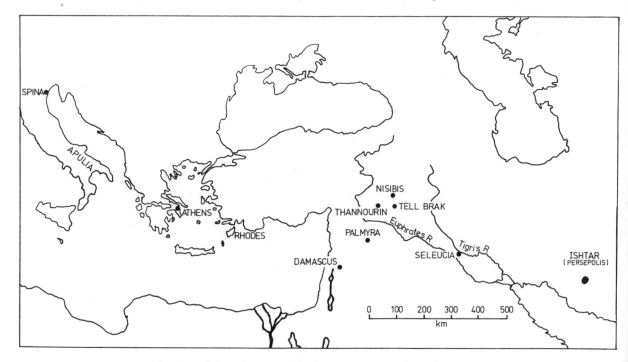

Fig. 13.1 Map of some of the locations covered in Chapter 13.

steps. Among these was Father Poidebard, a French cleric who carried out his work in Syria and Mesopotamia (Poidebard, 1934). Like Crawford, he made use of the long shadows cast by the early morning and late afternoon sun. He relied more on natural vegetation than on crops, and concentrated his efforts at the period when the autumn rains made the vegetation green almost overnight. Father Poidebard observed that the color of the vegetation would vary:

> . . . according to the permeability and undulations of the soil. The color remains lighter where the run is hidden underground, because the permeability is less, or because plant life is hindered by the dissolving of the lime in the old walls. The color is darker in the depressions due to an old gravel road or trench. A depression of a few centimeters is enough to increase the dampness of the soil.

A reverse reaction would occur in summer when the vegetation became parched in a few days and had a variable color that reflected the nature of the substrate. As reported by Deuel (1969), Poidebard carried out some of his earlier work in the Upper Euphrates near the ancient fortified town of Nisibis. He identified several Byzantine camps from an altitude of 1000 m. Later he discovered Tell Brak and its castellum. This latter discovery was made shortly after the onset of autumn rains and Poidebard was able to identify the castellum from the lighter vegetation covering the subterranean ruins of the ancient walls buried in the sand to a depth of 1 m.

After numerous further discoveries, Father Poidebard turned his attention to northern Syria, where in the mountains east of Damascus, he identified a part of the Roman road *Via Diocletiana* leading to Palmyra. One of his greatest feats was the discovery in 1928 of the ancient Byzantine city of Thannourin.

In further exploration, an aviator named E. F. Schmidt from the University of Chicago, discovered at least 400 ruined sites near the city of Persepolis in Iran (Schmidt, 1940). This city had been the ancient capital of the Persian kings Darius and Xerxes. One of his photographs taken in 1936 at Istakhar near Persepolis was judged to be completely confusing until Schmidt and his colleagues realized that they were dealing with photographic crop marks rather than natural vegetation and that these marks accurately delineated the plan of the city.

During World War I, several haphazard discoveries were made by pilots flying over Mesopotamia, Jordan and Syria. Among these was a dark line of vegetation marking the site of a former capital Seleucia, founded in 300 B.C. (Insall, 1927). As in his earlier discovery at Woodhenge, Insall used a simple box camera for his work at Seleucia.

13.3 AERIAL ARCHAEOLOGY IN ITALY

13.3.1 Northern Apulia

It is to be expected that Italy, with its wealth of discovered and potential archaeological sites, would be a favored target of aerial explorers. However, work in Italy began later than in northwest Europe and, like so many other projects, owed its origins to a world war. Shortly after World War II, two British army officers stationed in Apulia, J. S. P. Bradford and P. Williams-Hunt, had been amateur archaeologists. They were confident that the Foggia Plain in southern Italy would yield useful aerial data. Plate 13.1 shows one of their early discoveries, a Neolithic settlement (4500 B.P.) revealed by crop marks at Passo di Corvo near Foggia. Bradford continued his work in Rhodes and Attica (Bradford, 1956a,b), Dalmatia, southern France and in other parts of Italy. His findings were later published (Bradford, 1957).

The soil of northern Apulia consists of a thin layer overlapping porous limestone, conditions ideal for the display of crop marks or changes in natural vegetation. The region is known as the Tavoliere.

During a four-week period in the early autumn of 1945, Bradford and Williams-Hunt produced several thousand photographs of the area from an altitude of 3000 m. An enormous wealth of archaeological sites was revealed by the work, few of which were evident from the ground. Northern Apulia seemed to have the same favorable conditions of climate, soil, topography, and geomorphology which had led to Crawford's successes in Wessex some 20 years earlier.

Despite the rapidity at which the aerial photographs were taken in 1945, it was to be several years before significant excavations were carried out.

The Apulia expedition of 1949 (Bradford, 1950) was carried out under Bradford in the late summer when the land was free of crops. At this season he noted the occurrence of weed marks which obeyed the same laws as crop marks but which took: ". . . a far greater variety of forms. Above ancient ditches flowering species grew taller, more thickly and often more quickly and thus accelerated, had sometimes flowered, withered, and prematurely 'fall'n into the sear, the yellow leaf' before those not so advanced."

13.3.2 Etruria

Bradford carried out extensive aerial work in Etruria where he identified many ancient Etruscan tombs (Fig. 13.2) and ruins (Bradford, 1947, 1956c). He recorded dark wedges cutting into the periphery of tomb circles. These marked the entrances to the tombs (dromos) and were spots where the entrance steps had filled with soil to give deep water-retentive zones with more luxuriant vegetation. In one sector of the Cervetti Burial Ground, Bradford noted over 100 of such wedges. The proliferation of entrances to a single tumulus was explained by consecutive burials within the same mausoleum. Some of the tombs were so extensive that they were used as air raid shelters in World War II.

One of Bradford's greatest achievements was the discovery of over 600 buried tumuli at Monte Abbatone (Bradford, 1956c). Because of its thin topsoil, this site proved to be very useful for aerial archaeology. The tombs were identified mainly by weed marks in natural wild plants and grasses. The entrances to the tombs were invariably marked by luxuriant natural vegetation and occasionally by shrubs.

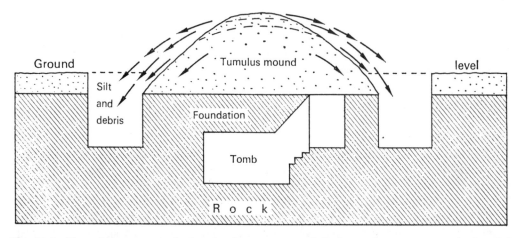

Fig. 13.2 Plan of Etruscan tomb showing how patterns of ditches and stairways can lead to differentiation in soils and vegetation. Source: Bradford (1957). By courtesy of Unwin Hyman Ltd.

13.3.3 The Po Delta

The exciting discovery of the lost Etruscan city of Spina (Fig. 13.3), along the Po delta south of Venice was made by the Italian aerial archaeologist Valvassori (Alfieri, 1957) in the 1960s. The success of the aerial work had been made possible by a reclamation project. The

Vale Pega (La Paganella) had been drained and high-stemmed marsh grass then grew on the area. Topographic analysis (Alfieri, 1957) had narrowed the search to La Paganella, and Valvassori's work had made it a certainty with the revelation of sharply-defined buried features of a city of perhaps 500 000 inhabitants covering an area of some 300 ha.

To quote Deuel (1969):

> ... The silted canals filled with detritus and fertile humus, besides retaining much moisture, were traced by dark-green ribbons of grass, while the squares and rectangles of the building blocks, which stood on what used to be barren sand, supported only a sparse yellowish vegetation. Thus, the basic physical make-up of lagoon settlements was itself a determinant in bringing out the geometric plan. One could not wish for greater contrasts.

Plate 13.2 shows Spina as a grid of canals and city blocks revealed by lighter and darker shades of marsh grass. The white lines are modern drainage channels.

Valvassori's aerial reconnaissance was augmented by *in situ* excavations by Alfieri who began to dig at the site of Spina. This work revealed wooden pilings that had been used by the Etruscans to support their houses (as was also done at nearby Venice). Further excavations also revealed ceramics dating back to the 4th or 5th Centuries B.C., an age in agreement with the nearby Etruscan necropolis.

Despite the large extent of the city of Spina, discoveries are not likely to rival those of the necropolis because most of the houses were made of timber and have not survived the long passage of time.

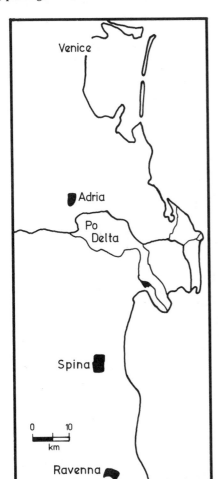

Fig. 13.3 Location map of ancient Spina with adjacent lagoons and present course of the River Po.

13.4 AERIAL ARCHAEOLOGY IN GREECE

Despite its wealth of archaeological remains, very few aerial archaeological surveys have been carried out over the Greek Peninsula and Aegean Islands. A well-known book by Schoder (1974); *Ancient Greece from the Air,* contains a wealth of aerial photographs but all of these are of obvious sites well elevated from the surrounding terrain. There is not a single example of the use of vegetation to identify these sites. This does not mean that crop marks and other vegetational indicators are not present, rather, it signifies that very little work has been done in this direction. We again turn to the early work of Bradford (1956a, 1956b) for a record of aerial phytoarchaeology in the Greek archipelago. His work was carried out in 1955 and was followed by a ground survey of two of the most promising sites on the island of Rhodes and in Attica near Athens.

The work of Bradford (1956a) at Rhodes was devoted to establishing the town plan of this ancient port, but did not rely to any great extent on vegetation patterns. However, his work on ancient field systems (Bradford, 1956b, 1957) on the slopes of Mt. Hymettos, near Athens was largely based on negative vegetational anomalies (soil marks). It was stimulated (as in Holland and Germany) by a study of Royal Air Force reconnaissance photographs taken during World War II. In 1943, he observed patterns which seemed to indicate field systems adjoining the sites of ancient demes that had had a long association of occupation during Greek and Roman times. These ancient fields (Fig. 13.4) are situated near the villages of Euonymus (Trachones), Halimous (Chasani), Aixone (Glyphada), Halai Aixonides (Palaiochori), and Anagyrous (Vari) (the names in parentheses are the modern equivalents). It is remarkable that these ancient field systems were preserved within 10 km of Athens. This happened largely because the area was given over to pastoral activities rather than cropping. An aerial photograph (Plate 13.3) reveals a system of ancient terraces facing the coast. The old terrace walls have in most places eroded down to ground level and appear as white soil marks devoid of vegetation. Insofar as soil marks can be considered as negative vegetational anomalies, they fall within the terms of reference of this book.

Plate 13.4 is a terrestrial photograph showing a line of stones (the remnants of an old retaining wall) forming a soil mark in the aerial shots.

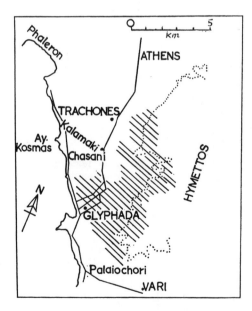

Fig. 13.4 Map of ancient villages and terraced fields in Attica near Athens. The dotted line marks the 250 m contour. Source: Bradford (1957). By courtesy of Unwin Hyman Ltd.

The ancient fields of Attica near Athens have now been partially destroyed by urban encroachment and revived agriculture in the area. From fragments of pottery, it appears that the fields date back to the 5th and late 4th Centuries B.C. This work in Attica again reveals the useful spin-off from wartime activities involving aerial photography originally used for a more sinister purpose.

13.5 AERIAL ARCHAEOLOGY IN SOUTHERN AFRICA

The discovery of the grass *Cenchrus ciliaris* as an indicator of Iron Age middens in southern Africa (Denbow, 1979) has already been described in Chapter 8. The previous treatment had however, concentrated on surface investigations and a brief summary of the aerial work is in order, this present chapter.

The investigations were carried out in eastern Botswana in the Serowe-Palapye area (see Fig.8.5). Aerial photographs at a scale of 1:40,000 were used for the investigation, and were examined for bald spots in surrounding woodlands. These sites appear as bald spots because they are covered with dense stands of *Cenchrus ciliaris*.

Ground reconnaissance of the sites revealed that all of the 100 or so locations marked as 'probable' were, in fact, Iron Age middens.

Plate 13.5 shows the location of some of these bald spots in the test area. The reliability of aerial photography for locating sites was dependent on the underlying geology and soils that influenced the density of the vegetation. Contrary to the conditions needed to identify stone walls by aerial photography, denser woodland vegetation rendered it easier to discern *Cenchrus* middens as discrete bare patches. In Plate 13.5 the hills in the southern section of the photograph support a denser vegetation because they are composed of siltstones and shales of the Waterberg system which are more easily weathered, and give more fertile soils, than the Waterberg diabases on the northern section.

Identification of middens according to Denbow (1979) was less reliable on the harder gneissic koppies (hills) of the basement complex to the east.

Reconnaissance of lowland areas showed the same occurrence of stands of *Cenchrus* with Iron Age midden sites, but disturbance of the natural vegetation by human activity produced many more bald spots not related to archaeological sites.

13.6 CHAPTER SUMMARY

This chapter describes aerial archaeology carried out in southern Africa, southern Europe, and the Middle East. Work in the Middle East dates back primarily to the interwar years and was carried out in Mesopotamia, Syria, Jordan, and Iran. One of the more remarkable of these investigations was the delineation of the site of the Persian city of Istakhar (near Persepolis) using crop marks in 1936.

Aerial archaeology in Italy was carried out after World War II and was centered primarily in Etruria and northern Apulia. The Etrurian work resulted in the identification of numerous Etruscan ruins and tombs as well as the discovery of the ancient Etruscan city of Spina just south of Venice.

Aerial archaeology in Greece has centered around ancient field systems near Athens as well as around known archaeological remains.

In southern Africa, Bronze Age middens in Botswana (see also Chapter 8) colonized by buffalo grass (*Cenchrus ciliaris*) have been identified by aerial photography.

REFERENCES

Alfieri, N. 1957. The Etruscans of the Po and the discovery of Spina. *Italy's Life,* pp. 92–104.

Bradford, J. S. P. 1947. Etruria from the air. *Antiquity* 21: 74–83.

———— 1950. The Apulia expedition: an interim report. *Antiquity* 24: 84–95.

———— 1956a. Fieldwork on aerial discoveries in Attica and Rhodes, Part I. *Antiquaries J.* 36: 57–69.

———— 1956b. Fieldwork on aerial discoveries in Attica and Rhodes, Part II. *Antiquaries J.* 36: 172–180.

———— 1956c. Mapping 2000 tombs from the air: how aerial photography plays its part in solving the riddle of the Etruscans. *Illus. London News* 16th June: 736–738.

———— 1957. *Ancient Landscapes.* G. Bell, London.

Crawford, O. G. S., and Keiller, A. 1928. *Wessex from the Air.* Clarendon Press, Oxford.

Denbow, J. R. 1979. *Cenchrus ciliaris:* an ecological indicator of Iron Age middens using aerial photography in Eastern Botswana. *S. Afr. J. Sci.* 75: 405–409.

Deuel, L. 1969. *Flights into Yesterday.* Macdonald, London.

Insall, G. S. M. 1927. Excerpts from letter in 'Notes and News'. *Antiquity* (March): 99–100.

Poidebard, A. 1934. *La Trace de Rome dans le Désert de Syrie.* Geuthner, Paris.

Schmidt, E. F. 1940. *Flights over Ancient Cities of Iran.* Chicago Univ. Press, Chicago.

Schoder, H. V. 1974. *Ancient Greece from the Air.* Thames, London.

Chapter 14

AERIAL ARCHAEOLOGY IN NORTH AMERICA

14.1 INTRODUCTION

Between the World Wars, North American aerial archaeologists lagged behind their European counterparts largely because they had not had the same experience of aerial reconnaissance for military purposes, and for the administration of large colonial empires. Among the Europeans, this reconnaissance had had a useful spin-off in aerial identification of archaeological sites. Archaeology therefore benefited from photographic data originally obtained for other purposes. A classic example is the use of Royal Air Force photographs of Germany and Holland during World War II that proved invaluable for German and Dutch aerial archaeologists long after the war had ended (see Chapter 12).

A useful historical summary of aerial archaeology in North America has been given by Schorr (1974). The first American article on aerial archaeology was published by MacLean (1923). A boost to the field was given by the pioneer aviator Charles Lindbergh who accidentally discovered the potential of aerial reconnaissance for archaeological research while pioneering the development of new air routes in the Caribbean for Pan American Airways. He had apparently been unaware of the earlier work of Crawford and others in Britain during the interwar years (e.g. Crawford and Keiller, 1928). Lindbergh later made a number of successful trials using aerial photography over Pueblo Indian sites in Arizona and New Mexico (Kidder, 1930: Weyer, 1929).

A distinction must be made between the use of aerial archaeology to detect buried ruins (the major consideration in this book) and the use of the airplane to detect larger physical traits of socioculturally-specialized populations (ethnography). In this wider canvas, the vegetational changes play a role other than the mere identification of vegetation patterns revealing archaeological sites and artifacts. A useful review of aerial photography and ethnography has been given by Vogt (1974). In aerial ethnography particular attention is paid to settlement patterns, land tenure, house type, cultivation cycles, irrigation and drainage, and the effects of seasonal variations. The pioneer in this field was Rowe (1953) who carried out most of his work in Colombia. A useful basic text for aerial archaeology and remote sensing is by Lyons and Avery (1977), with basic manual supplements for individual states such as that by Aikens et al. (1980) for Oregon.

There has already been some mention of the use of satellite imagery in aerial archaeology (Stringer and Cook, 1974, see also Chapter ll). The original study was carried out by the use of LANDSAT images and it appeared that the resolution (30 m) was such as to make the usefulness only marginal except for the largest sites. However, the development of the French SPOT system with a resolution as fine as 10 m should do much to enhance the potential of satellite imagery in archaeological exploration. For the present, however, we must remain content mainly with conventional aerial photography for the discovery of ancient ruins and sites.

14.2 AERIAL ARCHAEOLOGY IN OREGON

14.2.1 Introduction

Aerial archaeological research in Oregon has been summarized by Aikens et al.(1980); it is primarily ethnographic in its scope. The research has concentrated on sites with the required vegetational, geomorphological, and hydrological attributes that would render them favorable for human habitats.

What is now the state of Oregon was peopled in aboriginal times by many small groups who spoke languages of over 100 families. The initial occupation of Oregon occurred during the final stages of the last glaciation when the climate was cooler and moister than it is now. The earliest occupation is dated at 13 200 B.P. (Bedwell, 1973). All groups exploited the largest animals in their environment (deer, elk, bear, antelope, sheep, and bison), along with fish and smaller game animals. The two sites described below (Glass Butte and Coffeepot Flat) had been occupied by the Paiute and Klamath peoples. These were humans of the deserts in the southeast quarter of Oregon. The terrain is dominated by sagebrush-covered plains and valleys, with juniper and pine at higher elevations. The Northern Paiute occupied this vast territory at very low density and had to travel long distances to gather food. They relied heavily on wild seeds, roots, berries, rabbits, ground squirrels, fish, and waterfowl. Big game was too rare to be a staple item of diet. Summer dwellings consisted of small domed huts framed with willow and covered with brush or grass thatch. They were simple wind breaks open to the sky. During the winter several families congregated together (Stewart, 1939), but during the summer they were widely dispersed.

The Klamath people occupied primarily higher, forested country where the higher rainfall allowed them to have larger winter villages. They had a greater emphasis on fishing, fowling, and exploitation of the local environment than did the Northern Paiute. The Klamath culture dates back to about 6000 B.P. (Cressman, 1956) and the Paiute about a millenium earlier.

14.2.2 Glass Butte

Glass Butte rises 1950 m (6400 ft) out of the high lava plateau of central Oregon (Fig. 14.1). The soil is very thin (in places there is only bare rock) and the local vegetation is dominated by sagebrush (*Artemisia tridentata*) with juniper (*Juniperus communis*) on fault scarp ridges. According to Aikens et al. (1980):

> The local vegetation is dominated by sagebrush, but juniper trees are common on the fault scarp ridges and on Glass Butte itself. Native edible seeded grasses were formerly common: deer, pronghorn antelope, jackrabbit, cottontail and smaller mammals occur now, as do native sage grouse. Waterfowl, grasses and sedges occur on some of the smaller playa lakes, and at higher elevations, mountain mahogany, quaking aspen (*Populus tremuloides*) and willow (*Salix* sp.) stand sporadically in small groves.
>
> Glass Butte lies within the historic territory of the Northern Paiute, but its obsidian has been long and widely used by aboriginal people. Projectile points of ancient types, made of this obsidian, are found in the Glass Butte area itself. Obsidian from archaeological contexts on the lower Snake River over 200 miles away dating between 8000 and 10 000 B.P., has been identified as Glass Butte obsidian by trace element analysis.

A general survey showed that sites judged to be camps were found on terraces, on ridges, and at springs. Quarry sites, identified from aerial photographs by the lack of vegetation, occurred on eminences on the slopes of Glass Butte.

The heavy dependence of the Northern Paiute on water sources resulted in their camp sites being situated near springs. These were identified from aerial photographs as black spots surrounded by clumps of brush. The quaking aspen, which is a good indicator of water was readily distinguished from the darker toned juniper and pines. Plate 14.1 shows a ground photograph of an obsidian quarry on Glass Butte. The bare quarry area is surrounded by a stand of juniper.

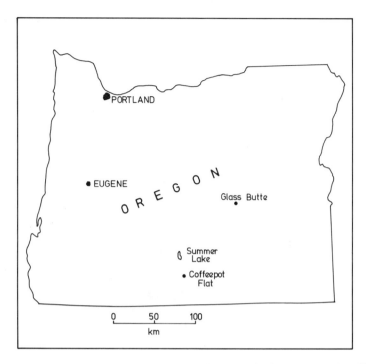

Fig. 14.1 Map of Oregon showing approximate locations of Glass Butte and Coffeepot Flat.

14.2.3 Coffeepot Flat

Coffeepot Flat (Plate 14.2) is situated 30 km south of Summer Lake (Fig. 14.1) in southcentral Oregon. Coffepot Flat and the Chewaucan Mts. lie close together on either side of a topographical and vegetational boundary separating wooded uplands from desert woodland (Aikens et al., 1980). This is also the ethnic boundary between the Northern Paiute and Klamath peoples. Two archaeological sites (A and B) are located on the tips of lightly-wooded ridges (Plate 14.2) and the third site (C) occurs on a terrace carrying a light clump of trees.

A ground survey preceded the aerial photography and revealed known springs as dark areas on the photographs and habitation sites as lighter areas. The lightness resulted from reduced survival of vegetation.

The search for additional sites was carried out by scanning the entire scene and concentrating on low ridges, terrace edges and the edges of the forest, while at the same time bearing in mind the necessity for a nearby water supply.

14.3 AERIAL ARCHAEOLOGY IN QUEBEC, CANADA

Richmond Gulf is situated in northeastern Quebec on the eastern shore of Hudson Bay (Fig. 14.2) and is the site of fairly recent archaeological discoveries (Harp, 1974). The territory has always been thinly populated. Before the arrival of European fur traders and colonists, its only known inhabitants were semi-migratory Indians and Eskimos. These primitive hunters had a minimal impact on their environment and left behind few artifacts. Such conditions are the antithesis of the rich archaeological sites of Roman Britain or of Greece and Italy. This case history therefore presents the outer limits of the potential use of the phytoarchaeological method.

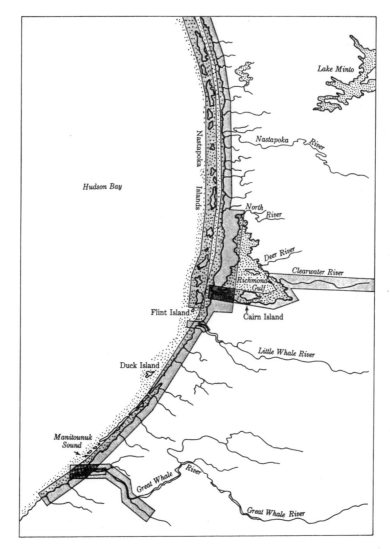

Fig. 14.2 Map of Richmond Gulf, Eastern Hudson Bay, Canada Source: Harp (1974). Reprinted by permission of Harvard University Press.

Richmond Gulf (Plate 14.3) is a large body of almost landlocked water connected to the outer bay only by the tidal Gulf Hazard. The face of the land is composed of barren rocky hills or mountains occasionally interspersed with patches of vegetation.

The landscape shows strong signs of previous glaciation being pockmarked with a myriad of basins and ponds. The valleys are filled with glacio-fluvial deposits of sands and gravels. Vegetation occurs only in the intermontane lowlands as the area is close to the limits of the northern tree line.

In certain well-protected areas, such as the southeastern slopes of Castle Peninsula, there are thin-to-moderate stands of conifers which can sometimes attain 10–15 meters in height. Some of the areas can be described as open lichen woodlands in which dense patches of *Cladonia rangiferina* (reindeer moss) replace ordinary grassland. Elsewhere there are dense stands of scrub dominated by Arctic willow (*Salix* sp.) or alder (*Alnus tenuifolia*). High well-drained soils support a heath vegetation with clumps of dwarf birch (*Betula nana*).

Aerial photography pinpointed the Gulf Hazard area as having the most potential for

MAG

N

#4 — _Dorset_ chipping station and lookout on N side of height of land.

#7

#8

1
2 #3
3

#1-Dorset

#5
2 3
1 4

5

Granite Outcrop

#9

#6

Modern
Recent

2
Contact Sites
#2

RICHMOND GULF

Narrows

Fig. 14.3 Field sketch of Gulf Hazard sites, Canada. Source: Harp (1974). Reprinted by permission of Harvard University Press.

archaeological sites after consideration of all the environmental factors (including vegetation) of the region. A field sketch of the Gulf Hazard sites (Harp, 1974) is shown in Fig. 14.3. Several features clearly not part of the natural environment were revealed in the photographs. Among these were circular pits (Complex 3 and 5) associated with subterranean Eskimo winter quarters of the late-period Dorset culture (prehistoric Eskimo culture of the Arctic zone of eastern Canada and Greenland—dated to 600–1300 B.C.)

These sites were not discovered solely by the vegetation patterns, but rather by a series of indicators which included vegetation. Where human intervention in the natural environment has been slight, as here, the only recourse is to consider a range of different indicators, including land forms, drainage patterns, erosion patterns, vegetation, and other components of the natural landscape.

Essentially these studies in Oregon and Quebec have illustrated the clear bond between phytogeomorphology (Howard and Mitchell, 1985) and phytoarchaeology. To quote from this latter work:

The importance of phytogeomorphology to archaeology lies in its use for recognizing and categorizing land types and improvement patterns as a means of identifying and reconstructing the past. The two distinct scales at which this can be considered are regional cultural units and local settings for families and small groups. Frequently the cultural units of the past can be observed on aerial photographs as being associated with recognizable land systems, land catenas, and land facets.

At a regional scale, groups of people have activity loci within districts somewhat analogous to the catchment areas of rivers within which movement, settlement, development and interchange take place rapidly. These activity loci are often lake or river basins or ancient plains that coincide with phytogeomorphic regions, land systems or specific land facets. The settled areas may have been eroded or buried as a result of tectonic or volcanic activity, the effects of which are especially conspicuous in coastal areas where there has been emergence or submergence.

The potentially large amount of archaeological data about many regions necessitates the use of a sampling program either to select areas representing a microcosm of the region as a whole, or purposive sampling of selected land facets, or else to sample a particular activity system such as agriculture, the crafts, trade, and communications wherever it occurs. In each type, the sampling patterns are stratified in terms of relevant landforms, plant communities, and water resources

Within regions, the individual sites may be visible or invisible at the surface, or visible on aerial photographs through expression in vegetal structures. In recent years there has been a rapid increase in the number of known sites, largely as a result of their expression in the form of vegetation patterns or occasionally in species distribution as observed on aerial photographs. To find these unknown sites, one starts from the assumption that as the surface indications of most ancient land uses resemble those of similar land uses today, their traces can usually be interpreted as related to recognizably homologous land units. Road layouts, village settlements, seafaring facilities and military constructions, for instance, are often associated with particular topographic conditions, and patterns of settlement and agriculture reflect the locations of fertile soils, water sources, vegetation types and ore-bearing rocks.

14.4   AERIAL ARCHAEOLOGY IN ALASKA

14.4.1   Introduction

There has already been some discussion of the potential of satellite imagery for the detection of archaeological sites. The main disadvantage of the technique is its poor resolution. Even the high resolution (10 m) of the French SPOT system is really only suitable for larger sites. Aerial photography has a much better potential resolution (i.e., 1 m) but suffers from the disadvantage that only a small area of ground is covered with a single photo. The work of Stringer and Cook (1974) in Alaska, though oriented specifically towards satellite imagery has equally valid applications to aerial photography. These applications will be considered with particular reference to sites in Alaska.

14.4.2   Old Fish Camp, Alaska

Archaeological sites in Alaska are fitting subjects for aerial exploration for the following reasons:

1) They are relatively large and are surrounded by large areas of disturbed vegetation.

2) The sites are usually inaccessible by road and hence are protected from modern intrusion.

3) The potential search area is so vast that aerial reconnaissance is a necessity rather

than added luxury.

4) Aerial reconnaissance is 'timely'. There is nothing more impact-making than an idea whose time has come.

To quote E. Harp from Stringer and Cook (1974):

> If archaeologists will exploit this kind of interpretation in depth (i.e. aerial archaeology), proceeding logically from the macro levels of regional, natural topography towards the micro-levels of man's social and cultural activity, I am convinced that we can learn to read minimal signs of past human activity on the earth's surface. The most primitive and ancient traces may have been obscured, perhaps entirely obliterated, by physiographic processes, but short of drastic elimination, any cultural activity with social magnitude is likely to have altered the surficial environment and established a chain of unnatural effects that will long endure. And as long as these do persist, they will inevitably be reflected in remote sensing imagery. Ultimately, I suggest, we may penetrate to the stage of aboriginal, preliterate societies, perhaps even to prehistoric levels of Paleolithic culture.

A feature of the Alaskan archaeological sites is the lush tall grasses that grow over them. These grasses are believed to be related to:

1) disturbance of the original flora, 2) ground disturbance, 3) increased soil nutrients, 4) economic pattern of the inhabitants, 5) the period of occupancy, and 6) the technological development of the occupants.

In order to test the potential of aerial remote sensing over these Alaskan sites, Stringer and Cook (1974) selected a site known as Old Fish Camp on the Khotol River (Fig. 14.4) near Kaltag (De Laguna, 1947). Carbon–14 dating of artifacts from the site established its age at about 490 B.P.

The site was studied thoroughly on foot before aerial photography and satellite imagery were used. A sketch of the site is given in Fig. 14.5. Two transects of the site were carried out in order to establish the species composition and to recognize distinct vegetation communities from the air at a later date. The vegetation of a lateral transect across the site is shown in Table 14.1.

In 1972 and 1974, Stringer and Cook (1974) carried out aerial reconnaissance across the Old Fish Camp site using a light aircraft. Many oblique color shots were taken and used to obtain spectral signatures for several vegetation types. After the initial aerial photography, the area was scanned with vertical-incidence multiband photography. The channels involved were single-band black-and-white photography, color and infrared photography, and double-band thermal imagery. The color and infrared images were the principal means of determining vegetation signatures.

The next stage in the procedure was to obtain LANDSAT satellite images (see Chapter 11) and to determine which pixels (picture elements of about 0.4 ha in area) represented the various surface and vegetation types. For this purpose, the MSS bands 5,6 and 7 (see Chapter 11) were used. Table 14.2 shows reflectance levels for pixels representing a specific surface feature. It will be remembered from Chapter 11, that reflectance levels in satellite imagery are digitalized on a scale of 0–255 where zero represents zero reflectance and 255 is the highest value. The table shows probable archaeological sites (1–7) based on a combination of the features in the same table. When this system of classification was used to identify possible archaeological sites, 7890 (3%) of 262 144 pixels in a LANDSAT scene were identified as being "archaeological." The most frequent classification was 6 (1.6%) on the scale of 1–7 where 1 is the most probable, and 7 the least probable archaeological site.

Clearly most of these sites were not archaeological at all. It was possible, however, to reduce the number very considerably by considering the lifestyle of the people who were highly dependent on fishing and water transport.

In a survey over the terrain surrounding Old Fish Camp, it was possible to discard all but 19 of 379 possible archaeological sites in a scene covering 1152 km^2. Only one quarter of these would have been identified by high-resolution aerial photography. Of these 19 sites however, 5 of 12 situated along the Khotol River had previously been identified by De Laguna (1947).

Plate 14.4 shows an area of the Yukon River close to the village of Kaltag. The top part of the plate is the aerial photograph with the village and airstrip clearly shown at the extreme left of the photograph. The bottom part of the plate shows the spectral signatures of the surface features. Blank spaces indicate areas whose spectral signatures had not been determined in previous exploratory work over test areas such as at Old Fish Camp.

Along the east bank of the Yukon River there are several pixels representing archaeological village sites. Three areas of high probability have been delineated on the printout and are close to a site named Khaltag discovered in 1887 by Schwatka (1900).

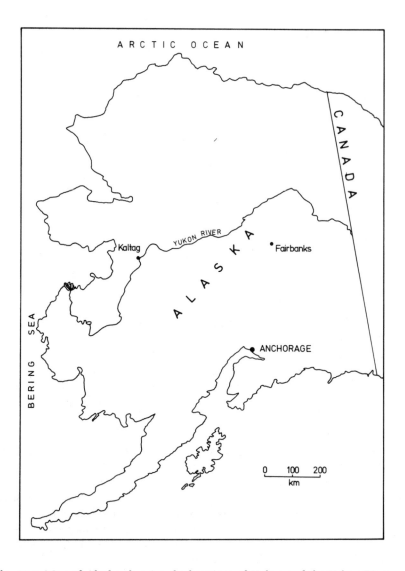

Fig. 14.4 Map of Alaska showing the locations of Kaltag and the Yukon River.

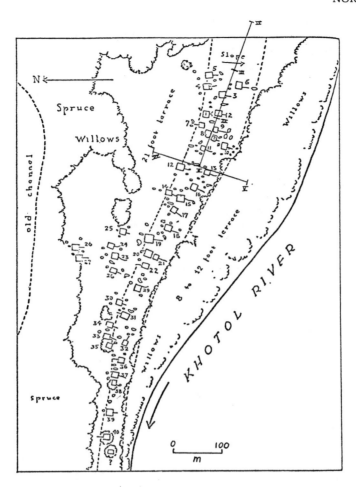

Fig. 14.5 Sketch of Old Fish Camp, Kaltag, Alaska. Source: De Laguna (1947).

TABLE 14.1 **Plant species recorded across a lateral transect (See Fig. 14.5) of Old Fish Camp, Kaltag, Alaska. Values expressed as % cover.**

Species	Station		
	V	I	VI
Polygonum alaskanum	1	15	0
Mertinisia paniculata	5	5	10
Calamagrostis canadensis	2	68	55
Echinopanax horridum	0	2	0
Rubus idaeus	10	2	5
Erysimum cheiranthoides	0	1	2
Galium boreale	0	2	0
Epilobium angustifolium	1	5	2
Salix sp.	40	0	10
Picea glauca	3	0	10
Betula sp.	0	0	5
Equisetum arvense	1	0	1
Populus balsamifera	37	0	0

Source: Stringer and Cook (1974).

TABLE 14.2   Code used for reflectance levels representing surface features of the Old Fish Camp area, Kaltag, Alaska. Pixels on satellite images were correlated with ground truth (see also Plate 14.4).

Symbol	Classification
1–7	Signatures characteristic of former archaeological sites. (1 = most probable, 7 = least probable)
K	Khotol Slough
L	Lake
Y	Yukon River
P	Stands of large spruce
T	Large trees (spruce, birch and aspen)
B	Bank of slough (average of slough and vegetation)
F	Vegetation characteristic of old burnt areas
X	Small black spruce, willow and grass
Z	Willows, grass and bare ground
Q	Water puddles, wet bare ground and grass
O	Bare grass
+	Submerged sand bar
*	Sand bar
.	Average of general vegetation, sandy bare ground and water

Source: Stringer and Cook (1974)

14.5   CHAPTER SUMMARY

This chapter, concerned with aerial phytoarchaeology in North America, details specific case histories in Oregon, Quebec, and Alaska. The work in Oregon was largely ethnographic (locating sites favorable for settlement, whether or not they were actually settled). Favorable sites for Paiute Indian settlement were identified at Glass Butte and Coffeepot Flat in Oregon.

Ethnographic work in the Richmond Gulf region of northeast Quebec revealed several sites favorable for Eskimo occupation, many of which contained archaeological remains and artifacts.

In Alaska, work was carried out over aboriginal sites at Kaltag near the Yukon river, using aerial photography and satellite imagery. Of 379 possible sites identified by aerial methods, only 19 were considered to be favorable after consideration of the lifestyles of the people and their dependence on fishing and water transport. Of these 19 sites, 5 were found to have been settled previously and to have archaeological remains.

REFERENCES

Aikens, C. M. Loy, W. E. G. Southard, M.D., and Hanes. R. C. 1980. *Remote Sensing, Suppl. #4.* National Park Service, Washington, D.C.

Bedwell, S. F. 1973. *Fort Rock Basin: Prehistory and Environment.* Univ. Oregon Press, Eugene.

Cressman, L. S. 1956. Klamath prehistory. *Trans. Am. Philosoph. Soc.* 46, Pt. 4:

Crawford, O. G. S., and Keiller, A. 1928. *Wessex from the Air.* Clarendon Press, Oxford.

De Laguna, F. 1947. The Prehistory of Northern North America as seen from the Yukon. *Mem. Soc. Am. Archaeol.* #3.

Harp, E. Jr. 1974. Threshold indicators of culture in air photo archaeology: In, E. Z. Vogt [ed.]

Aerial Photography in Anthropological Field Research. Harvard Univ. Press, Cambridge, Mass.

Howard, J. A., and Mitchell, C. W. 1985. *Phytogeomorphology.* Wiley, New York.

Kidder, A. V. 1930. Colonel and Mrs. Lindbergh aid archaeologists. *The Master Key* (January): 5–7.

Lyons, T. R., and Avery, T. E. 1977. *Remote Sensing: A Handbook for Archeologists and Cultural Research Managers.* National Park Service, Washington, D.C.

MacLean, R. A. 1923. The aeroplane and archaeology. *Am. J. Archaeol.* 27:68–69.

Rowe, J. H. 1953. Technical aids in anthropology: a historical survey. In, A. L. Kroeber [ed.] *Anthropology Today.* Univ. Chicago Press, Chicago.

Schoor, T. S. 1974. A bibliography with historical sketch. In, E. Z. Vogt [ed.] *Aerial Photography in Anthropological Field Research.* Harvard Univ. Press, Cambridge, Mass.

Schwatka, J. 1900. Compilation of narrative of exploration in Alaska. *Senate Rep. ±1023,* US Govt. Printing Office, Washington, D.C.

Stewart, O. C. 1939. The North Paiute Bands. *Univ. Calif. Anthrop. Rec.* 2: #3.

Stringer, W. J., and Cook, J. P. 1974. *Feasibility Study for Locating Archaeological Village Sites by Satellite Remote Sensing Techniques.* Tech. Rep. Geophysics Inst. Univ. Alaska, Fairbanks.

Vogt, E. Z. (ed.). 1974. *Aerial Photography in Anthropological Field Research.* Harvard Univ. Press, Cambridge, Mass.

Weyer, E. M., Jr. 1929. Exploring cliff dwellings with the Lindberghs. *Worlds Week,* (December): 52–57.

Chapter 15

AERIAL ARCHAEOLOGY IN CENTRAL AND SOUTH AMERICA

15.1 INTRODUCTION

One of the most notable of the early American pioneers of aerial archaeology was Charles Lindbergh. After his successful solo flight across the Atlantic in the late 1920s he turned his attention to North and Central America where he made several important discoveries. In collaboration with A. V.Kidder, he obtained backing from the Carnegie Institute to carry out an unsystematic aerial survey of the Yucatan Peninsula (Kidder, 1929, 1930a, 1930b; Ricketson and Kidder, 1949; Madeira, 1931; Mason, 1931). Although these early efforts were not very successful, they stimulated further aerial photography in Central and South America, principally in Peru (Johnson and Platt, 1930; Shippee, 1932a, 1932b; Ford and Willey, 1949; Schaedel, 1951; Willey. 1959; Kosok, 1965).

There has already been some mention in Chapter 14 of the field of ethnographic exploration. One of the first ethnographic studies in the New World was carried out by J.Rowe in the late 1940s (Rowe, 1953), when he photographed the region occupied by the Guambiano Indians near the town of Silvia, Department of Cauca, Colombia.

In Central America, the Harvard Chiapas Project, to quote Schorr (1974):

> ... got underway in 1956 (Vogt, 1969; Vogt and Romney, 1971) To the north, the Teotihuacan Valley Project together with the Teotihuacan Mapping Project, combining archaeology with ethnography, began in 1960 (Millon, 1964; Sanders, 1965) ... These projects included contract aerial reconnaissance, photogrammetry, cartography and photointerpretation by commercially-specialized firms, and provided opportunities for students of anthropology to receive training in the method and its techniques.

Several case histories of the use of aerial phytoarchaeology in Central and South America are described and discussed here; the locations of the sites mentioned are shown in Fig. 15.1.

15.2 AERIAL ARCHAEOLOGY IN CENTRAL AMERICA

15.2.1 The Yucatan Peninsula

The Yucatan Peninsula has been a favorite target of the aerial archaeologist since the pioneering days of Charles Lindbergh. A map of the peninsula together with principal Maya Classic Period (250–900 A.D.) sites is shown in Fig. 15.2.

The area has been surveyed by Adams (1980) who used radar imagery to "strip" the soil, water and vegetation from the land surface (see also Chapter 11). This revealed the presence of numerous canals around the city of Tikal (Fig. 15.3). It is debatable whether stripping the vegetation cover by radar is indeed a form of aerial phytoarchaeology, nevertheless, we believe its inclusion is justified, as this radar imagery drew attention to surface vegetational features that revealed the canals *per se*. The canals around Tikal and other cities in the Yucatan had been used to drain the swamps in order to use the sites for agriculture. It had previously been believed that the Maya had used a primitive slash-and-burn form of agriculture but this assumption did not tie in with the large populations of some of the Maya cities, for example, 50 000 at Tikal.

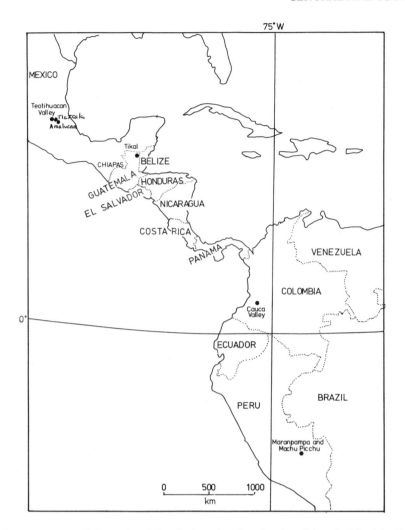

Fig. 15.1 Map of Central and South America showing localities cited in this chapter.

In his radar-assisted imagery of the Yucatan Peninsula, Adams (1980) suggested that the Maya of the Classic Period used a "drained-field" form of agriculture, similar to that of the Fenlands of East Anglia or the polders of the Netherlands. This would have supplied sufficient food for the large populations of the region.

Plate 15.1 shows the locality of an ancient canal system as revealed by the lusher vegetation growing above the feature. Although the vegetation pattern had been revealed after the radar imagery, there is no reason why the canals would not have been revealed by phytoarchaeology if the aerial explorers had known what to look for.

15.2.2 Ancient Canals and Mounds at Amalucan, Mexico

The town of Amalucan ("Place Found Near The Water") is situated near the ancient city of Teotihuacan in the Mexican state of Puebla (Fig. 15.1). The culture which colonized this site dates back to about 2500 B.P. and has been classified by Noguera (1945) as belonging to the Formative (Archaic) Period. The site has also been investigated by Fowler (1987) who discovered a Formative canal system on the valley floor (see also Fowler, 1968, 1969). The original discovery of the canal system was made by the observation of a dark line on a black-and white photograph taken in 1955. This dark line was due to the more luxuriant vegetation (crop mark) growing over the site of the ancient canals. The canal system intersects the larger of two burial/ceremonial mounds found over the site.

Low-oblique infrared photography (Plate 15.2) taken by Fowler (1987) revealed strong traces of the Formative canal system by crop marks in the agricultural land above the site. The key in Plate 15.2 shows details of the archaeological features later identified by ground truth established by digging and trenching. The purpose of the canal system apparently was to carry away runoff water. It has striking similarities with a similar system at Tlaxcala some 30 km to the northwest. The astonishing feature of this similarity is that the Amalucan site is 2000 years older than that at Tlaxcala. This shows that the formative people of the Puebla Valley had devised a very sophisticated adaptation to land use and reclamation and to water management.

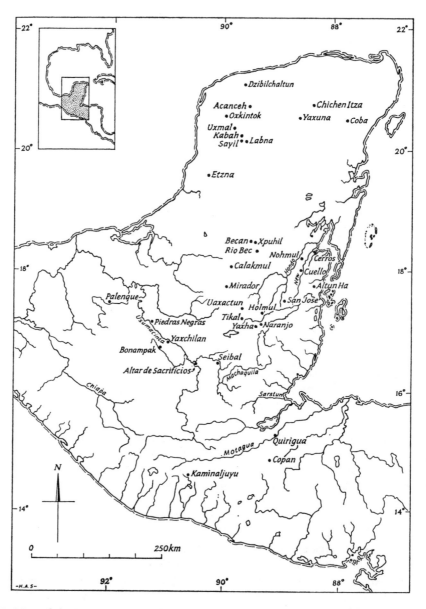

Fig. 15.2 Map of the Yucatan Peninsula, Mexico, showing location of Tikal and other sites of the Maya Classic Period (250–900 A.D.). Source: Adams (1980). By courtesy of the editor of *Antiquity*.

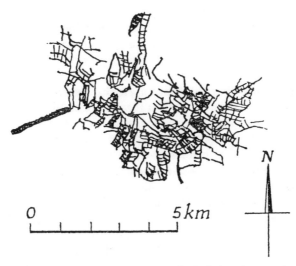

Fig. 15.3 Radar image of the region of the Maya city of Tikal showing canal systems. Source: Adams (1980). By courtesy of the editor of *Antiquity*.

15.3   AERIAL ARCHAEOLOGY IN SOUTH AMERICA

15.3.1   The Cauca Valley of Colombia

The Cauca Valley of Colombia (Fig. 15.1) was one of the first archaeological sites to be studied by North American aerial archaeologists (Rowe, 1953). As part of an ethnographic survey of the region, Schorr (1974) carried out aerial photography of the region in order to investigate the pattern of adaptive changes occurring among present-day descendants of the pre-Colombian inhabitants of the valley. The photographs identified Spanish-founded communities by clear grid systems of streets and central plazas with nearby civil and religious buildings. The pattern of pre-Columbian communities was revealed by veinlike tracings of trails and roadways bare of vegetation that followed the principal run-off channels and conformed to the topographic relief.

The riverside settlements were not static as those of the uplands. Major floods occurred on average once every 9 years, and when the settlements were rebuilt, their positions were changed to accommodate the changing course of the river. Some of the original field boundaries are still evident from crop marks and other changes in the vegetational patterns.

15.3.2   Machu Picchu

The Machu Picchu region of Peru is an area which has been studied more extensively than any other in South America. The ruins of Machu Picchu (Plate 15.3) are located on the eastern side of the Andes on the Cordillera Vilcabamba between the Urubamba and Apurimac rivers (13°09'S, 72°32'W) at an altitude of 2340 m.

The Machu Picchu site was first discovered by Hiram Bingham in 1911; he returned in 1912 and 1915 to clear the vegetation and draw a plan of the city (Bingham, 1930). Chohfi (1988) has used radiocarbon dating to establish the age of the Machu Picchu ruins at about 1000 B.C. for the first (pre-Inca) period of occupation and at about 1450 A.D. for the second (Inca) period.

The settlement pattern of the Machu Picchu region has been described by Chohfi (1988). Archaeological sites are primarily of agricultural, pastoral, and mixed character. They can be further subdivided into temporary and permanent sites. The sites cluster according to their ecological setting.

Sites located at ecotones such as at Machu Picchu played an administrative role. The agricultural sites are located on alluvial terrace configurations at the confluence of major rivers or near water sources. The pastoral sites are found within glacial valleys and near glacial lakes.

15.3.3 Aerial Phytoarchaeology over the Machu Picchu Region

A remote sensing project over the Machu Picchu region (Fig. 15.1) was carried out by Chohfi (1987a). Several remote sensing techniques were emphasized including:

1) LANDSAT satellite images (1973–1987), 2) SPOT satellite images (1987 and 1988), 3) SLAR radar images (1976), and 4) black-and-white photographs taken by SAN (Servicio Aerofotografico Nacional) of Peru. These methods were combined with field work on the ground in order to map archaeological sites, mainly from vegetational patterns. A flow chart for operations carried out by Chohfi (1987a) is given in Fig. 15.4.

Chohfi's work showed that the actual area of the Machu Picchu ruins is greater than was originally thought (Fig. 15.5). Some 94 new sites potentially of archaeological interest were mapped (Fig. 15.6), bringing the total to 138. These sites were determined from the typical signatures of pre-Hispanic settlement patterns and land use (Fig. 15.7). One of these sites (Maranpampa) was of particular significance as will be discussed further (15.3.4).

The results of the above surveys combined with the distribution of archaeological sites, showed that these sites cluster according to their type and to the ecological zones within the Machu Picchu region.

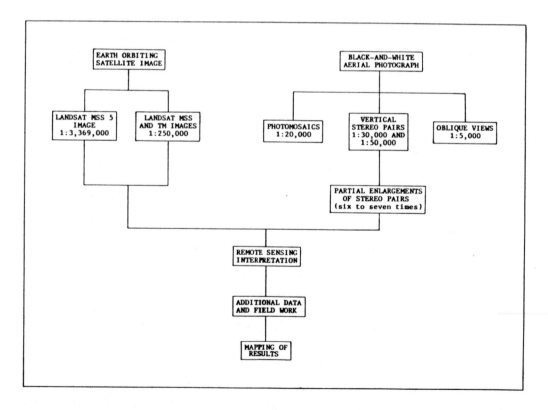

Fig. 15.4 Flow chart for remote sensing procedures carried out in the Machu Picchu region of Peru. Source: Chohfi (1987a). By courtesy of the author.

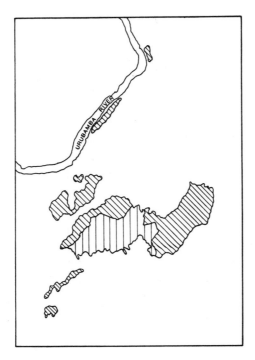

Fig. 15.5 Total extent of the Machu Picchu ruins. Vertical hatching indicates the original known area. Source: Chohfi (1987a). By courtesy of the author.

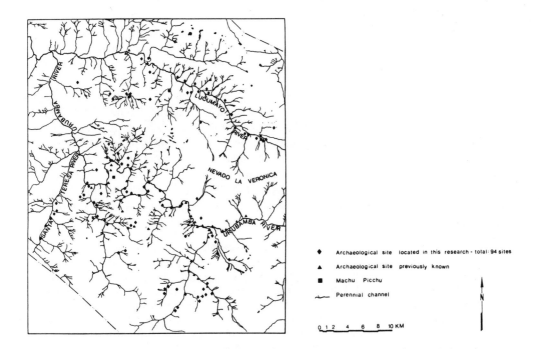

Fig. 15.6 Location of new and potentially archaeological sites in the Machu Picchu region. Source: Chohfi (1987a). By courtesy of the author.

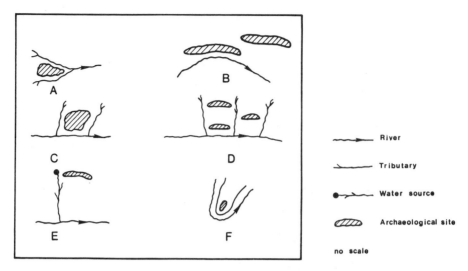

Fig. 15.7 Typical signatures of land use and topographic features near archaeological sites in the Machu Picchu region. Source: Chohfi (1987a). By courtesy of the author.

15.3.4 Maranpampa

One of the most spectacular phytoarchaeological discoveries of recent years is the settlement of Maranpampa near Machu Picchu (Chohfi, 1987b). Chohfi (1987c) concluded that Machu Picchu, perched on a rocky cliff, could not have had sufficient resources to grow the crops needed for its population and at the same time allow trading for other products, and must therefore have been supported by other nearby agricultural resources.

The area northeast of Machu Picchu (Fig. 15.8) initially attracted the attention of Chohfi (1987b) because of the patterns of vegetation seen in the aerial photographs (e.g. Plate 15.4). He was able to identify three very promising sites in the area later to be known as Maranpampa. These sites were located from the presence of 35 distinct signatures in the vegetation and topography. These signatures ranged in color from light to dark green. The light green represented land with very little native vegetation, the middle zone of color was a terrain of small trees and bushes, and the dark green represented a zone of tall trees.

On an enlarged scale, several distinct lineaments were visible in the vegetation cover over the site. Maranpampa was distinguished from its surroundings principally by a series of trees growing in a straight line and by several other rectilinear signatures. These linear features indicated buildings and agricultural terraces or walls.

In company with Octavio Fernandez of the Peruvian Instituto Nacional de Cultura (INC), Chohfi visited the Machu Picchu region for field reconnaissance. To quote from his paper (Chohfi, 1987b):

> We walked along the railroad that parallels the Urubamba River, to the Mamdor Farm. Mamdor Farm is located on a flood plain northeast of Machu Picchu at an altitude of 1650 m. We saw a young girl who showed us an abandoned trail—a short cut. It took us another two hours to hack our way through the dense vegetation alive with mosquitos, snakes and other vermin, and climb to the alluvial terrace at 1900 m. There we found archaeological evidence which was well exposed and easily identifiable. Our exploration was limited to the eastern 10% of the site shown in the aerial photograph. The western area by the Urubamba River was not surveyed.
>
> The following features were uncovered: two mortars with a single cup, one

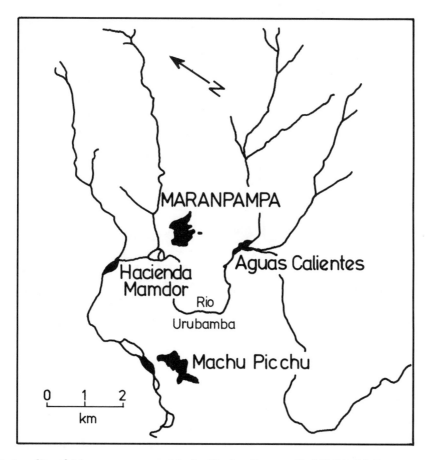

Fig. 15.8 Locality of Maranpampa near Machu Picchu. Source: Chohfi (1987b). By courtesy of the author.

grinding stone, a mortar with two cups and pottery sherds, walls 1.1 m high resembling agricultural terraces, a massive wall 3.5 m high, 2.8 m. thick, and at least 250 m long, remains of two rectangular rooms, 2.8 × 4 m built of granite on terraces, as well as several carefully-cut rectangular granite blocks. A thick layer of black humus, the topsoil, covered much of the site. No archaeological excavation was carried out.

Maranpampa may have been important because of its abundance of wood, water, and good topsoil on a gentle slope. It could have been Machu Picchu's production site, situated on the right bank of the Urubamba River. There is little doubt that the two sites were connected in the past, possibly by a bridge spanning a narrow gorge, about 50 m across. The direct distance between the two sites is only 1.6 km.

On our way back, we discussed a possible name for the site. We settled on *Maranpampa*—combination of two Quechua words meaning 'a level field with mortars' (*maran* = mortar; *pampa* = level field with good soil). INC was informed about this find in a written report two days after the field survey was completed. The INC will oversee all future research at the site.

A sketch of linear features observed at Maranpampa is shown in Fig. 15.9. Maranpampa remains one of the most significant phytoarchaeological discoveries of recent times. When it is explored in detail, it will surely shed further light on the mysteries of the Inca civilization that disappeared so quickly and so dramatically after the arrival of the conquistadores.

Fig. 15.9 Linear features observed in the vegetation above Maranpampa. Source: Chohfi (1987b). By courtesy of the author.

15.4 CHAPTER SUMMARY

This chapter describes aerial archaeology in Central and South America. In the Yucatan Peninsula, radar imagery has revealed the presence of numerous canals near the Maya city of Tikal. This is an example of negative aerial phytoarchaeology (i.e., "stripping" the vegetation from the surface using radar). The canals were later shown to have a more luxuriant vegetation, once their presence had been highlighted by radar.

At Amalucan in Puebla State, Mexico, the presence of burial sites and ancient Formative Culture canals has been revealed by crop marks in agricultural fields near the ancient city of Teotihuacan.

Among several aerial archaeological studies in South America, particular mention must be made of a recent significant discovery near the ancient Inca city of Machu Picchu in Peru. An ancient city now named Maranpampa, located only a few kilometers from Machu Picchu, was recognized by linear features on aerial photographs of the forest cover. These features were linked to boundary walls and the foundations of buildings.

REFERENCES

Adams, R. E. W. 1980. Swamps, canals and the locations of ancient Maya cities. *Antiquity* 54: 206–212.

Bingham, H. 1930. *Machu Picchu, a Citadel of the Incas.* Yale Univ. Press, New Haven.

Chohfi, R. E. 1987a. Remote sensing of the Machu Picchu region, Peru: an interdisciplinary approach. *Proc II Latin Am. Rem. Sens. Symp.* 1987, Bogota, 35 pp.

_____ 1987b. Maranpampa: its discovery and significance. *Backdirt* (Newsl. Inst. Archaeol. Univ. Calif. Los Angeles) 1: 1–3.

_____ 1987c. Maranpampa: the discovery of a lost city. *Architect. of Planning* (Univ. Calif. Los Angeles Grad. Sch. Architect. Urb. Planning), (Fall): 2–3.

_____ 1988. Radiocarbon dating of Machu Picchu. *Radiocarbon J.* (In press).

Ford, J. A., and Willey, G. R. 1949. Surface features of the Viru Valley, Peru. *Anthrop, Pap. Am. Mus. Nat. Hist.* 43: #1.

Fowler, M. L. 1968. *Un Sistema Preclasico de Distribucion de Agua en la Zona Arqueologica de Amalucan, Puebla.* Inst. Poblano de Antropologia e Historia. Puebla, Mexico.

_____ 1969. A Preclassic water distribution system in Amalucan, Mexico. *Archaeology* 22: 208–215.

_____ 1987. Early water management at Amalucan, State of Puebla, Mexico. *Nat. Geogr. Res.* 3: 52–68.

Johnson, G. R., and Platt, R. R. 1930. Peru from the Air. *Am. Geogr. Soc. Spec. Pub.* #12.

Kidder, A. V. 1929. Air exploration of the Maya country. *Bull. Pan-Am. Un.*: 12–1205.

_____ 1930a. Colonel and Mrs. Lindbergh aid archaeologists. *The Masterkey* (January): 5–17.

_____ 1930b. Five days over the Maya country. *Scient. Monthl* (March): 193–205.

Kosok, P. 1965. *Life, Land and Water in Ancient Peru.* Long Island University Press, New York.

MacLean, R. A. 1923. The aeroplane and archaeology. *Am. J. Archaeol.* 27: 68–69.

Madeira, P. C. Jr. 1931. An aerial expedition to Central America. *Philad. Mus. J.* 22: 95–153.

Mason, J. A. 1931. The air survey in Central America. *Philad. Mus. Bull.* 2: 73–75, 78–79.

Millon, R. 1964. The Teotihuacan mapping project. *Am. Antiq.* 29: 345–352.

Noguera, E. 1945. Excavaciones en el estado de Puebla. *Anal. INAH* (Austin) 1: 31–75.

Ricketson, O. G. Jr., and Kidder, A. V. 1930. An archaeological reconnaissance by air in Central America. *Geogr. Rev.* 20: 177–206.

Rowe, J. H. 1953. Technical aids in anthropology: a historical survey. In, A. L. Kroeber [ed.]. *Anthropology Today.* Univ. Chicago Press, Chicago, 895–940.

Sanders, W. J. 1965. *The Cultural Ecology of the Teotihuacan Valley.* Spec. Rep. Penn. State. Univ. University Park, Pennsylvania.

Schaedel, R. P. 1951. Lost cities of Peru. *Scient. Am.* 185: 18–23.

Schorr, T. S. 1974. A bibliography and historical sketch. In, E. Z. Vogt [ed.]. *Aerial Photography in Anthropological Field Research.* Harvard Univ. Press, Cambridge, Massachusetts.

Shippee, R. 1932a. Great Wall of Peru and other aerial photographic studies by the Shippee-Johnson Peruvian expedition. *Geogr. Rev.* 22: 1–29.

_____ 1932b. Lost valley of Peru: results of the Shippee-Johnson Peruvian expedition. *Geogr. Rev.,* 22: 562–581.

Vogt, E. Z. 1969. Chiapas Highlands. In, R. Wauchope [ed.] *Handbook of Middle American Indians,* v.7. Univ. Texas Press, Austin 133–151.

Vogt, E. Z., and Romney, A. K. 1971. The use of aerial photographic techniques in Maya ethnography. *Proc. 7th Int. Congr. Anthrop. Ethnogr. Sciences, Moscow,* 1964, 2: 156–171.

Willey, G. R. 1959. Aerial photographic maps as survey aids in the Viru Valley. In, R. F. Heizer [ed.] *The Archaeologist at Work.* Harper Row, New York. pp. 203–207.

Chapter 16
AERIAL ARCHAEOLOGY IN OCEANIA

16.1 AERIAL ARCHAEOLOGY IN AUSTRALIA

16.1.1 The Peopling of Australia

Australia and New Zealand have had very different patterns of human settlement. Man reached Australia much earlier than New Zealand which was only colonized about 1000 years ago.

In Pleistocene times the whole of southeast Asia (Sundaland) was essentially one land mass due to the lower sea levels at that time, caused by locking up of vast amounts of ice in the polar ice caps. This land mass may have been separated from what is now Australia (Sahul Shelf) by only a narrow area of sea. The climate of the Sundaland-Sahul mass was much less humid than today, and the terrain was covered with tropical savanna, an environment favorable to Early man who was a creature of the savanna rather than the forest.

The Australian aborigines arrived by canoe or raft across the narrow seas separating the Sahul Shelf from Sundaland. They brought with them the dingo (domesticated dog) which later became feral in Australia.

The aborigines were not agriculturalists and since the new territory contained no animals suitable for herding, they existed by food gathering and hunting. These activities were limited by distance from fresh water. As their numbers increased, subgroups set out to discover other sources of water. Trade routes indicate the direction of the migrations.

When Australia was settled by Europeans in 1788, the aboriginal population was estimated at about 350 000. Archaeological finds indicate an original settlement at about 40 000 B.P.

Hallam (1985) has discussed various theories accounting for the peopling of Australia and has summarized the following models:

1) The first (static) theory (Bowdler, 1981) envisages settlement at the moist margins of the country and little change thereafter.

2) The second (dynamic) theory (Horton, 1981 Jones, 1969) envisages a movement of populations under climatic and other environmental changes.

3) A third theory (Birdsell, 1953) suggests that population density was proportional to rainfall, with densities lowest in the arid center of the territory. It is suggested that there was a limited fanwise spread bringing populations up to the carrying capacity of the land.

4) A fourth theory (Hallam, 1985) proposes that the high aborigine population of the coastal rim was a result of amelioration of environmental conditions by human activities such as the opening up of the coastal forests by burning, and hence converting them to the savanna favored by the aborigines.

Although the physical remains of this hunter-gatherer society are both few and small in area, they have not been destroyed to any great extent by European colonization. This is due to the sparse population of Australia, and is in marked contrast to Europe where dense populations have destroyed much of the archaeological past. Australia is clearly the world's most favorable locality for archaeological research into hunter-gatherer societies.

16.1.2 The History of Aerial Archaeology in Australia

Over 30 years ago Mulvaney (1964) observed features in Australia that he considered could be revealed by aerial photography as easily as had been those in Britain. His comments were to some extent motivated by the writings of McPherson (1884) who observed from a train window that:

... owing to the drought... the green mantle of grass had disappeared, leaving the black patches of the oven-mounds very easily distinguishable from the bare surface of the soil.

Some of the earliest photographs of archaeological sites were taken by McBryde (1962) and Webster (1962) when photographing a prehistoric quarry near Tamworth, New South Wales. The first systematic aerial archaeology was undertaken by G. Connah who surveyed an area in New South Wales (Connah, 1978). This early work demonstrated that aerial photography could be used to identify and evaluate sites of both historic (early European) and prehistoric (aboriginal) significance.

In collaboration with A.Jones, Connah carried out a far more ambitious program of aerial archaeology during the period 1980–1982. This project has been reported by Connah and Jones (1983), in a work which is the source for much of the material in this chapter.

The early work by G. Connah consisted mainly of oblique photography using a hand-held camera focused through an open window. In 1979, A. Jones joined the expeditions and photographs were made with a hand-held 70 mm Hasselblad camera and also with vertically-mounted Vinten cameras. The geographical coverage of this and other work is shown in Fig. 16.1.

The main hurdle that Connah had to surmount in obtaining funding for his work was the widely-held belief that prehistoric aborigines, being hunter-gatherers, would have left no traces of their occupation of the land. It is true that primitive communities would have left fewer traces of their culture than advanced European communities, but it is also true that sparsely-populated Australia has had fewer archaeological sites destroyed by urban development.

Fig. 16.1 Map of Australia showing sites mentioned in the text.

Many of the permanent structures left behind by aborigines were stone or earth monuments of ceremonial significance such as bora rings (ceremonial earthworks), or more practical structures such as stone fish traps. These were semicircular stone walls built around the shore so that fish were trapped with the falling tide. None of these structures, however, bears a specific vegetative cover and will not be considered further.

One of the main problems with aerial archaeology in Australia is the very small size of aboriginal prehistoric remnants, a problem illustrated somewhat whimsically in Fig. 16.2. The use of helicopters rather than fixed-wing aircraft would seem to be the answer To this problem. For example, Walsh (1981) has been able to photograph aboriginal rock shelters actually inside the Carnarvon Gorge in Queensland by use of a helicopter.

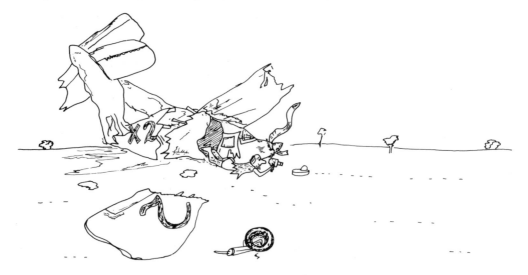

Fig. 16.2 Cartoon illustrating the problems of aerial photography of small archaeological features in Australia. Reproduced by courtesy of J. Urry, Wellington, New Zealand.

There are two types of vegetation-related structures that can be detected by aerial photography in Australia. These are: areas bare of vegetation such as ancient tracks and quarries, and areas of luxuriant vegetation such as above shell middens where the high lime content of the soil has favored plant growth.

Both types of structure will now be described.

16.1.3 Shell Middens in Australia

The discovery of aboriginal shell middens in Australia is largely due to the work of Connah (1978) and Connah and Jones (1983). The former carried out extensive work in New South Wales (Fig. 16.3). The Clybucca 3 site (Plate 16.1 and location 7 in Fig. 16.3) in northern New South Wales (Connah, 1978):

> . . . is situated on a former shoreline some 10 km inland from the present shoreline. This midden consists of oysters and cockles and dates from 3500–5000 B.P. The site excavated by myself (Connah, 1975), contains indications that prehistoric man actually camped on the midden. In the photograph the midden shows clearly due to the presence of different vegetation from the surrounding area. In the left foreground is part of the drained swamp which was formerly the edge of the sea, and behind and to the right of the midden rises a former coastal peninsula. Between this old landform and the midden lies a small body of water surrounded by white-trunked paper-bark trees (*Melaleuca* sp.). A windmill and circular water trough are situated near the left extremity of the midden.

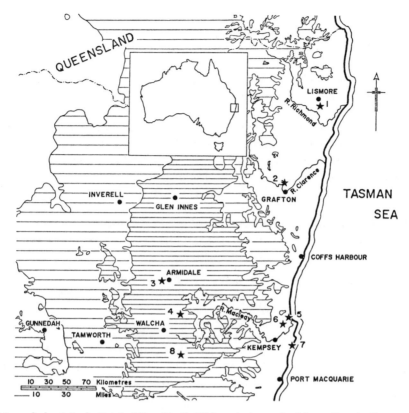

Fig. 16.3 Map of aboriginal sites in New South Wales photographed from the air. Source: Connah (1978). By courtesy of the editor of *Antiquity*.

The Stuarts Point Midden (Plate 16.2 and location 6 in Fig. 16.3, Connah, 1978) is:

> . . . an even more remarkable midden. This oyster and cockle midden runs for some 2.5 km and is in places 2 m high. It is situated near a former estuary of the River Macleay, on the inner edge of a former coastal sand barrier which has now been separated from the sea by a salt-water lagoon. Excavations have provided a radiocarbon date for the lower part of the midden of over 9000 B.P. (Connah, 1976). Excavated hearths indicate that man camped on the midden from time to time. In the aerial photograph (Plate 16.2), the foreground is occupied by a partly-drained swamp and a narrow belt of trees grows immediately in front of the midden itself. . . . Beyond the midden, the old sand barrier is fairly heavily timbered and the edge of the present lagoon is just visible at the top of the photograph.

16.1.4 Aboriginal Features Denuded of Vegetation

The proposition that absence of vegetation as opposed to an unusual vegetation cover is a valid category of phytoarchaeology, leads us to consider a number of aboriginal structures in Australia revealed by this absence of plant growth.

A prominent feature of aboriginal culture was the erection of ceremonial stone arrangements whose true purpose is not fully understood. Because these stony trackways provide an environment unfavorable to vegetation, particularly in an arid environment, they are prominent among the surrounding and more luxuriant plant growth. An example of this has been shown by Connah and Jones (1983) at the Pindera Downs near Tibooburra (Fig. 16.1). This feature (Plate 16.3) is 38 m long.

Another example of negative phytoarchaeology is provided by soil marks left behind after drought had stripped the vegetation cover. This is a peculiar feature of the Australian environment where drought can be so severe as to leave virtually no vegetation. In Europe by contrast, such conditions are seldom encountered. Plate 16.4 shows a prehistoric oven mound at Glenhope Mound near Hay, New South Wales (Fig. 16.1) revealed by soil marks on a drought-stripped landscape (Connah and Jones, 1983). This low-level oblique shot was taken from an altitude of 250 m.

A third example of negative phytoarchaeology is the presence of quarry sites whose excavations have covered the ground with rocky debris unfavorable for plant growth. Aboriginal quarries were usually situated at existing outcrops and as such are difficult to pinpoint. Nevertheless, Connah and Jones (1983) were able to find several such localities such as at Moondarah (Plate 16.5) near Mt. Isa in Queensland (Fig. 1).

16.1.5 Conclusions Concerning Aerial Archaeology in Australia

It is appropriate to quote from Connah and Jones (1983) in order to summarize the role of aerial photography in archaeology in Australia:

> It is clear from our work, that aerial photography of Australian historical sites is just as useful as aerial photography of historical sites in Britain or western Europe. Aerial photography of Australian prehistoric sites, however, raises problems about the application of aerial archaeology to hunter-gatherer sites that seem not to have been adequately investigated elsewhere in the world and which can be very suitably studied in Australia. We find that the ceremonial earthworks known as *bora rings,* the larger examples of stone arrangements, fish traps, oven-mounds and perhaps shell middens and quarries are susceptible to aerial study. On the other hand, rock shelters, open settlement sites, burial sites and art sites are rather less suitable subject matter . . . The situation is complicated, however, by the nature of the ground surface and of its vegetational cover. For example in the arid and semi-arid plains of western New South Wales, one can see things from the air that become invisible in the wooded hilly country of the eastern seaboard. Indeed quite minor variations in surface cover can drastically affect the extent to which sites are visible. Also the small size of many prehistoric features is a very real problem that will probably be solved only by the use of helicopters. . . . there must be many thousands of prehistoric sites scattered over the huge continent of Australia that would be worthy of aerial archaeological study. If such study is not attempted soon . . . it may mean that Australians will miss a unique opportunity of world-wide significance to investigate hunter-gatherer sites from the air.

16.2   AERIAL ARCHAEOLOGY IN NEW ZEALAND

16.2.1   The Peopling of New Zealand

New Zealand (Fig. 16.4) represents the southernmost limit of Polynesian expansion some 1000 years B.P. The main wave of immigrants arrived from from the Pacific Islands (probably Tahiti) in the mid 14th century in what is now known as the Great Fleet. The earlier original inhabitants were known as the Tangata Whenua (People of the Land) and were descended from Toi-Kai-Rakau, a Polynesian immigrant of about 1150 A.D. The newcomers gradually overcame the early settlers by warfare and intermarriage and these newcomers brought with them the kumara (sweet potato), taro, yam, and other cultivated plants. Like the Australian aborigines, they also brought their dogs, and a native rat known as kiore.

The natives, now known as Maoris, lived in villages (kainga) usually protected by a fort (pa) nearby. In the north of New Zealand the warmer climate and suitable soil allowed for the cultivation of the kumara, the main source of starch. On the coast, the main source of protein

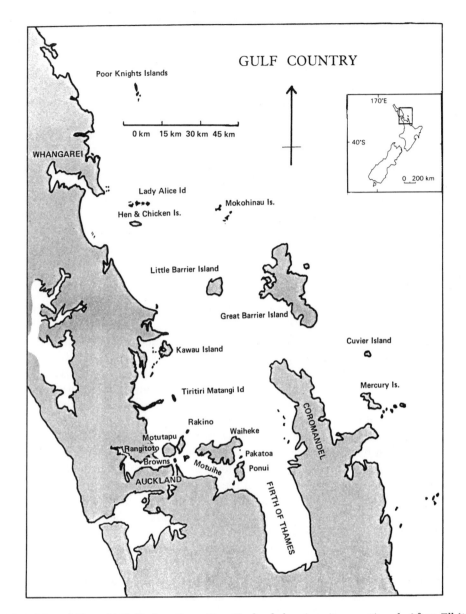

Fig. 16.4 Map of Hauraki Gulf of northern New Zealand showing sites mentioned. After: Ell (1982). By permission of the author.

was fish, but inland snared birds and native rats were the main source of meat.

Unlike the aborigines of Australia, the early Maoris were not purely a hunter-gatherer society. They were agriculturalists and, as such, formed permanent settlements throughout New Zealand.

16.2.2 Maori Fortifications

The Maori colonists of New Zealand left behind numerous relics of their occupation of the land. The most prominent of these was the fortification (pa) which protected the local villages and fields. According to Ell (1985) there were some 5500 of these pas in North Island and a further 100 or so in the more sparsely-settled South Island.

Since the human history of New Zealand is very short, perhaps 1000 years, there has not been sufficient time for early Maori settlements and relics to be covered with soil (which accumulates at a mean rate of Perhaps 25 mm per century). These Maori relics are therefore not revealed by crop marks as in western Europe, but are evident mainly from shadow marks in aerial photographs, or on foot from the ground.

Plate 16.6 shows an aerial photograph of Mt. Eden (Maungawhau Pa) situated in the center of Auckland, New Zealand's largest city. The terraces and trenches are extremely well preserved.

The purpose of the pa was twofold: to protect the two most valuable possessions of the tribe, its women and its food supply. The circle of walls enclosed a citadel (tihi) where the chief and his daughters lived. The less fortunate members of the tribe lived outside the walls of the pa, among the gardens or surrounding hillsides.

The early pas were constructed mainly of wood. However, when contact was made with Europeans at the end of the 18th century, the advent of the musket, used for intertribal warfare as well as for fighting the Europeans, enforced a radical change of design of the pas. They were now surrounded by a ring of trenches as used in World War I.

16.2.3 The Kumara

Very little aerial phytoarchaeology has been carried out in New Zealand because most sites are so well delineated by historical records. There is, however, one vegetational feature that can be recognized from aerial photography. This is the kumara pit.

When the early Polynesians arrived in New Zealand, they brought with them tubers of the kumara or sweet potato (Ipomoea batatas), a staple item of diet in the Pacific Islands. The kumara was a key element in Polynesian culture, though its origin was in South America, and its cultivation in New Zealand forced the Maoris to remain in more-or-less static communities. A relatively fixed abode, and regular supply of food gave more time for arts and crafts, and resulted in the development of the "Classic" Maori culture expressed in ornate carvings and hand woven garments. When these settlers first attempted to grow kumaras in their new homeland, they found that they would not survive the frosts of winter except in a few favored localities. They soon discovered, however, that kumaras could be stored underground and the protected stock replanted in the spring. Storage was carried out in kumara pits dug to a depth of about 2 m. These pits were oblong in shape (Plate 16.7) and were covered with a roofing of bark of the (Podocarpus totara), or thatch of the nikau palm (Rhopalostylis sapida). Their temperature never fell below the critical 11°C below which the tubers would not remain edible and below which the seeds would not survive for the spring planting.

The roofing of disused kumara pits soon collapsed and filled with loose soil and water over which a more luxuriant vegetation, rich in rushes (Juncus, sp.) grew and served to identify the position of these pits. These are readily identifiable in aerial photographs of pa sites where they tend to occupy the highest points of the structures (Plate 16.6).

16.2.4 Early Polynesian Gardens

There was only one place in New Zealand where the kumara would grow the whole year round without storage. This was at Tamawera Pa on Great Mercury Island. Growth of the kumara was encouraged by dividing the fields by a series of stone walls at right angles to the contours of the hillsides. The purpose of the walls was twofold: to mark ownership of individual fields, and to produce a microclimate of warmth from the heat of the sun radiated from the stones. These stone structures are illustrated in Plate 16.8. They have been C-14 dated at about 1000 B.P. Like the ceremonial structures of the Australian aborigines, the walls are an example of "negative phytoarchaeology." Though mainly low in elevation, they have not permitted the growth of vegetation and are as prominent today as they were 1000 years ago.

The Maoris did not grow only kumara. They brought with them the taro and yam from

Polynesia and cultivated native plants where they could. A special mention must here be made of the karaka tree (*Corynocarpus laevigatus*). This bears a golden fruit whose flesh is edible and whose kernel is highly poisonous, though it can be treated to render it edible. The golden fruit was eaten by the Maoris and more importantly, attracted the native pigeon and other birds that were then readily snared. The orchards, often planted by the Maoris around their pas are readily recognizable from the air because they were often planted in straight lines rather than haphazardly. A typical karaka plantation near a Maori settlement is illustrated in Plate 16.9.

Aerial photographs of high quality are available for the whole of New Zealand, but they have not, as yet, been used very much of phytoarchaeological purposes. There is the potential use of finding as yet undiscovered sites through the subtle approach of examination of vegetational anomalies.

16.3 AERIAL ARCHAEOLOGY IN FIJI

16.3.1 Pre-European Ring-ditch Sites

Several important aerial phytoarchaeological studies have been carried out in Fiji (Fig. 16.5) by J. T. Parry (Parry, 1977, 1979, 1982, 1984).

At the time of the first contact with Europeans at the beginning of the 19th century, Viti Levu (the main island of the Fijian Group) supported a dense population of Melanesians who occupied circular fortified villages surrounded by a ring-ditch system. These fortifications served as a defense against surprise attack. They were not designed for a long siege as the attackers usually withdrew when the first assault failed. Around the settlements were gardens of the giant swamp taro (*Cyrstosperma chamissonis*), the staple food crop. The Rewa delta (Fig. 16.5) contained several large settlements and cultivated areas and was notorious

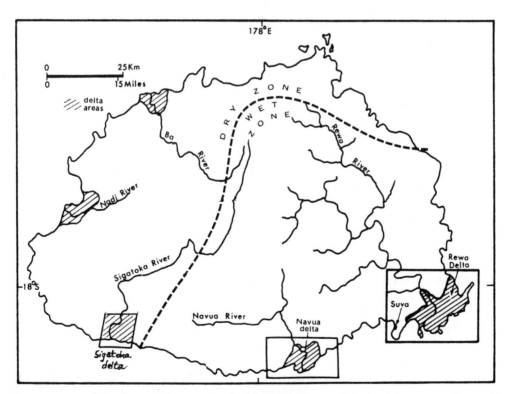

Fig. 16.5 Map of Viti Levu, the largest island of the Fijian Group, showing delta areas with extensive ring-ditch fortifications and taro gardens. Source: Parry (1984). By courtesy of the editor of the *New Zealand Journal of Archaeology*.

for the almost continuous local warfare which led to even more elaborate fortifications around the larger settlements. The labour for the construction of these fortifications was usually derived from subject peoples who carried out the work as a form of tribute to their conquerors.

Plate 16.10 shows a typical ring ditch fortification at Vewara, Nadi Bay, Vanua Levu. It is based on a painting by J. G. Wilson made during a visit by HMS "Herald" in 1856. Fig. 16.6 shows a plan of one of these structures with a circular water-filled ditch surrounding an inner palisade erected on top of the inner bank of the ditch. Access to the enclosure was effected by a causeway in the form of a narrow earthen bank leading to gateways in the fence. In some cases the ditch was continuous and access was provided by logs of coconut that served as a drawbridge that could be removed when the settlement was under attack.

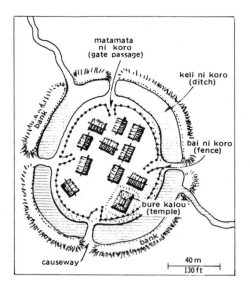

Fig. 16.6 Plan of ring-ditch fortification of Viti Levu, Fiji. Source: Parry (1984). By courtesy of the editor of the *New Zealand Journal of Archaeology*.

In air photograph analysis of ring-ditch systems, Parry (1977, 1982) studied over 600 aerial shots of the Navua and Sigatoka deltas (Fig. 16.5). Although many of the structures were identified by shadow marks, there were several whose presence was indicated only by crop and vegetation marks at different seasons of the year (Plate 16.11; Parry, 1984). The upper photograph was taken in March 1966 and clearly shows ring-ditch fortifications (designated by white arrows to the left of the plate). The lower photograph, taken in January 1973, shows no sign of the structures due to changes in the vegetation cover and a different season of the year.

Using crop marks and other vegetational changes such as the presence or absence of forest, and other variables such as relief and moisture status of the terrain, Parry (1984) was able to show that differences in the vegetation signatures could be used to detect traces of human occupation dating back to the 18th century. For earlier dates, the signatures became indistinct due to the re-establishment of the climax vegetation.

16.3.2 Pre-European Gardens

The swamps of the Fijian deltas were a valuable source of food for the early Melanesian inhabitants of the area. In limited well-drained areas it was possible to grow yams, plantains, and several tree crops. However, over most of the terrain, conditions precluded cultivation of all except hygrophilous plants such as the giant swamp taro

Cyrstosperma chamissonis. The taro, known locally as via kau or via kana, was preferred because of its flavor. It is one of the ancient plants of the Indo-Pacific region and has an extensive range in Melanesia and western Polynesia.

The taro gardens, known as *vuci* by the Melanesians, were abandoned after the European conquest. In the traditional method of cultivation, the vuci were prepared by creating a number of small plots separated by ditches. The effect of ditching was to raise the level of these plots, and the material extracted from these ditches helped To maintain their fertility. The raised fields also helped in the harvesting of the tubers which could weigh as much as 40–80 kg.

The Pre-European vuci are difficult to identify from the ground because of infilling of the ditches with grasses, guavas and other vegetation. They can, however, be readily detected from aerial photographs because of the darker tones of the ditches, resulting from the denser growth of shrubs and grasses in these damper localities.

Two types of pattern are found in these aerial photographs (Plate 16.12). These are of the reticulated type (left of plate) and gridiron form (right of plate). It is significant that the gridiron type of field is found elsewhere in the world, notably in Colombia (San Jorge River), Bolivia (Llanos de Mojos), Mexico (Lake Texcoco), and in New Guinea.

As emphasized by Parry (1984), the significance of the via as a staple food crop of the Melanesians of Fiji can be judged by the occurrence of the word as a component of several place names in the area such as Koronivia, Tumavia, and Natavia, and also by the practice of referring to the people of the area as the *bata via*. The work of Parry in showing the application of aerial phytoarchaeology to the study of this highly specialized and labour-intensive agricultural system is a particularly good example of the value of this aerial technique.

16.4 CHAPTER SUMMARY

This chapter is concerned with aerial archaeology in Australia, New Zealand, and Fiji. Although the Australian aborigines were a hunter-gatherer society, they did leave some permanent traces of their occupancy of the land. These include shell middens in New South Wales, readily identified by aerial photography due to their specific calciphile plant community. Other aboriginal remains can be identified by negative phytoarchaeological features such as *bora rings* and stone trackways, both of ceremonial significance. Aboriginal quarry sites can also be identified from negative features.

In New Zealand, Maori fortifications (*pas*) can be identified from shadow marks and unusual plant communities over *kumara pits* (food stores). Early Polynesian gardens in New Zealand have been identified from lines of stones serving to radiate heat and forming boundaries of plots. Maori settlements are also visible from the air by straight lines of the karaka (*Corynocarpus laevigatus*) planted near settlements to attract the native pigeons and render them easier to capture.

In Fiji, there are numerous precolonial ring ditch sites serving as fortifications. These have been identified from shadow marks and crop marks by photographs taken at different times of the year. Native gardens known as *vuci* were demarcated by ditches which have since filled in. These former ditches support a more luxuriant vegetation due to the higher water status of the soils, and can readily be identified by aerial photography.

REFERENCES

Birdsell, J. B. 1953. Some environmental and cultural factors influencing the structure of the Australian aboriginal population. *Amer. Naturalist* 87: 171–207.

Bowdler, S. 1981. Hunters in the highlands: aboriginal adaptations in the eastern Australian uplands. *Archaeol. in Oceania* 16: 99–111.

Connah, G. 1975. Current research at the Department of Prehistory and Archaeology, University of New England. *Austral. Archaeol.* 3: 28–31.

_____ 1975. Archaeology at the University of New England 1975–76. *Austral. Archaeol.* 5: 1–6.

_____ 1978. Aborigine and settler: archaeological air photography. *Antiquity* 52: 95–99.

Connah, G., and Jones, A. 1983. Aerial archaeology in Australia. *Aerial Archaeol.* 9: 1–30.

Ell, G. 1982. *Wild Islands.* Bush Press, Auckland.

_____ 1985. *Shadows over the Land.* Bush Press, Auckland.

Hallam, S. J. 1985. The tropical peopling of temperate Australia: coastal colonization or savannah spread ? *Proc. ANZAAAS Conf. August 1988:* 27 pp.

Horton, D. R. 1981. Water and woodland: the peopling of Australia. *Austral. Inst. Aborig. Stud. Newslett.* 16: 21–27.

Jones, R. 1969. Firestick farming. *Austral. Nat. Hist.* 16: 224–228.

McBryde, I. 1962. Archaeological field survey work in northern New South Wales. *Oceania* 33: 12–17.

McPherson, P. 1884. The oven-mounds of the aborigines in Victoria. *J. Proc. Roy. Soc. N.S.W.* 18: 49–59.

Mulvaney, D. J. 1964. Prehistory of the basalt plains. *Proc. Roy. Soc. Vict.* 77: 427–432.

Parry, J. T. 1977. Ring-ditch fortifications in the Rewa delta: air photo interpretation and analysis. *Bull. Fiji. Mus.* #3, 90 pp.

_____ 1979. Pre-European ring-ditch fortifications and taro gardens in the Rewa delta, Viti Levu, Fiji. *Rev. Photo Interpret.* #3: 47–50.

_____ 1982. Ring-ditch fortifications in the Navua delta, Fiji: air photo interpretation and analysis. *Bull. Fiji Mus.* #7: 84 pp.

_____ 1984. Air photo interpretation of fortified sites: ring-ditch fortifications in southern Viti Levu. *N.Z. J. Archaeol.* 6: 71–93.

Walsh, G. 1981. Site location by helicopter in Queensland's central highlands. *Austral. Inst. Aborig. Stud. Newslett.* 15: 73–78.

Webster. W. J. E. 1962. Techniques of field plotting for archaeological purposes. *Oceania* 33: 139–142.

GLOSSARY OF TERMS

adits—horizontal mining shafts or tunnels

advertent colonization—intentional colonization of ecological niches by plants, often as a result of human agriculture and trade.

Alliance (phytosociology)—hierarchical classification unit in phytosociology.

anthropogenic—caused by activities of man.

artifacts—man-made archaeological remains.

Association (phytosociology)—hierarchical classification unit in phytosociology.

auriferous—bearing gold.

barrows—ancient burial sites and tombs.

basiphilous—plants preferring a lime-rich soil.

biogenic—caused by biological activity.

biogeochemical prospecting—prospecting for minerals by chemical analysis of vegetation.

biomass index—term used in aerial photography and satellite imagery. Measures the contribution of vegetation to the spectral signature.

bora rings—Australian aborigine stone ring structures of ceremonial significance.

cadmia—old Roman name for zinc ores.

calcifuge—pertaining to plants which will not tolerate lime-rich soils.

calciphile—pertaining to plants which prefer lime-rich soils.

castellum—fortress.

chert—flinty igneous rock.

chlorosis—yellowing of plant leaves due to iron deficiency sometimes caused by excess of other heavy metals in the soil.

Class (phytosociology)—hierarchical unit in phytosociology.

conquistadores—Spanish conquerors of Central and South America in the 16th and 17th centuries.

croisettes—copper crosses used as currency in precolonial central Africa.

crop marks—marks in crops indicative of buried archaeological remains.

cupricolous plants—plants which tolerate high copper levels in soils and which are confined to them.

cupules—cup-shaped parts that partially enclose ripening fruit as in acorns.

damp marks—changes in the appearance of soils caused by moister conditions. These are often indicative of buried archaeological remains.

demes—land subdivisions of ancient Greece.

dendrochronology—dating of trees from their annual rings.

density in plant mapping—density of plant species.

dwarfism—reduction in plant size due to stress that could be caused by buried archaeological features.

ecotypes—plants adapted to a particular geological substrate.

edaphic properties—chemical properties of the soil.

ethnography—the study of favourable sites for human occupation.

eutrophy—reduction of the oxygen supply in natural waters, caused by abnormal growth of certain species or by runoff from the land.

factor analysis—a statistical technique which reduces a large number of variables to a much smaller number of factors, each accounting for several of these variables.

festucoid phytoliths—siliceous remains of grasses.

frost marks—preferential deposition of frost in hollows related to buried archaeological features. These are recognizable from the air.

gangue—the non-economic waste remaining after ore extraction.

gigantism—enhanced growth in plants

caused by environmental factors such as enhanced levels of phosphate or nitrate near archaeological sites.

gossan—the surface expression of a buried ore deposit.

heliophile—pertaining to plants preferring open sunny growth sites.

hyperaccumulator—a plant that contains over 1000 mg/kg (0.1%) of heavy metals such as copper, cobalt, and nickel.

inadvertent colonization—unintentional colonization of ecological sites by plants, usually by human agency.

indicator geobotany—the relationship between plant communities and geology.

jacal structures—hovels.

kumara pit—a storage pit for kumaras (sweet potatoes) used by New Zealand Maoris.

layering in plant mapping—the concept of plants occupying different layers in an ecological system.

line transects—a form of plant mapping in which a long measuring tape is laid across the terrain and a record is made of plants touching it or near to it.

lithic scatters—stoney flakes used for cutting meat in primitive societies.

lynchet—an ancient field division in Northwest Europe consisting of raised banks, particularly in the so-called "Celtic Fields."

macroplant remains—plant remains such as seed, stems etc. that are larger than pollen size.

metallicolous plants—plants that will tolerate mineralized soils and that are confined to them.

metallophytes—plants that grow on mineralized soils.

midden—a rubbish dump of primitive societies. These often contain sea shells that provide calcium-rich soils upon which calciphile plants can grow.

mine tips—mine dumps remaining after extraction of ores.

minimal area in plant mapping—the minimum area that provides a representative number of plant species of the site.

monoband aerial imagery—aerial imagery using only a single wavelength band.

multiband aerial imagery—aerial imagery using several wavelength bands. In the LANDSAT series, four bands are used: one in the infrared and three in the ultraviolet/visible range.

nanism—see dwarfism above.

necrosis—death of plant tissue.

Order (phytosociology)—a hierarchical unit in phytosociology.

pa—Maori fortress.

paleoethnobotany—the use of plant remains to reconstruct ancient agricultural systems and food gathering customs.

palynology—the use of pollen to date ancient relics and to reconstruct their original climate and botanical environment.

panicoid phytoliths—siliceous remains of flower clusters.

pedology—the study of soils.

periodicity in plant mapping—a study of flowering times.

phyllodes—small narrow leaves or needles.

pixel—picture element. A unit in satellite imagery. In the LANDSAT series of satellite, a pixel represents an area of about 80 × 80 meters.

plant opal phytolith (POP)—the siliceous residue after the organic matter of a plant has decayed.

polder—a field recovered from the sea. Common in Holland.

pueblo—village.

quadrat—a square measuring area used in plant mapping.

red edge—reduction of the wavelength at which light is reflected from vegetation in the near infrared part of the spectrum. This can be caused by geochemical stress or by the influence of buried archaeological remains upon the plant's health.

remote sensing—assessment of terrestrial features by aerial photography or by satellite imagery.

satellite imagery—remote sensing by use of satellites (see above).

scoria—loose gravelly material often of volcanic origin.

scree—loose gravelly material on hillsides.

seed rain—natural fall of seed upon a given site.

shadow marks—shadows cast by archaeological features. These are usually recognizable from the air.

snow marks—marks in snow caused by archaeological features. Often this involves selective fall of snow, or early or late melting.

sociability in plant mapping—degree to which plant species will mix with others.

soil marks—marks in soils caused by buried archaeological remains.

spacing in plant mapping—spacing of plants in plant communities.

spoil heap—heap of uneconomic material left behind after ore extraction.

steppe—open grassland.

supervised maps—maps produced by aerial photography in which "ground truth" has been established by on-foot observations.

tangata whenua—people of the land (Maori).

tell—raised artificial hill.

tessarae—pottery tiles used in the Roman Empire.

thermography—remote sensing using far infrared imagery.

trepanging—smoking meat and fish for food preservation. Used in Southeast Asia. Visitors from this area left traces in Northern Australia.

ultramafic (serpentine) soil—a soil derived from ultramafic rocks which have high levels of nickel, chromium, iron, and magnesium. Only specialized plants can grow over such soils.

unsupervised maps—maps prepared from aerial surveys only. i.e., with no "ground truth" obtained from on-foot observations.

vegetation dominance types (VDT)—dominant vegetation determined by statistical tests.

vexillation fortress—a fortress built by, or for, veteran auxiliary soldiers of the Roman Empire.

vitality in plant mapping—assessment of plant health.

BOTANICAL INDEX

GEOGRAPHICAL INDEX

SUBJECT INDEX

Robert R. Brooks is Professor in the Department of Chemistry and Biochemistry at Massey University, Palmerston North, New Zealand. He is the author of *Serpentine and Its Vegetation*, also published by Dioscorides Press.

Dieter Johannes is Assistant Managing Director of the Fachvereinigung Auslandsbergbau e. V. (Association of International Mining) in Bonn, West Germany.